The Kingfisher Book of the Universe

The Kingfisher Book of the Universe

KINGFISHER

KINGFISHER

Kingfisher Publications Plc
New Penderel House, 283-288 High Holborn,
London WC1V 7HZ

Authors David Lambert, Martin Redfern
Senior Editor Clive Wilson
Editors Rebecca Fry, Charlotte Hurdman
Design Jacqueline Palmer, Traffika Publishing Ltd
Picture Research Veneta Bullen, Jane Lambert
Pre-Press Manager Caroline Jackson
DTP Co-ordinator Nicky Studdart
Indexer Hilary Bird

First Published by Kingfisher Publications Plc 2000

2 4 6 8 10 9 7 5 3 1
1TR/0600/TWP/(MAR)/130SMA

Copyright © Kingfisher Publications Plc 2000

All rights reserved. No part of this publication may be reproduced, stored in a retrieval system or transmitted by any means, electronic, mechanical, photocopying or otherwise, without the prior permission of the publisher.

A CIP catalogue record for this book is available from the British Library.

ISBN 0-7534-0385-4

Colour separations by Newsele
Printed in Singapore

CONTENTS

DYNAMIC PLANET

- 8 Birth of the Earth
- 10 Spaceship Earth
- 12 Sky and Sea
- 14 Mantle Mysteries
- 16 Changing Continents
- 18 Under the Sea
- 20 Earth Revealed
- 22 The Living Core

THE RESTLESS EARTH

- 24 Eruption!
- 26 Anatomy of a Volcano
- 28 Hot Spots
- 30 Blowing its Top
- 32 Volcanoes and People
- 34 Earthquake!
- 36 Earthquakes and People
- 38 Prediction and Prevention
- 40 Mountains

AIR AND WATER

- 42 The Wind
- 44 The Weather
- 46 Weird Weather
- 48 The Climate
- 50 Climate Threat
- 52 Water Power
- 54 Floods and Droughts
- 56 Lands of Ice

LIFE STORY

- 58 Changing Times
- 60 The Dawn of Life
- 62 Wonderful Life
- 64 The Fossil Sky
- 66 Invasion of the Land
- 68 The Real Jurassic Park
- 70 Kingdom of the Giants
- 72 Extinction
- 74 The Birds and the Bees
- 76 Creatures of the Ice
- 78 Our Ancestors

PEOPLE AND THE PLANET

- 80 Fuel from the Earth
- 82 Metals from the Earth
- 84 Gems from the Deep
- 86 Human Creators
- 88 Human Destroyers
- 90 The End of the Earth

THE CHANGING OCEANS

- 92 Planet Ocean
- 94 The Invisible Landscape
- 96 Tides
- 98 Waves

OCEAN LIFE

- 100 Fish
- 102 Sea Mammals
- 104 Coral Reefs
- 106 Life in the Depths
- 108 Rocky Shores
- 110 Sand and Pebbles

PEOPLE AND THE OCEANS

- 112 Early Ocean Explorers
- 114 The Age of Exploration
- 116 Advances in Navigation
- 118 The Sea and the Arts
- 120 Food from the Sea
- 122 Hidden Dangers
- 124 Future Prospects

EXPLORING SPACE

- 126 A Place in the Cosmos
- 128 Looking Up
- 130 Looking Out
- 132 Rise of the Rocket
- 134 Race to the Moon
- 136 The Space Shuttle
- 138 Living in Space
- 140 Using Space
- 142 Earthwatch

THE SOLAR SYSTEM

144 The Solar System
146 Mercury
148 Venus
150 The Moon
152 Mars
154 Mission to Mars
156 Asteroids and Meteorites
158 Jupiter
160 Jupiter's Moons
162 Saturn
164 Saturn's Moons
166 Uranus
168 Neptune
170 Pluto
172 Comets

STARS

174 The Active Sun
176 Outside the Sun
178 Star Birth
180 Star Life
182 Star Death
184 Black Hole!

OUT IN SPACE, BACK IN TIME

186 The Milky Way
188 Our Local Group
190 Expanding Universe
192 The Galactic Zoo
194 Violent Galaxies
196 Echoes of Creation
198 The Big Bang
200 The Great Unknown

COSMIC QUESTIONS

202 Beyond Time
204 The Search for ET
206 Impossible Questions

REFERENCE

208 Universal Facts
212 Glossary

218 Index
224 Acknowledgements

DYNAMIC PLANET

Birth of the Earth

Five billion years ago, there was no planet Earth and no Sun. But the Universe was already in full swing and whole generations of stars had already used hydrogen to create the atomic building blocks – carbon, oxygen, silicon and others – that would later make up the planets. In a spiral arm of what is now our galaxy, clouds of these atoms started to condense, pulled together either by gravity or by shock waves from exploding stars. As they contracted, they began to rotate, forming a swirling disk at the heart of which lay a small, young star. And so the Sun began its life.

△ *Every culture has developed its own story of the Creation. This illustration from the Luther Bible (1530), shows God making the world and the Universe.*

Heat and dust

As the young Sun warmed, it blew a wind of energetic particles through the dusty disk, driving the remaining gases outwards to form the giant planets Jupiter and Saturn. Other dust grains accumulated into rocky lumps which bumped into each other, sometimes joining together. Slowly, the remaining material was swept up into a few large planets. One of these was the beginnings of the Earth.

Fire and brimstone

The new Earth was a hot young planet, warmed by atoms spewed out by an earlier generation of stars and by its own gravity. It suffered heavy bombardment from large asteroids and comets which rained down upon it, melting its surface. One of these impacts was so large that it created the Moon.

◁ *Hindu theory sees the Universe as an egg created by Brahma. Brahma emerged from the egg and split himself into two people.*

8

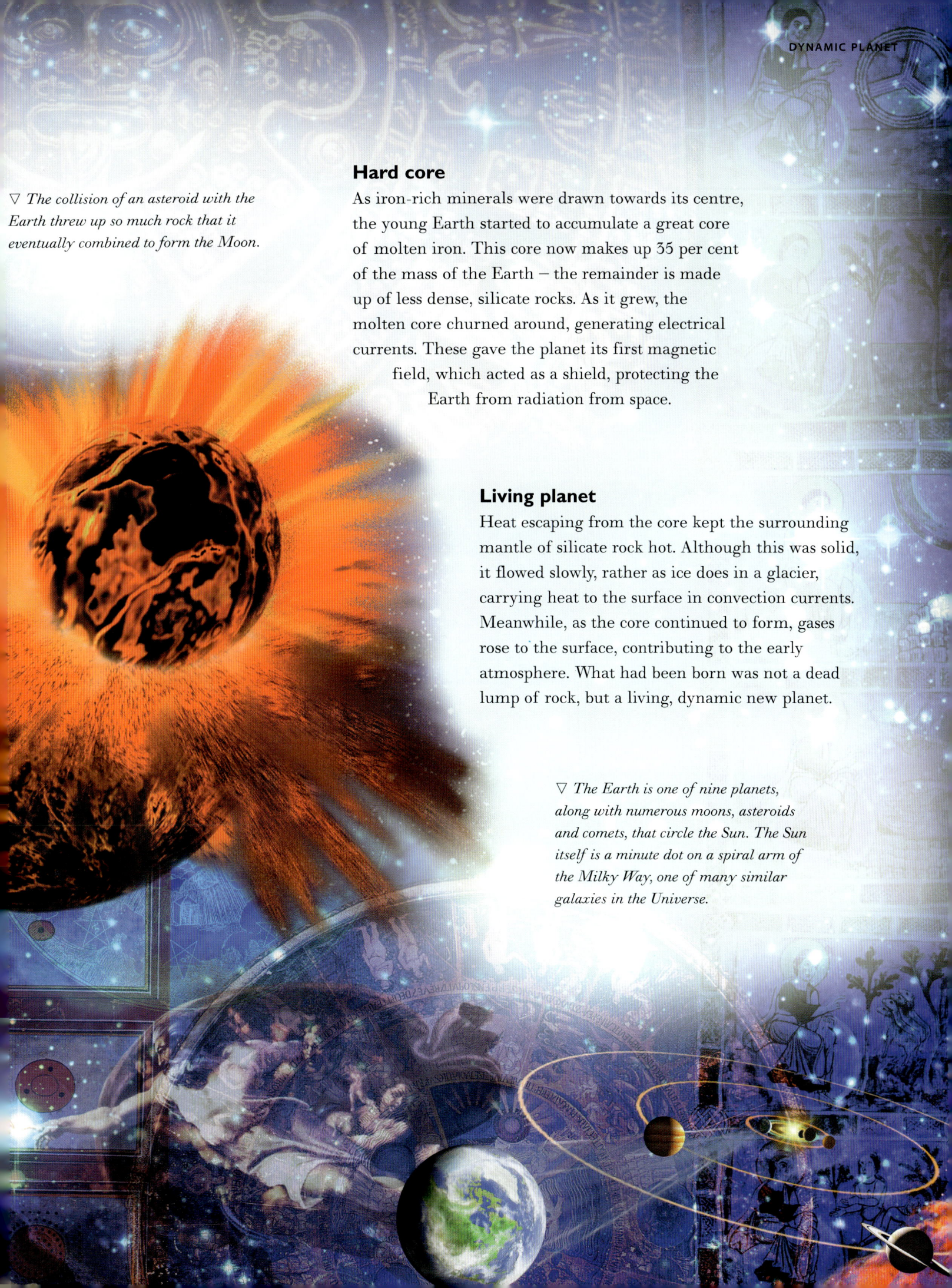

▽ *The collision of an asteroid with the Earth threw up so much rock that it eventually combined to form the Moon.*

Hard core

As iron-rich minerals were drawn towards its centre, the young Earth started to accumulate a great core of molten iron. This core now makes up 35 per cent of the mass of the Earth – the remainder is made up of less dense, silicate rocks. As it grew, the molten core churned around, generating electrical currents. These gave the planet its first magnetic field, which acted as a shield, protecting the Earth from radiation from space.

Living planet

Heat escaping from the core kept the surrounding mantle of silicate rock hot. Although this was solid, it flowed slowly, rather as ice does in a glacier, carrying heat to the surface in convection currents. Meanwhile, as the core continued to form, gases rose to the surface, contributing to the early atmosphere. What had been born was not a dead lump of rock, but a living, dynamic new planet.

▽ *The Earth is one of nine planets, along with numerous moons, asteroids and comets, that circle the Sun. The Sun itself is a minute dot on a spiral arm of the Milky Way, one of many similar galaxies in the Universe.*

DYNAMIC PLANET

Spaceship Earth

If an alien spaceship approached our Solar System and began scanning the planets for signs of life, it would soon detect that one planet was special. The atmosphere of the Earth is different from that of all the other planets. It contains plenty of oxygen but very little carbon dioxide. Closer examination would also reveal a protective layer of ozone, and traces of the pigment chlorophyll on land and in the sea – confirmation of the existence of life. The alien space probe might even pick up the incessant babble of radio and television transmissions, suggesting that the Earth's life is intelligent.

△ Satellite sensors tuned to detect the pigment chlorophyll in plankton and plants were used to build up this image of life on land and in the sea.

▽ Infrared sensors reveal growth of new vegetation on the volcanic island of Fogo, near West Africa. The blue is surrounding sea, white the clouds and red the vegetation.

Third rock from the Sun

The Earth is one of three planets that must have started their lives under similar conditions. Venus is about the same size as the Earth and a little nearer to the Sun. Mars is slightly smaller and further away. All three began with water vapour and carbon dioxide in their atmospheres. During their lifetime, the Sun has warmed. On Venus, this gave rise to a runaway greenhouse effect that boiled away any water. On Mars, the free-flowing water froze or escaped into space. Today, the surface temperature of Venus is over 400°C, while that of Mars is typically −100°C.

A living planet

Only on the Earth can life survive. The planet is a delicate ecosystem, maintained in a precarious balance between freezing and overheating. Yet, somehow, that balance has been maintained for billions of years, even while the Sun's heat has steadily increased. Many scientists now believe that the custodian of the planet is life itself. Thanks to life, the Earth's climate has not been disrupted by the warming Sun. Bacteria and algae, as well as plants, have consumed the carbon dioxide blanket that once enveloped the planet, and liberated the oxygen. In this way, they have sustained a perfect atmosphere for life to flourish – so far, at least. This concept is termed Gaia, after the ancient Greek Mother Earth goddess.

◁ *An alien space probe would pick up all the signs of life on our planet – water, air and chlorophyll, as well as radio, TV and satellite signals.*

The first view from space

The Apollo astronauts were the first to comment on the impact of seeing their home planet from space. In various ways, they all described it as breathtakingly beautiful, a fragile blue jewel in a star-studded sea of blackness. The first photographs of our planet from space also heralded a new understanding of the Earth from a global perspective.

Keeping an eye on the planet

The Earth is being observed from space at this minute – not by aliens (as far as we know), but by orbiting satellites. Remote sensing, as it is called, can reveal geological features too large to notice on land. The satellites can prospect for minerals in remote areas, monitor the atmosphere and watch weather systems forming. They can spot environmental damage and help us do our planetary housekeeping.

▷ *Earth is one of nine very different planets. Mars (top left) is frozen under a thin, dry atmosphere. Venus (top right), by contrast, is hot under its thick, acidic atmosphere. Jupiter (bottom right) is a swirling bag of hydrogen with a small rocky core. And Saturn (bottom left), the other gas giant, has a ring of icy particles around it.*

DYNAMIC PLANET

Sky and Sea

From a single swirling cloud of gas and dust, the Sun and planets emerged about 4.5 billion years ago. At first, the young Earth may have had a thick atmosphere of hydrogen, similar to that of Jupiter. But if it did, it was very soon swept away as the new Sun began to shine. Volcanoes on the hot Earth were belching out gas and steam, but that too may have evaporated in the heat, or been stripped away by the solar wind and constant bombardment by asteroids. The Earth probably then resembled Jupiter's moon Io, with little atmosphere and a rash of volcanoes renewing its surface. Slowly, the atmosphere and oceans that we know today emerged.

△ Comets brought water to the Earth in their icy cores, and volcanoes released gases into the atmosphere.

△ Active volcanoes on Jupiter's closest moon Io are similar to those that formed the Earth's first crust more than four billion years ago.

How the sea fell from the sky

The sky we know today probably came out of the ground and the sea must have fallen from the sky. Volcanoes were constantly adding nitrogen and carbon dioxide to the new atmosphere. And the Earth's oceans were created by icy comets returning from the outer Solar System and raining down on the Earth's surface. Even today, many thousands of tonnes of water fall to the Earth from space every year.

The changing air

When it was first formed, the Earth's atmosphere had no oxygen, only a lethal mixture of hydrogen, methane, ammonia and hydrogen cyanide. It must have been the worst case of pollution in history! But the hydrogen escaped into space and ultraviolet radiation from the Sun broke down the larger molecules, leaving a mixture of nitrogen and carbon dioxide. Only when life emerged and photosynthesis began did oxygen first appear on the Earth about 3.4 billion years ago. It probably was produced by organisms called cyanobacteria in colonies known as stromatolites, which can still be found today at low tide.

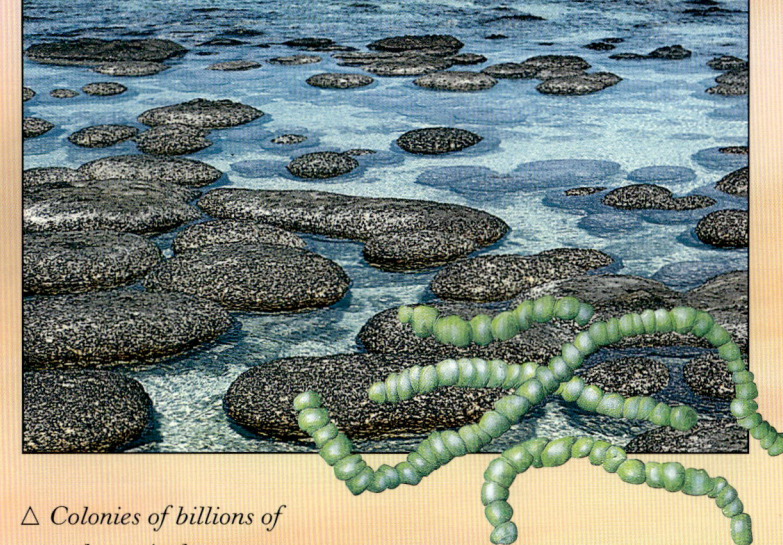

△ Colonies of billions of cyanobacteria, known as stromatolites, grow in Shark Bay, Western Australia. Ancient stromatolites may have released the first oxygen on the Earth.

△ Filaments of many tiny algal cells probably once filled the oceans, releasing oxygen into the young atmosphere.

A climate for life

By two billion years ago, the levels of oxygen were rising fast as algae filled the oceans. To produce the oxygen, the algae were consuming the carbon dioxide blanket that had kept the planet warm. But the planet did not freeze, as the Sun was also steadily warming. The two kept pace with each other, maintaining a suitable climate for life.

DYNAMIC PLANET

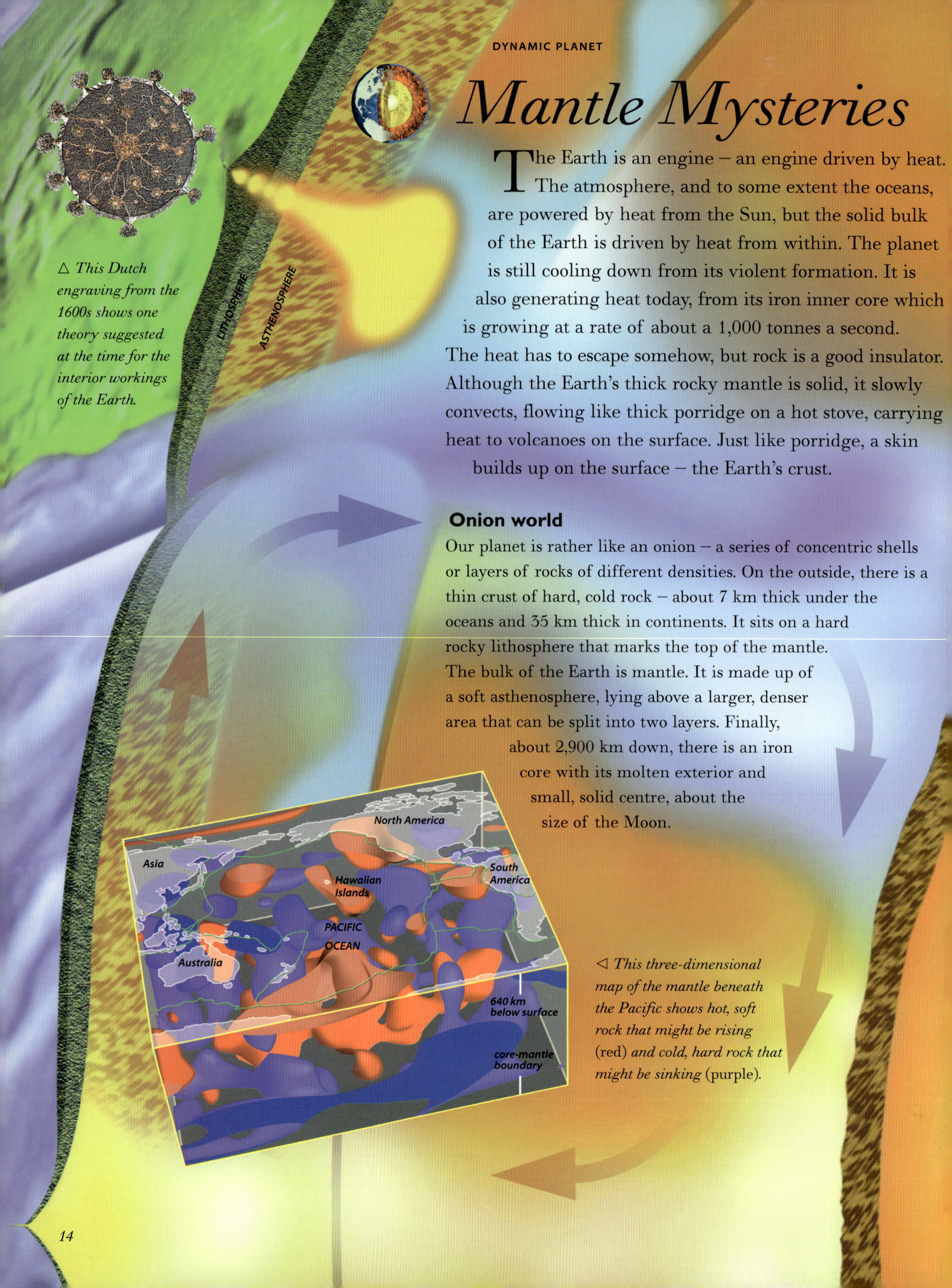

Mantle Mysteries

The Earth is an engine – an engine driven by heat. The atmosphere, and to some extent the oceans, are powered by heat from the Sun, but the solid bulk of the Earth is driven by heat from within. The planet is still cooling down from its violent formation. It is also generating heat today, from its iron inner core which is growing at a rate of about a 1,000 tonnes a second. The heat has to escape somehow, but rock is a good insulator. Although the Earth's thick rocky mantle is solid, it slowly convects, flowing like thick porridge on a hot stove, carrying heat to volcanoes on the surface. Just like porridge, a skin builds up on the surface – the Earth's crust.

Onion world

Our planet is rather like an onion – a series of concentric shells or layers of rocks of different densities. On the outside, there is a thin crust of hard, cold rock – about 7 km thick under the oceans and 35 km thick in continents. It sits on a hard rocky lithosphere that marks the top of the mantle. The bulk of the Earth is mantle. It is made up of a soft asthenosphere, lying above a larger, denser area that can be split into two layers. Finally, about 2,900 km down, there is an iron core with its molten exterior and small, solid centre, about the size of the Moon.

△ This Dutch engraving from the 1600s shows one theory suggested at the time for the interior workings of the Earth.

◁ This three-dimensional map of the mantle beneath the Pacific shows hot, soft rock that might be rising (red) and cold, hard rock that might be sinking (purple).

DYNAMIC PLANET

Endless cycle

The Earth is constantly changing. New material is being added to the surface only to be worn away and removed again. Hot rock is rising up from the Earth's mantle, while slabs of cold rock are sinking back down into it. The entire rock cycle is powered by heat from within and sunshine from above.

▷ *Lava erupting on the surface of the Earth may contain rock that has risen from the very base of the mantle – having begun its journey many hundreds of millions of years before.*

OUTER CORE

Lumps and bumps

As we travel over the surface of the Earth, we see all sorts of different features. There are continents and oceans, mountains and valleys. In some places the rocks are hard and dense, in others they are soft and light. Similarly, deeper down, within the mantle and core there are also differences from place to place including lumps and bumps and temperature variations.

Secrets of the Earth's interior

About 670 km down in the Earth's mantle, there is a boundary. Old, cold slabs of ocean lithosphere descend towards it. Hot, soft rock rises from it, towards volcanic hot spots on the surface. Beneath it, the hot rocks also circulate. But does the whole mantle circulate, or is heat passed between the upper and lower mantle, without getting mixed up together? The answer could be that both are true. Material sinking in the upper mantle comes to a halt at the boundary, and spreads out for hundreds of millions of years before avalanching on through the lower mantle, almost to the top of the core.

INNER CORE

◁ *Though made of solid rock, the mantle is slowly circulating. Boundaries at some depths cause the hot or cold rock to spread out before journeying on.*

◁ *In the centre of the Earth is a solid iron core about the size of the Moon. Around it is a slowly churning molten iron outer core. Electric currents circulating in it generate the planet's magnetic field.*

15

DYNAMIC PLANET

Changing Continents

As mantle rocks slowly circulate, they bring lighter rocks to the Earth's surface like a scum. This has built up to form the continents, the planet's great landmasses. Like icebergs, there is much more to a continent than is visible. Continental crust can be 30 or 40 kilometres thick, compared to ocean crust which is only 6 or 7 kilometres thick. Although it is hard to find ocean crust older than 400 million years, the continents have been slowly accumulating ever since the Earth's surface solidified. Part of Australia, for example, is more than 3 billion years old.

△ *This granite boulder, one of the so-called Devil's Marbles, is in northern Australia. Granite is made from sediments which have melted at great depths and risen to the surface.*

Flotsam and jetsam

For billions of years, the continents have been tossed about on the mantle. Where they have crashed into each other, mountain ranges have formed. Where they have been pulled apart, oceans have opened up. When hot mantle rock rises under a continent, it can inject layers of volcanic rock, stretching the continent.

The rise of granite

As continental rocks pile up, the base of the continent gets buried deeper and deeper. As it descends, it heats up and the rocks at the base begin to melt and rise towards the surface. Huge bubbles of molten rock bake the surrounding rock which cools slowly, forming crystals. Eventually, the surrounding rock wears away to reveal a new material – granite.

▷ *A technician from the US Geological Survey checks a 'creep' meter on the San Andreas Fault in California. It is sensitive enough to detect Earth movements the thickness of a human hair.*

16

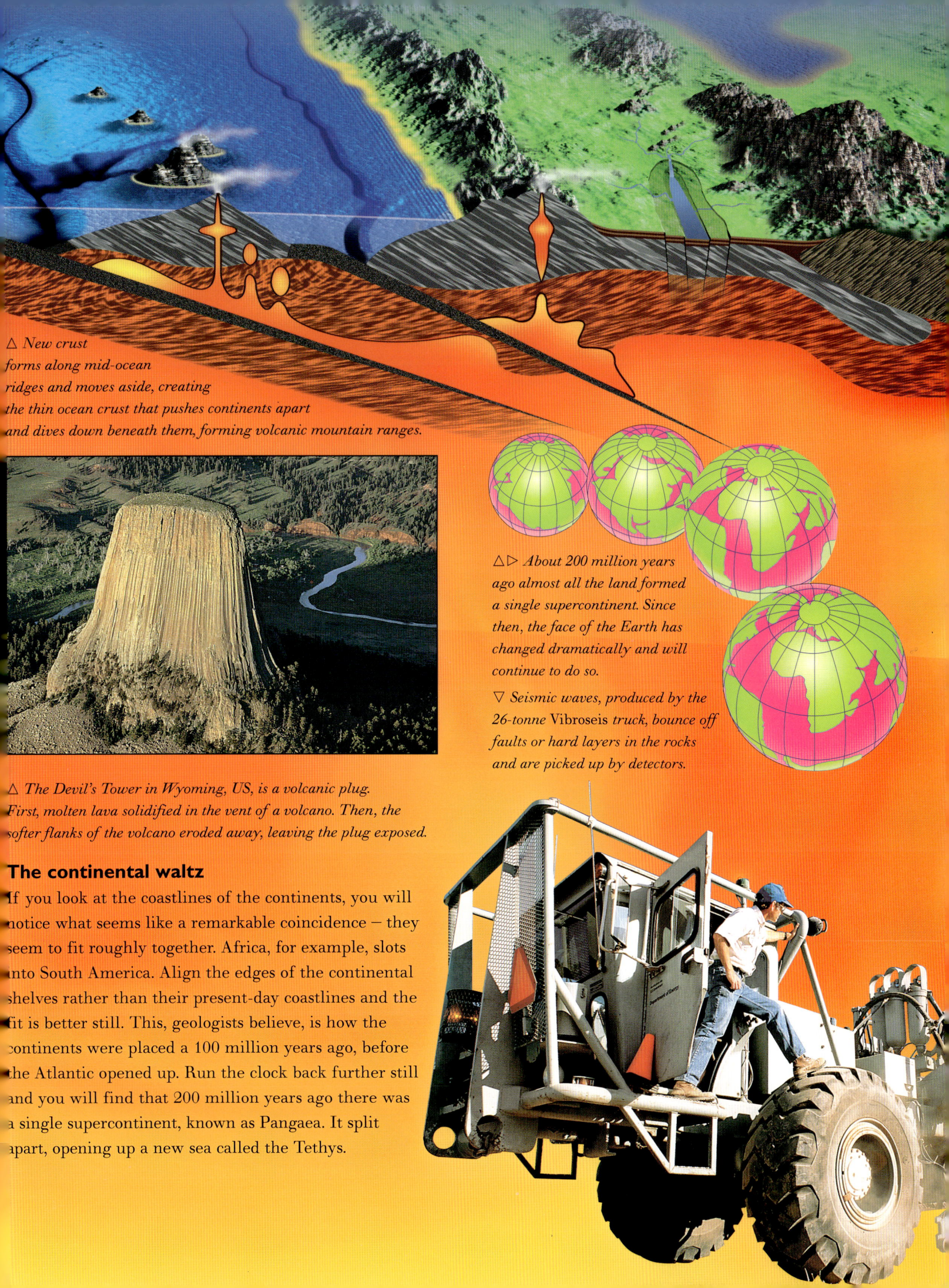

△ *New crust forms along mid-ocean ridges and moves aside, creating the thin ocean crust that pushes continents apart and dives down beneath them, forming volcanic mountain ranges.*

△▷ *About 200 million years ago almost all the land formed a single supercontinent. Since then, the face of the Earth has changed dramatically and will continue to do so.*

▽ *Seismic waves, produced by the 26-tonne* Vibroseis *truck, bounce off faults or hard layers in the rocks and are picked up by detectors.*

△ *The Devil's Tower in Wyoming, US, is a volcanic plug. First, molten lava solidified in the vent of a volcano. Then, the softer flanks of the volcano eroded away, leaving the plug exposed.*

The continental waltz

If you look at the coastlines of the continents, you will notice what seems like a remarkable coincidence — they seem to fit roughly together. Africa, for example, slots into South America. Align the edges of the continental shelves rather than their present-day coastlines and the fit is better still. This, geologists believe, is how the continents were placed a 100 million years ago, before the Atlantic opened up. Run the clock back further still and you will find that 200 million years ago there was a single supercontinent, known as Pangaea. It split apart, opening up a new sea called the Tethys.

DYNAMIC PLANET

Under the Sea

More than 70 per cent of our planet's surface is covered by oceans. Their average depth is more than 4,000 metres — far too deep for sunlight to reach the ocean floor. Yet it is in the oceans that one of the most important clues to how the Earth works has been found. In the 1960s, as the ocean floors began to be surveyed by sonar, magnetometers and submersibles, it soon became clear that there is a whole system of ridges running down the middle of the world's oceans. This system is the longest continuous mountain chain on the planet — a network over 70,000 kilometres long, like the seam on a baseball. As the oceanographers discovered, the ridges are quite literally the seams of the planet, and the boundaries of creation.

△ *Twenty Thousand Leagues Under the Sea was written in 1870 by French science-fiction writer Jules Verne. It tells of a powered submarine*, Nautilus, *whose crew discovers weird and wonderful creatures at the bottom of the sea. One hundred years later, fiction became fact.*

Volcanoes beneath the waves

Mid-ocean ridges are peppered with active volcanic vents, from which dense, black basalt oozes like toothpaste into round lumps called pillow lava. The eruptions are not usually violent, but sometimes are accompanied by small earthquakes.

Black smokers

Water sometimes seeps into the volcanoes, where it dissolves minerals and then rises out of hydrothermal vents known as black smokers. The water can reach temperatures as high as 200° or 300°C, but it does not boil because of the enormous pressure.

◁ *A mid-ocean ridge is the dividing point between two pieces of the Earth's crust. Hot magma from deep within the mantle forces its way up through the crack, continually creating new ocean crust.*

Life around the vents

Amazingly, a whole ecosystem of organisms has been discovered around such vents. Bacteria that take energy from sulphur provide food for giant tube worms, clams, fish and blind white shrimps.

DYNAMIC PLANET

Recycling the ocean floor
If mid-ocean ridges are constantly spewing out new sea floor, does this mean that the Earth is expanding? The answer is no – the old ocean crust is sinking into the mantle. As the ocean crust cools, it becomes more dense and either dives into an ocean trench or under a continent, throwing up volcanic islands or mountain chains as it goes.

0 million years 180

△ This magnetic map reveals the symmetry of the rocks on either side of the Mid-Atlantic Ridge, where rising magma has pushed the continents apart.

◁ The sulphur and dissolved minerals released at hydrothermal vents allow creatures to exist without sunlight.

DYNAMIC PLANET

Earth Revealed

A journey to the centre of the Earth was once a dream of science fiction. Today, it is possible in science fact. Humans themselves can only burrow a few thousand metres underground in the deepest mines. Boreholes can only drill into the crust of the Earth — to date the deepest hole is just over 12 kilometres. Science, however, can take us beyond the crust and deep into the planet. Using observations from the surface and from satellites in space, together with laboratory simulations, geologists now have a clear understanding of how the Earth works.

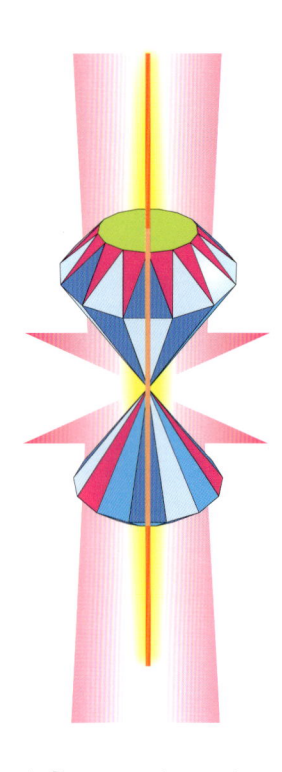

△ *The characters in Jules Verne's* Journey to the Centre of the Earth *(1864) discovered living dinosaurs inside the Earth.*

▽ *The satellite* LAGEOS II *reveals variations in the Earth's gravity caused by different rock densities.*

△ *By squeezing a tiny sample of rock between the polished faces of two diamonds it is possible to re-create the pressures at the centre of the Earth.*

Squashed Earth

The Earth is very slightly squashed — its diameter at the equator is about 38 km greater than at the poles. This is because the planet is spinning, forcing material out towards the equator. Overall, however, the Earth is very smooth. If the planet were scaled down to the size of a one-metre ball, the difference between the highest mountains and the deepest valleys would only be a few millimetres.

Freefall

When Isaac Newton saw an apple fall, he realized that the force of gravity was pulling objects towards the centre of the Earth. What he did not know was that apples fall slightly faster in some parts of the world than others — although you cannot measure the difference using apples! Satellites, however, can measure the variations. The gravitational pull of a region of dense rock will make a satellite speed up. Over a region of lower gravity, it will slow down.

Split-second timing

The Earth is slowing down. We know from daily growth lines in fossil shells 180 million years ago that there were about 400 days in a year and each day lasted only 22 hours. This slowing down is caused mainly by energy lost as the Moon's gravity pulls on the Earth. There are also variations, of billionths of a second, that take place over days and hours, caused partly by currents in the core.

DYNAMIC PLANET

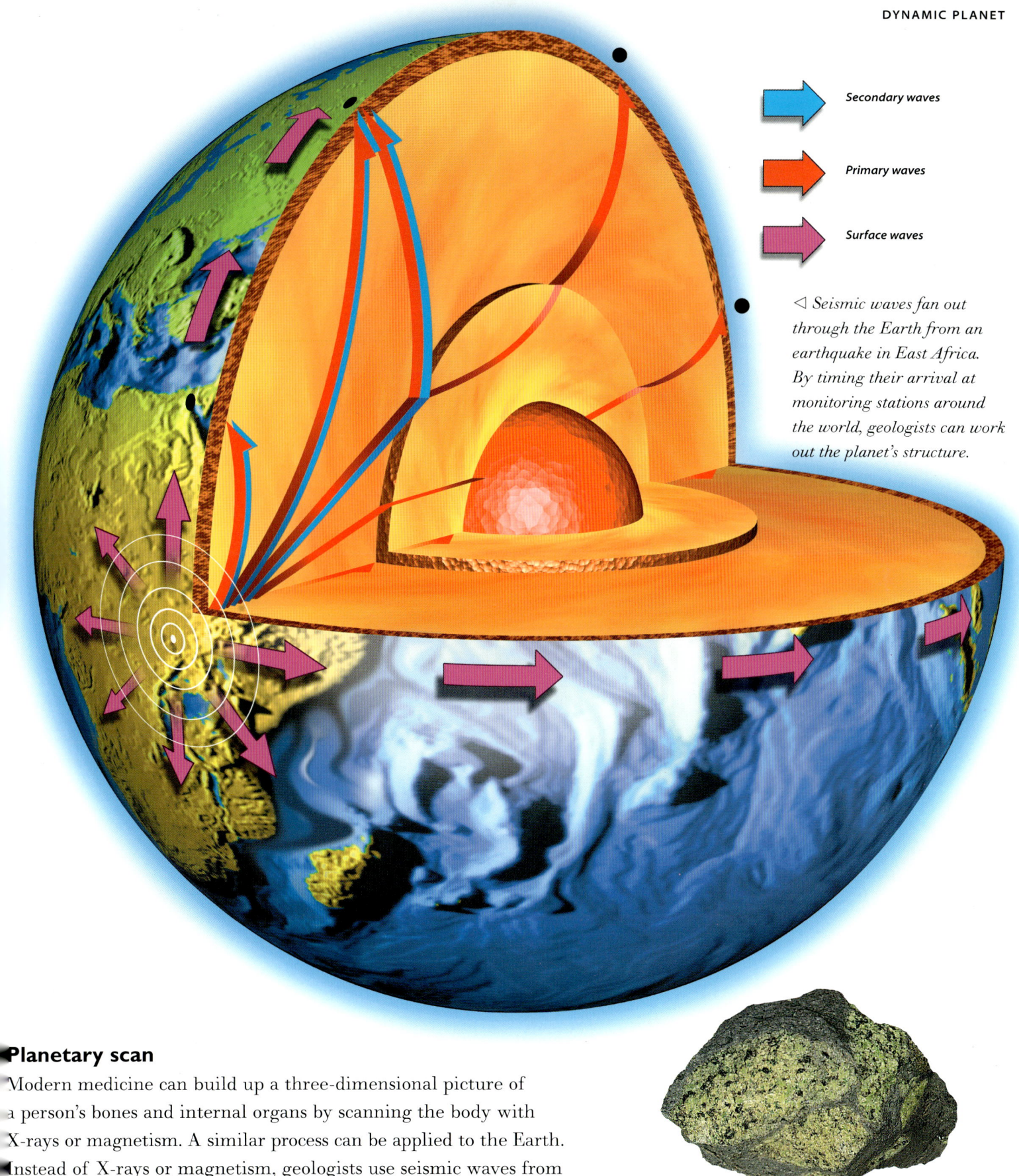

⬅ Secondary waves

⬅ Primary waves

⬅ Surface waves

◁ *Seismic waves fan out through the Earth from an earthquake in East Africa. By timing their arrival at monitoring stations around the world, geologists can work out the planet's structure.*

△ *This dense rock, made of the mineral olivine, is a sample of the mantle. It was brought to the surface in a volcanic eruption.*

Planetary scan

Modern medicine can build up a three-dimensional picture of a person's bones and internal organs by scanning the body with X-rays or magnetism. A similar process can be applied to the Earth. Instead of X-rays or magnetism, geologists use seismic waves from earthquakes and nuclear bomb tests. The waves move quickly through hard, dense rock, but more slowly through soft rock. Computers then build up a detailed picture of the planet based on the routes the waves take through the Earth.

DYNAMIC PLANET

The Living Core

By tracking the paths of seismic waves as they travel through the Earth after an earthquake, geologists have discovered some surprising facts about the planet's core. It seems to have a liquid outer layer that is churning like cement in a mixer at a speed of several millimetres a second. And right at the centre of the Earth there could be a crystal the size of the Moon! The pressure is so great at such depths that the only substance capable of behaving in this way is iron, perhaps with traces of nickel, sulphur, oxygen and silica. But geologists are puzzled by the discovery of a crusty boundary between the molten outer core and the mantle rocks above. What is this upside-down landscape 2,900 km beneath our feet?

Lost oceans

This mysterious boundary is not continuous — in some places it is 200 km thick and in others absent completely. It could be an iron and silicate scum that has risen like continents to the top of the core. Or, perhaps, more likely, it is the final resting-place of old, cold ocean crust that has sunk down through the mantle — a lost ocean.

Upside-down mountains

The result is a subterranean landscape with mountains and valleys that dwarf any found on the surface of the Earth. Beneath Alaska is a liquid mountain taller than Mount Everest, and under the Philippines is a valley in the core that is twice the depth of the Grand Canyon.

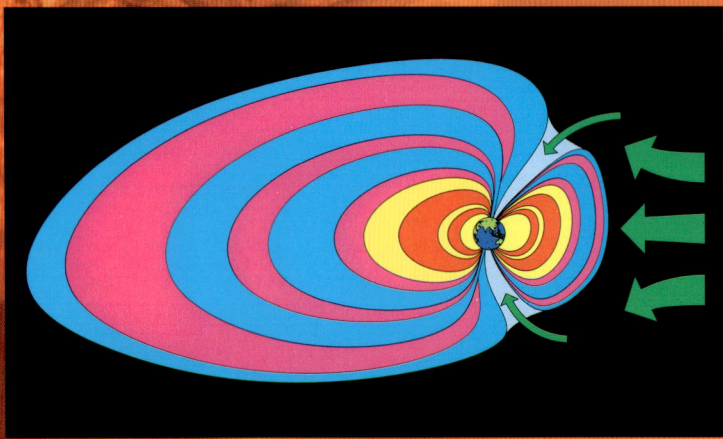

△ *The Earth's magnetic field is rooted in the core but reaches far out into space. It envelops the Earth and protects us from harmful radiation and particles, especially those emitted by the Sun.*

DYNAMIC PLANET

△ *As charged particles from space stream in along magnetic lines over the poles, they strike the atoms and molecules in the Earth's upper atmosphere and cause spectacular light shows called auroras.*

Magnetic dynamo

The Earth's magnetic field originates in the outer core. It is far too hot down there for a permanent magnet. Instead, the field is generated by electric currents in the churning metal. Like any magnet, the Earth has two poles – North and South. At present, they lie in the Arctic and Antarctic, but evidence in the rocks shows that they have reversed positions many times in Earth's history.

Frozen in time

The inner core is about the size of the Moon, and growing! Iron is freezing onto it at the rate of about a 1,000 tonnes a second. Yet only about 4 per cent of the total core has frozen in 4.5 billion years. This change to a solid releases a lot of heat, which combines with radioactive decay to keep the outer core churning, the magnetic field working and the mantle moving.

▷ *If we could pull the mantle away from the core, a strange subterranean landscape of valleys and mountains would be visible on the underside of the mantle. The outer core – a liquid metal furnace, churning at temperatures of 5,000°C – pushes against these features, and affects the rotation and magnetism of the planet.*

THE RESTLESS EARTH

Eruption!

Chains of volcanoes encircle the globe. Dotted along the edges of the plates that make up the Earth's crust, they are evidence that the interior of our planet is hot and active. When two continents move apart, material from the Earth's mantle rises to fill the gap. As the rock rises and the pressure drops, it partly melts to form liquid basalt. This lava emerges in huge quantities from fissures and vents – volcanoes – under the newly forming ocean. Occasionally, the ridges where the ocean crust is growing rise to the surface to form islands – Iceland is one example. Fresh volcanic land makes a rich and fertile home, but it can also be a risky place to live.

△ *The Giant's Causeway in Northern Ireland was formed from volcanic basalt which erupted as Europe split from North America 60 million years ago. The lava cooled to form these hexagonal columns, each up to half-a-metre across.*

An explosive history

The relatively sudden eruption of vast quantities of basalt must have taken place many times during the history of the Earth. There is evidence of other such events on the floor of the Pacific and sometimes on land, for example in Siberia and Argentina.

◁ *This spectacular firework display is in fact a volcanic explosion, caused as a flow of lava enters the sea off the Hawaiian coast. This lava has already flowed more than 10 km, yet its temperature is still 1000–1,200°C.*

Sticky lava

When lava is rich in silica, it is sticky and does not flow easily. This causes pressure to build up in a volcano, until it erupts in a violent explosion of super-heated steam, ash and molten rock. This kind of volcano is the most dangerous, and its eruption hard to predict.

Types of volcano

It is tempting to try to classify volcanoes according to the way they erupt, but the geological record shows that any one volcano can change during its history. It may begin fairly gently, producing runny basalt at first. Over time, it will build up and gradually become unstable. Eventually, it will start to crack and fall in onto itself which causes explosive eruptions of viscous, silica-rich lava.

THE RESTLESS EARTH

Big bang
The biggest volcanic eruption in recent history occurred on the island of Krakatoa, Indonesia. The volcano had been silent since 1680 and the crater was plugged with solidified lava. Then, on August 27, 1883, the volcano exploded, blowing the entire island into the sky. Tidal waves up to 40 m high resulted – hundreds of villages were destroyed and up to 36,000 people died.

△ *This eight-legged robot was developed to explore other planets. But it has also been used on the Earth to collect samples of gas and rock from volcanoes too hazardous for humans to approach.*

THE RESTLESS EARTH

Anatomy of a Volcano

Mount Etna is one of the most active volcanoes on the Earth. It has erupted at least 40 times in the last 20 years and shows no signs of stopping. Towering 3,300 metres above the Mediterranean in the east of Sicily, the volcano has four summit craters. During an eruption some of these craters can fill with red-hot lava. Seen from aircraft that pass overhead, these look like giant eyes in the night. Scientists have walked over every centimetre of the volcano with a variety of instruments. Seismographs measure the slightest shaking of the Earth while gravity meters and magnetometers measure the gravitational pull of rocks and their magnetic effects underground. Finally, scientists survey and measure how the mountain swells and contracts as the lava rises and falls within it.

△ Carrying whatever they can, the population of a Sicilian village flees ahead of an advancing lava flow in this illustration from 1910.

▽ During the 1971 eruption of Mount Etna, a stream of lava slowly advanced down the slopes and engulfed the volcano observatory.

Underground plumbing

From all these measurements, it is clear that molten rock collects in a wide, flat chamber about 20 km beneath the mountain and rises up a single pipe. Towards the top, perhaps 1,000 metres beneath the summit, the pipe splits, leading to four different summit craters and various other cracks and fissures. There is always molten rock at some depth in the central pipe, and this gives off bubbles of sulphurous gas, as if the volcano is breathing.

△ During the 1983 eruption of Mount Etna, lava surrounded the Sapienza Hotel. The flow moved slowly enough to allow people to be evacuated, and the building survived.

Story of an eruption

The 1971 eruption of Mount Etna began like many others before and since. Magma in the central pipe reached the top of one of the summit craters, sending a fiery fountain of lava and hot rocks into the air. Lava then began to creep downhill at a slow walking pace. Then, about two months later, a minor earthquake opened up several vents lower down the mountain, draining magma away from the summit towards villages. Luckily, no one was hurt.

THE RESTLESS EARTH

A change of mood

In the early 1990s, survey teams on the slopes of Mount Etna noticed a disturbing change. Not a rising bulge, as might be expected before an eruption, but a dip in the ground. Was this the prelude to a catastrophic collapse of one side of the mountain? If it was, then a landslide might follow, sending pressurized magma towards the city of Catania. Fortunately, the slope stabilized. But it showed how a volcano can change character dramatically.

△ *There are several types of volcano – a fissure, or crack in the ground* (A); *shield volcano* (B); *dome volcano* (C); *conical peak* (D); *composite volcano – like Mount Etna* (E); *and collapsed volcano or caldera* (F).

◁ *Beneath Mount Etna, rising magma pushes through a network of vents and fissures, leading to four summit craters and many cracks on its sides.*

△ *Mount Etna has been active since its birth, half a million years ago. On average, its lava flows are 12 m thick and can reach 7.5 km in length*

27

THE RESTLESS EARTH

Hot Spots

Around the Pacific Ocean is the Ring of Fire — a circle of volcanoes that marks the boundaries of the Pacific Plate. But not all volcanoes lie on plate boundaries. In the middle of the Pacific Ocean is the biggest volcano of all — Hawaii. The island sits on top of a hot spot — a spring of rising magma that has burst through the Earth's crust from the mantle below. The hot spot has been in the same place for millions of years. But during that time, the Pacific Plate has moved slowly to the northwest, passing over the top of the hot spot and creating a string of volcanic islands. The oldest of these was active more than 20 million years ago. The youngest is a submarine volcano called Loihi, lying beneath the waves, southeast of Hawaii.

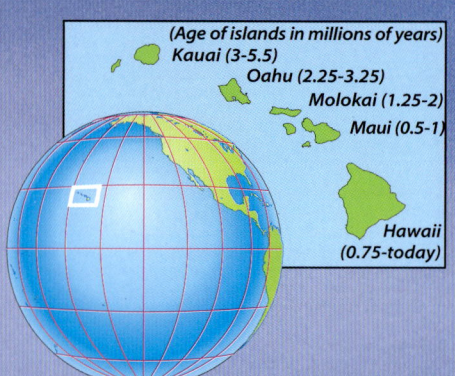

△ This is a statue of the Hawaiian fire goddess, Pele, who is said to live in the crater of Kilauea.

(Age of islands in millions of years)
Kauai (3-5.5)
Oahu (2.25-3.25)
Molokai (1.25-2)
Maui (0.5-1)
Hawaii (0.75-today)

△ The slow, northwesterly journey of the huge Pacific Plate can be seen in the increase in age of the islands as they move away from the hot spot.

◁ A night view reveals lava erupting along a fissure on the flanks of Kilauea and pouring into the sea.

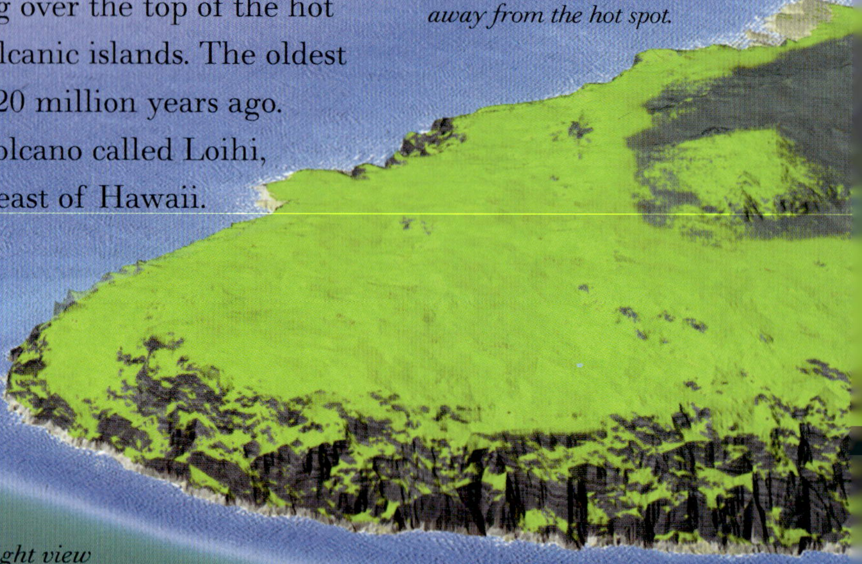

△ Hawaii is entirely volcanic, with the peaks of Mauna Kea and Mauna Loa towering to 4,200 m. Kilauea is one of the world's most active volcanoes.

A Hawaiian eruption

Hawaiian volcanoes have their roots at a depth of 50 km or more. Lava rises up a pipe which broadens into a storage area a few thousand metres beneath the volcano. Tourists flock to Kilauea, the most active crater on the main island, to see an eruption. This usually begins with a curtain of fire as gas sprays up lava along a fissure. After a while, the runny basalt builds a cone around a single vent. Sometimes, lava streams towards the sea, crossing roads in its path.

Cooking a continent

There are many hot spots on the Earth. Some are beneath continents. One example is Yellowstone National Park in the US. Here, the continent is too thick for volcanic forces to break through, but heat still escapes, producing the famous sulphurous hot springs and geysers of the park. Another hot spot under East Africa is slowly cooking the continent. It has already created the Great Rift Valley of East Africa, and one day it may split the continent in half.

THE RESTLESS EARTH

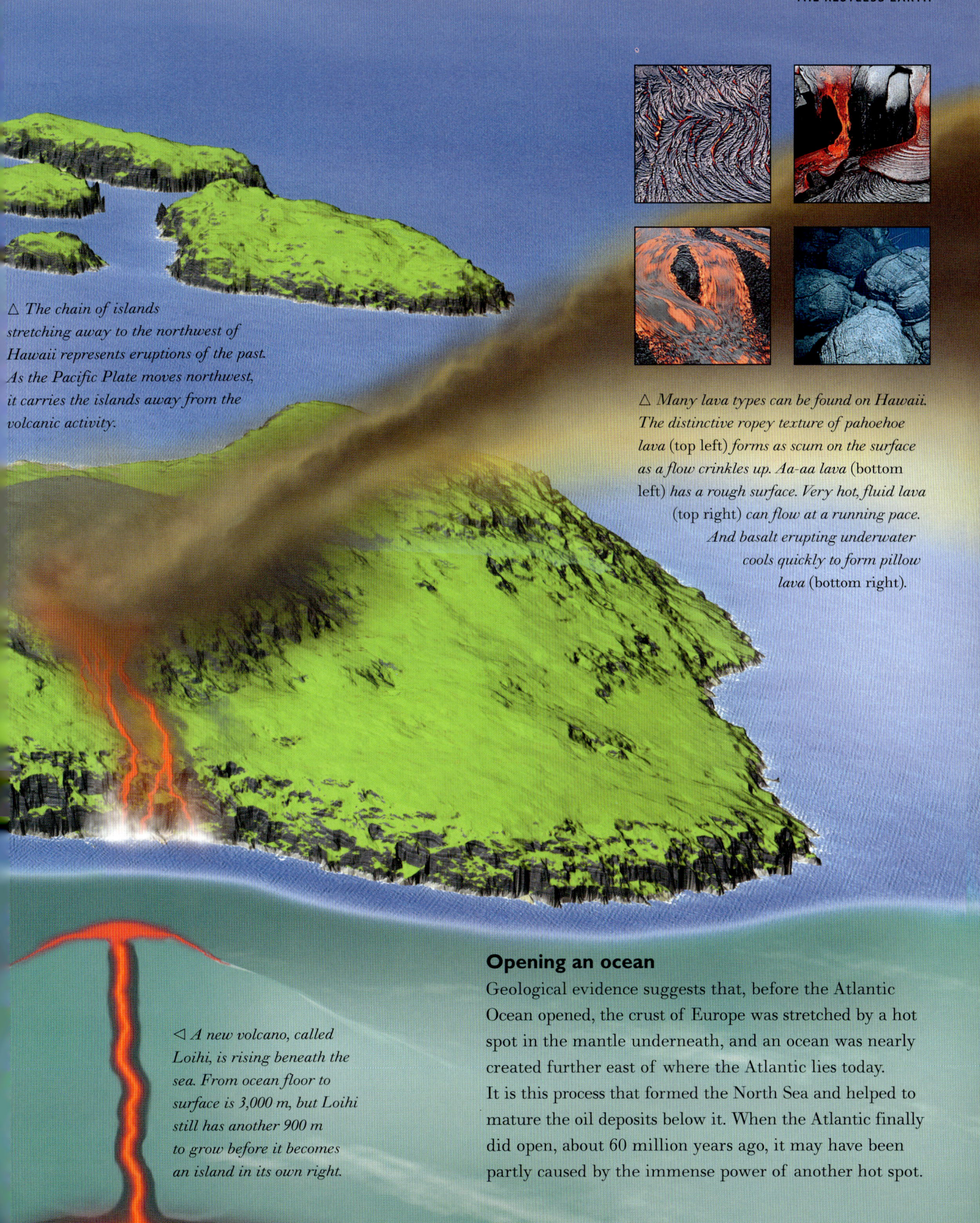

△ *The chain of islands stretching away to the northwest of Hawaii represents eruptions of the past. As the Pacific Plate moves northwest, it carries the islands away from the volcanic activity.*

△ *Many lava types can be found on Hawaii. The distinctive ropey texture of pahoehoe lava* (top left) *forms as scum on the surface as a flow crinkles up. Aa-aa lava* (bottom left) *has a rough surface. Very hot, fluid lava* (top right) *can flow at a running pace. And basalt erupting underwater cools quickly to form pillow lava* (bottom right).

◁ *A new volcano, called Loihi, is rising beneath the sea. From ocean floor to surface is 3,000 m, but Loihi still has another 900 m to grow before it becomes an island in its own right.*

Opening an ocean

Geological evidence suggests that, before the Atlantic Ocean opened, the crust of Europe was stretched by a hot spot in the mantle underneath, and an ocean was nearly created further east of where the Atlantic lies today. It is this process that formed the North Sea and helped to mature the oil deposits below it. When the Atlantic finally did open, about 60 million years ago, it may have been partly caused by the immense power of another hot spot.

THE RESTLESS EARTH

Blowing its Top

When old ocean crust dives down under a continent, it carries water with it. The rocks heat up, begin to melt and magma rises. But the water turns it into a giant pressure-cooker, waiting to blow its steam valve. On April 2, 1991, a nun walked into the Philippine Institute of Vulcanology and, begging their pardon, pointed out that the mountain behind her village had just blown up. Mt Pinatubo had lain dormant for 600 years and was covered with lush vegetation. The first earth tremors were followed by a plume of ash and gas, rising several kilometres into the sky. A rapid response force from the US Volcano Disaster Assistance Program rushed to the Philippines to monitor the eruption and warn the hundreds of thousands of people at risk.

Ring around the Earth

Two months later, a mighty explosion shot steam and ash more than 30 km into the sky above Mt Pinatubo. Nearly 300 people died, but had there been no early warnings or evacuation, the death toll would have been catastrophic. Following the eruption, a cloud of ash from the volcano spread out around the Earth, blotting out enough sunlight to lower global temperatures by half a degree over the next three years.

△ When Mt Pinatubo in the Philippines blew its top in June 1991, about two cubic kilometres of rock were turned to dust and sent high into the atmosphere, darkening the sky. Some dust spread around the world, creating spectacular sunsets and affecting the climate. But most rained down on nearby towns and villages leaving a thick layer of ash over everything.

▽ Super-hot pyroclastic flows of gas and lava raced down the flanks at 100 km/h, sending those people not already evacuated racing for safety. Here, journalists in a jeep flee from a giant cloud of noxious gases and dust.

THE RESTLESS EARTH

Eleven years earlier
One of the reasons why scientists could react so quickly to Mt Pinatubo lay on the other side of the Pacific, in Washington State, US. Eleven years earlier, in March 1980, Mount St Helens had also begun gushing steam and ash. Residents and loggers were evacuated and geologists flocked to the site. Instead of erupting out of the summit crater, a bulge began to appear in the northern flank. It grew to over 100 metres high and, at one stage, was rising by two metres a day.

Burning avalanche
At 8:30 in the morning of May 18, 1980, two sightseers watched as the entire bulge fell away during a mild earthquake. The lid was off the pressure-cooker! The volcano exploded sideways, sending a mixture of super-heated gas, steam and ash racing along a valley at more than 150 km/h. In all, a cubic kilometre of rock disappeared from the top of Mount St Helens. The two sightseers escaped with their lives and their camera, although 57 people died during the eruption.

▷ *Until May 18, 1980, Mount St Helens was a serene volcanic peak. But the pressure beneath was mounting.*

▷ *After the eruption, the mountain was 400 metres lower. About 540 million tonnes of ash and lava had erupted.*

▷ *As far as 30 km from the volcano, trees were stripped of branches, flattened like matchsticks or swept away.*

◁ *Molten magma inside Mount St Helens pushed a bulge out on one side of the volcano. When that collapsed, hot magma shot out sideways in what is known as a pyroclastic eruption.*

△ *When heavy rain follows an eruption — as happened in the Philippines in 1995 — dust and ash turn to rivers of mud, adding to the disaster.*

△ *In AD79, hot ash from Mt Vesuvius buried thousands of citizens in the city of Pompeii. Casts of their bodies remain.*

△ *Later eruptions of Mt Vesuvius have been less violent. This painting from the 1700s shows sightseers enjoying the pyrotechnic display.*

THE RESTLESS EARTH

Volcanoes and People

Few people have ever seen the birth of a volcano. One exception is a Mexican farmer called Dionisio Pulido. On February 5, 1943, while preparing a cornfield for planting near his home in Paricutin, Pulido noticed that a strange pit in the corner of a field had a crack running across it from which gas was escaping. When glowing rocks were hurled out and nearby trees caught fire, he hurriedly departed. A day later, there was a cinder cone 50 metres high. After a year, this had risen to 325 metres, and eruptions of lava had covered two villages, leaving only a church tower rising above them. But this case is unusual. Most active volcanoes have been in existence for thousands of years, and lie in easily identifiable and comparatively small areas of the world. Yet people have always lived in their shadows and many still die in their eruptions every year.

▷ *This map of recent volcanic eruptions shows how many volcanoes lie along plate margins where one plate is diving beneath another. Others occur where the crust is splitting, or over a hot spot in the Earth's mantle.*

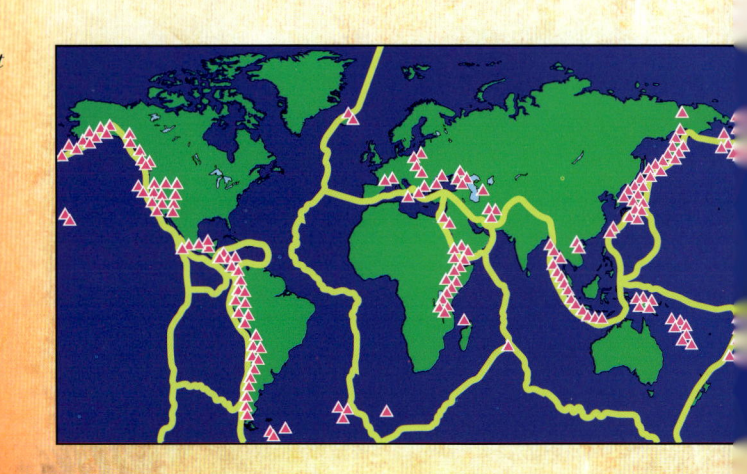

▷ *In 1902, when Mount Pelée, on the Caribbean island of Martinique, began to give out sulphurous fumes, people in the port of St Pierre did not evacuate because of local elections. A month later, the entire city and its population of 29,000 were destroyed (top right), apart from a condemned prisoner awaiting execution in his cell. On Montserrat (right), over 30 residents have died in eruptions since 1995 because they would not leave their homes.*

Pompeii revisited

The excavated remains of the crouched and huddled citizens of Pompeii are a grim reminder of the speed with which a volcano can overwhelm a population. In AD79, a 20-metre-thick blanket of burning ash and dust from Mt Vesuvius buried about 16,000 people living on its flanks. If the same were to happen today, three million people in and around the Italian city of Naples would be at risk.

Dangerous waters

Fire and water are a dangerous combination. Volcanic peaks are often covered in snow and the resulting mudflows, or lahars, can be more damaging than the eruption itself. At Nevado del Ruiz in Columbia in 1985, 22,000 people died as a 40-metre-high wave of mud burst down a canyon above the town of Armero.

Stopping volcanoes

There is no stopping a volcanic eruption, but the power can be redirected, away from humans. In Iceland in 1973, water was pumped into lava erupting from Helgafell, causing it to solidify before reaching the harbour and village. And in Sicily in 1983, explosives diverted a lava flow from Mt Etna away from tourist facilities.

△ *Volcano-watching can be an extremely hazardous profession. Here, a vulcanologist in protective clothing ventures to within metres of lava fountaining from a fissure in Iceland.*

THE RESTLESS EARTH

Earthquake!

The surface of the Earth is paved with slabs of crust, floating on the dense, soft rocks of the mantle. But each slab is constantly on the move, as oceans open or disappear and continents drift like great ships on the mantle. Sometimes, one piece of crust dives down beneath another, or it grates alongside and gets stuck. Most spectacularly, two pieces may crash head-on. Where these mighty slabs meet, stresses gradually build up under the ground, and whole networks of cracks, known as faults, can appear. As the pieces suddenly slip into a new position, years of strain are released as an earthquake.

△ As the tension created by two plates rubbing together is released, shock waves ripple outwards from the hypocentre (A), causing an earthquake. The epicentre (B) is the point above where the waves hit the surface.

Tracking continents

The drifting continents can be tracked by flashing laser beams from them to orbiting satellites and measuring how long the beams take to reflect back to the ground. Typically, continents move at the same pace as your fingernails grow — a few centimetres every year.

▽ A nearby earthquake measuring over 7 on the Richter scale will damage the foundations of buildings, rupture pipes, tear cracks in roads and even topple skyscrapers.

▽ The surface of the Earth may roll and heave for many days following a quake as aftershocks reverberate through the rocks.

THE RESTLESS EARTH

◁ A row of cars in a basement parking bay in Northridge, California, is squashed as the building collapses in 1994 during a quake, measuring 7 on the Richter scale.

◁ The San Andreas Fault stretches like a giant scar across the Carrizo Plain between Los Angeles and San Francisco.

The most famous crack in the world

Californians are used to living with the possibility of earthquakes. Their state is split north to south by a huge crack in the Earth's surface – the San Andreas Fault. To the west of the fault lies the Pacific Plate which is moving northwards, grating past the great North American Plate.

Earthquake intensity

Earthquakes can be measured on two scales. The Richter scale measures the energy of the ground waves produced by an earthquake. The Mercalli scale monitors physical effects on the surface. At the bottom end of both scales, the tremors are scarcely noticeable. At 5 on the Mercalli scale, doors swing open and liquids spill. By 8, masonry starts crumbling, roads crack and walking is difficult.

Changing places

The motion across the San Andreas Fault adds up to 34 mm per year, although it is far from smooth. Geological evidence shows that the fault moves during some quakes by up to 12 metres at a time. In 1906, San Francisco was devastated by such a quake. At the present rate of movement, Los Angeles will be as far north in 10 million years' time as San Francisco is today.

◁ *Crowds gather in the streets of San Francisco on April 18, 1906, to survey the damage to their quake-struck city. Many people were afraid to return to what remained of their homes.*

▷ *Underground pipes are frequently ruptured during earthquakes. Here, a massive fireball erupts from a gas main near Los Angeles in 1994. Cracked water pipes often make it more difficult to extinguish the fires.*

THE RESTLESS EARTH

Earthquakes and People

Many small earthquakes happen every day. Big ones make headlines several times a year, and every so often an earthquake kills tens of thousands of people. No one knows precisely when a quake will happen, but we do have a good idea where. Some high-risk areas, such as California and Japan, are as well prepared as they can be. They have strict building codes, a well-educated public and emergency services which are constantly on alert. In Japan, some skyscrapers have heavy weights in the roof that can be quickly moved to cancel out the shaking during a quake. But in many earthquake-prone areas of Asia and South America, buildings are still poorly designed and there are few resources available to cope with a major earthquake.

△ *Devastating earthquakes this century include the San Francisco quake in 1906, the Kobe quake in Japan in 1995, and the Loma Prieta quake in California in 1989.*

▽ *A giant crane lifts cars and debris from under the toppled Hanshin expressway in Kobe, Japan, after the quake in January 1995.*

▽ *This aerial view of Kobe reveals the devastation caused by the quake which measured 7.2 on the Richter scale. Black smoke rises above burning buildings. Fires can often cause more damage than the earthquakes that start them.*

◁ **Richter below 3/Mercalli I**
Detected by seismographs, but not by people. Over 500,000 each year.

◁ **Richter 3-3.4/Mercalli II**
Detected by instrument and a few people. Delicate objects may shake.

◁ **Richter 3.5-4/Mercalli III-IV**
Obvious shaking felt indoors, walls creak, hanging items swing.

◁ **Richter 4.1-4.8/Mercalli V**
Felt by most people. Some windows may crack and loose objects fall over.

◁ **Richter 4.9-6/Mercalli VI-VII**
Felt by all. Furniture moves. People run outdoors. Some chimneys topple.

◁ **Richter 6.1-7/Mercalli VIII-IX**
General panic. Some houses collapse, roads crack and pipes rupture.

◁ **Richter 7.1-8.1/Mercalli X-XI**
Large cracks open up in the ground, landslides, few buildings remain.

◁ **Richter over 8.1/Mercalli XII**
Total destruction. The ground rises and falls in waves.

△ *The Richter and Mercalli scales plot the magnitude of earthquakes. The former measures wave energy, while the latter charts the effects.*

△ *Earthquake zones cluster along plate boundaries, which makes it possible to predict the location of earthquakes.*

Creating waves

By the time the San Andreas Fault reaches South America, it lies 200 km out at sea. This should be good news for the people living along the coast, but in May 1960, several big earthquakes along the fault line created one metre-high ripples in the ocean. As they travelled towards land, they grew to 10-metre-high *tsunamis*, or tidal waves. Three such waves hit the Chilean city of Valdiva, toppling buildings like sandcastles and tossing ships out of the harbour.

As safe as houses

Whether a building falls down in an earthquake depends on the strength and duration of the quake, and also on the building's design. In small buildings, flexible materials are better than rigid ones, and lightweight structures kill fewer people when they do fall. The most dangerous buildings are made of brick or stone, or have poor-quality reinforced concrete frames. They are often found in poorer countries.

Fire! Fire!

One of the greatest dangers during an earthquake is fire. Both in San Francisco in 1906 and Tokyo in 1923, more people died in fires than in the quakes themselves. Once fires start, they are often fuelled by cracked gas pipes. In San Francisco, 'smart pipes' are being developed that automatically shut off sections where a break is detected.

Urban dilemmas

When an earthquake strikes, the safest place to be is in flat, open countryside. The worst thing to do is panic. Nowadays, most people live in towns or cities, where falling glass and masonry outside can pose a real threat, so it is safer to stay indoors under strong structures such as stairways.

◁ *During the 1989 Loma Prieta quake, the flexible structure of the Golden Gate Bridge kept it standing, while more rigid bridges collapsed under the strain.*

THE RESTLESS EARTH

Prediction and Prevention

Long before the age of scientific instruments, people watched for early warnings of earthquakes. The Chinese still look out for traditional warning signs such as strange animal behaviour or sudden changes of water levels in wells. Using such indicators, the city of Haicheng was evacuated in 1975, hours before a massive earthquake, saving hundreds of thousands of lives. A year later, 240,000 people died in Tangshan, where no warnings were given. There are many signs of an imminent quake, but the most reliable indicator may be the pattern of seismic waves that travel through the ground.

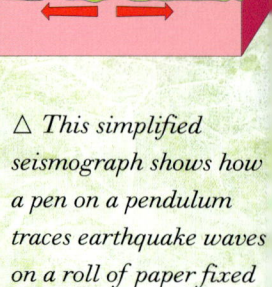

△ *This is the very first earthquake detector, made in China, AD132. Earth tremors caused one of the balls to fall into a frog's mouth.*

△ *This simplified seismograph shows how a pen on a pendulum traces earthquake waves on a roll of paper fixed firmly to the ground.*

High stakes!

Most big earthquakes are preceded by foreshocks. But nobody knows whether a minor earth tremor is an isolated event or the prelude to a major quake. From historical records, a big earthquake is predicted in the next 100 years — putting the chance of it occurring tomorrow at 1 in 36,500. However, the detection of minor tremors — suppose there are 10 of these a year — shortens the odds of a big quake in the next 24 hours to 1 in 1,000.

Real time warnings

Predicting earthquakes is difficult. But detecting them is easy. This fact was turned to an advantage in California, US, in 1989. Following the Loma Prieta earthquake, rescue workers were trying to free motorists trapped beneath a section of the Nimitz freeway. Debris was unstable and any aftershocks potentially devastating. At the focus of the quake, almost 100 km away, sensors transmitted a warning at the speed of light, so it reached the scene 25 seconds ahead of the shock waves, which travel at the speed of sound. This gave people time to scramble clear.

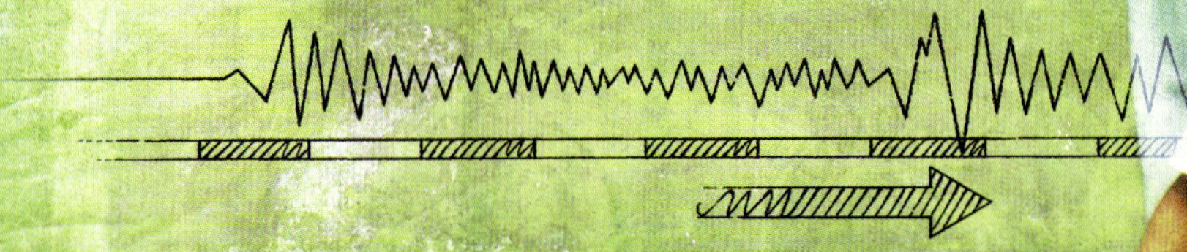

▽ *Tokyo school children, in fireproof headgear, emerge from their classrooms during a quake drill.*

△ *These Chinese government posters warn people of the strange animal behaviour to watch out for before an earthquake.*

THE RESTLESS EARTH

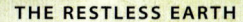

◁ John Milne designed the first practical seismograph when he lived in Japan. On retiring with his Japanese wife to Britain in 1895, he set up the world's first seismic monitoring headquarters.

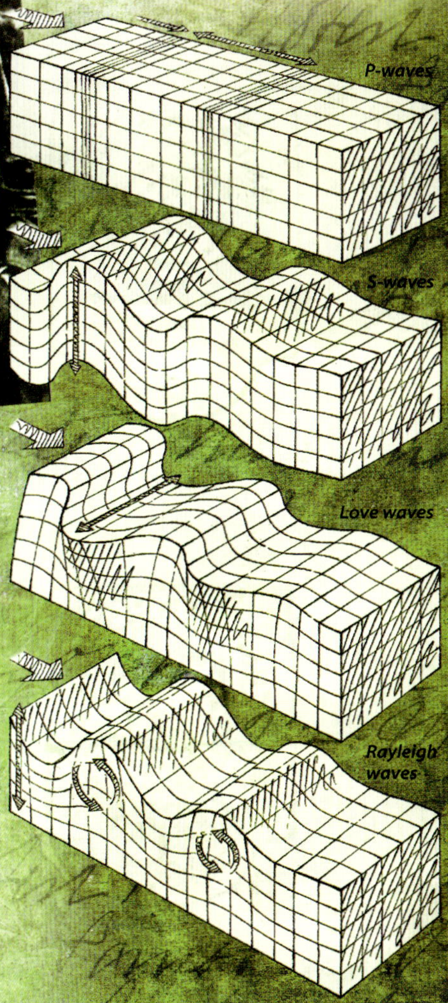

P-waves

S-waves

Love waves

Rayleigh waves

▷ There are two types of body wave produced in an earthquake – Primary (P-waves) and Secondary (S-waves). These travel from the focus under the ground to the surface by either compressing and stretching, or shearing from side to side. Love waves and Rayleigh waves are L-waves, which cause surface effects.

Oiling the joints

No one can stop the relentless drift of the continents, and this results in earthquakes. But it may be possible to stop a big earthquake by causing lots of little ones. The longer an active fault line goes without a quake, the bigger the quake is likely to be when it happens. So if a fault line can be kept moving, a big quake may be avoided. The idea is to lubricate faults and this has been tested on a small scale at an old desert oil field in the US. By pumping water down abandoned oil wells, minor earth tremors were triggered, but not in the places expected. This makes it unlikely that this trick will be repeated in a densely populated area!

▷ Laser beams shine out from this hilltop monitoring station near Parkfield in California. Timing the flashes as they bounce off a network of 18 reflectors on the other hills can reveal shifts of less than a millimetre over six kilometres.

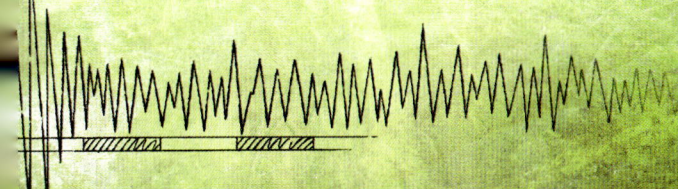

THE RESTLESS EARTH

Mountains

The mighty continents are continually colliding with one another, but like a well-designed vehicle, they have crumple zones which buckle under pressure. Although made of hard rock, the layers in the continental plates fold on impact like a rucked blanket, rising from the Earth's surface to form mountains. These collisions take place over millions of years, as if being played out in extremely slow motion. As each layer piles onto the next, the mountains grow into great ranges.

△ *These Jurassic limestone rocks at Stair Hole, on the south coast of England, are the result of Africa's collision with Europe 18 million years ago.*

Mountains in the making

The continents are still slowly colliding, and the newest ranges continue to rise. Just 18 millon years ago, Africa drove Italy like a ramrod into Europe, creating the Alps. The Himalayas rose 5 million years ago during India's collision with Asia, and are still rising. This range contains Mount Everest (8,848 m), the world's highest mountain.

The birth of the Himalayas

Around 65 million years ago, huge volcanic eruptions caused the Indian sub-continent to split away from the other southern continents and to head northwards, pushing the great Tethys Ocean ahead of it. The dense ocean floor was pushed under Asia while the lighter seabed sediment was scooped up and squeezed between the continents, rising up like a multi-layered cake to become part of the Himalayan range.

△ *Standing 4,808 metres high, Mount Blanc in the French Alps shows how much rock can be thrown up by an intercontinental collision.*

THE RESTLESS EARTH

Ancient collisions

The Himalayas and the Alps are the results of the most recent mountain-building activity. But there is also plenty of evidence of more ancient continental collisions. North America's Appalachian chain, eastern Greenland, the highlands of northern Scandinavia, and parts of Scotland were once joined in a huge range, the result of a collision that took place over 250 million years ago.

Completing the cycle

What goes up must come down, as the saying goes, and the Earth's crust records the history of a constant battle between the uplift of mountain-building and the forces of weathering and gravity. Little by little, the mountains crumble and, carried by rivers and glaciers, the sediment returns to the oceans. There it settles, only to be scooped up again several hundred million years later as a new mountain range is formed. And so the cycle continues.

◁ *The Himalayas continue to grow upwards. But the taller a mountain, the more prone it is to landslides and erosion. After they stop growing, these mountains will eventually be reduced to the size of hills.*

△ *The Indian subcontinent heads north, 35 to 45 million years ago (1). Ocean sediments are scooped up and the ocean crust is forced under Tibet (2). The continents finally meet 5 million years ago, creating the Himalayas (3).*

AIR AND WATER

The Wind

If left to itself, the air in the Earth's atmosphere would not change in pressure or temperature. But it is not left to itself. The Earth revolves, the Sun rises and sets, ocean currents warm or cool the air, clouds gather and scatter and mountains block the way. All this powers the atmosphere like a giant dynamo. As pockets of air become warm and expand, their pressure increases. This fuels winds which then blow to regions of lower pressure. At times, a wind can become so intense that it spins itself into a tornado or carves up the surface of the planet.

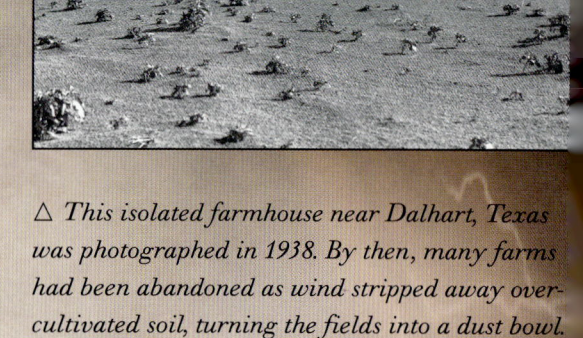

△ *When two wind systems travelling at different speeds and in different directions clash, a tornado ensues. As the storm begins to spin, a funnel of warm air descends to the ground and a spiralling updraft sucks up debris.*

△ *This isolated farmhouse near Dalhart, Texas was photographed in 1938. By then, many farms had been abandoned as wind stripped away over-cultivated soil, turning the fields into a dust bowl.*

Carved with sand

Air by itself may not seem like a powerful force, but when the wind whips up sand, it can cut like a chisel. Desert landscapes are almost entirely sculpted by wind. As well as carving rocks, the wind can pile sand up into dunes hundreds of metres high which advance slowly, engulfing villages and pasture.

Dust bowl

Away from desert sands, the soil is usually held fast by vegetation. But careless farming practices can change all that. In the Midwest of the US, it took centuries for prairie plants to evolve that could withstand the region's droughts and strong winds. Yet, within decades of the arrival of settlers, new crops and overgrazing had created a vast dust bowl.

Twister!

The most violent of all wind storms are tornadoes. They can reach speeds of 480 km/h, yet can last less than 30 seconds and strike in a small area. They usually form inside thunderclouds, as fast-moving warm air meets slower-moving cold air. Cars, houses, and even people may be picked up like toys in the vortex and flung far away.

△ *Bryce Canyon National Park in Utah, US, is a jagged, wind-eroded landscape. Great columns of rock have been carved over time by windblown sand, leaving needles of harder rock behind.*

Tearing across the states

'Tornado Alley' in the US Midwest earned its name because hundreds of tornadoes strike the area each year as hot, humid air from the Gulf of Mexico hits cold, dry, polar air from Canada. In April 1965, 37 tornadoes tore through six states for nine hours, killing 271 people and injuring 3,000.

AIR AND WATER

The Weather

While the climate is all about the broad changes that occur from season to season and year to year in different regions of the world, the weather concerns local variations, from day to day and hour to hour. The world's weather systems are driven by the Sun which transforms our planet into a global solar-powered heat engine. Constantly warmed by the Sun, especially near the equator, air is pushed around the planet – it is this movement that creates weather. The world has three major circulation cells, systems where hot air rises continuously, cools and then descends. The first of these, the Hadley cell, is located over the equator. Hot air rises from this central band, moves to the north and south, then loses heat and drops. The second cell is found over the Tropics and the third over polar zones.

△ *A satellite wind-speed map of the Pacific shows slow winds in blue, medium-speed winds in pink and purple, and winds over 44 km/h in red and orange.*

The front line

Weather is governed by regions of low or high pressure which form when masses of cold and warm air meet. When warm air rises, it leaves a low pressure hole, which is then filled by cold air. This is called a cold front. As the warm air rises, it also cools. The water vapour it holds condenses into clouds and the system starts to rotate. Each of these stages brings different weather.

Land and sea

The land and the sea have a major influence on the weather. When warm air passes over the ocean, it picks up moisture. If the warm air rises above the land during the day, it will draw in air from the sea, creating sea breezes. Then, as the air moves inland it passes over mountains or hills, where it cools. This causes clouds to form and eventually the moisture falls as rain or snow. In Asia, monsoons are caused by hot air rising over the Himalayas.

△ *High in the atmosphere, where there is no friction with the surface of the Earth, jet streams blow around the rotating globe. This jet stream is shown by a line of high-altitude cirrus clouds.*

44

△ *Modern meteorology uses readings from an international network of land-based weather stations, atmospheric balloons and space satellites. Research aircraft such as this C130, nicknamed* Snoopy, *can fly into storm clouds and measure conditions at the heart of the storm.*

When the wind blows

Sometimes, in late summer when tropical sea temperatures are at their highest, hundreds of storm systems come together and rotate in a great low pressure system known as a hurricane. As the wind speed picks up, a hurricane will tend to move away from the equator, gathering force and whipping up high waves in the sea until it meets the coast, often with devastating results.

DIY forecasting

Anyone can forecast the weather. Simply look at what sort of day it is today and predict exactly the same for tomorrow. In mid-latitudes you will be right about 70 per cent of the time. But of course you will never predict the times when the weather changes. To do that, you need to observe the weather on one day in thousands of different places, understand the processes at work and calculate all the interactions that are likely to take place.

Predicting the unpredictable

Meteorologists enlist the help of supercomputers to forecast the weather. Using data from weather stations around the world they calculate what will happen up to ten days ahead. Even so, they are often wrong. This is because of tiny, unpredictable changes that eventually have dramatic effects somewhere else in the world.

△ *These light aircraft were overturned and tossed into trees by powerful winds of over 160 km/h during Hurricane Gilbert, which struck Kingston, Jamaica in September 1988.*

45

AIR AND WATER

Weird Weather

The weather must be the most widely discussed natural phenomenon on the Earth. Usually, people are complaining about the cold, heat, drought or rain. In fact, our climate is remarkably constant and hospitable when compared to the extremes of heat and cold on Venus and Mars, or the 1,800 kilometre per hour winds on Saturn. Most of the surface of the Earth is a few degrees above the freezing point of water. Without that constancy, life on the planet would not continue so easily. Even so, the Earth's weather does create some strange, varied and often beautiful phenomena.

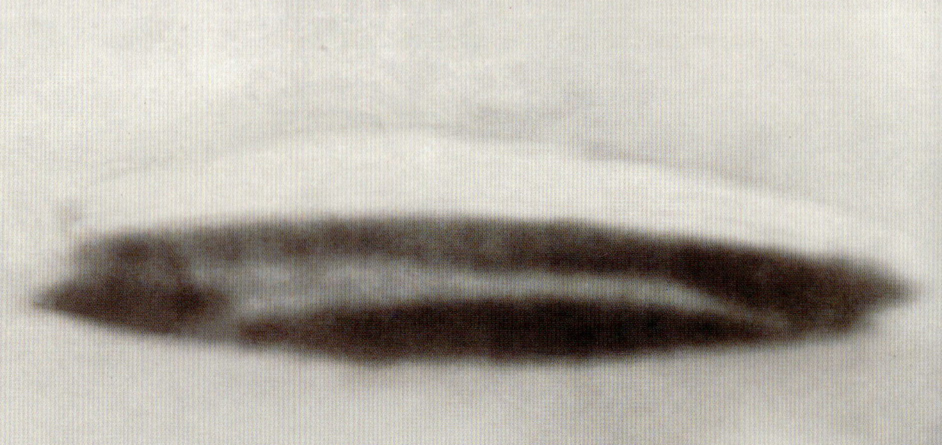

▷ *These may look like flying saucers, but in fact they are lenticular cloud formations photographed in Brazil in 1969.*

△ *This is one of many buildings in the French Pyrenees damaged when hailstones the size of tennis balls fell in June 1991.*

The clear light of day

Light waves of all colours shine from the Sun, but air molecules scatter mostly blue light, so the sky appears to be blue. When the Sun sets, its light travels through the dusty lower atmosphere which scatters more red light, making the sky look red. Light also travels at different speeds through air of different temperatures. Where cold air hangs above a layer of hot air, the light is bent and a heat haze is created. Occasionally, this will also magnify the image of a distant scene so that it appears as a mirage.

◁ *Layers of air of different temperatures spread light to produce this double image of an island. This sort of mirage is called a* fata morgana.

AIR AND WATER

▽ *On crossing mountains, layers of air rise, then fall to create a series of waves. As water condenses around each wave, layers of cloud are formed.*

Flying colours
Falling raindrops can act like tiny lenses and will scatter white light into its spectrum of colours. So, if the Sun is shining on a showery day, we may see a rainbow. Anyone searching for gold at the rainbow's end will have a hard task since, were it not for the horizon getting in the way, a rainbow would form a circle and have no end. Sometimes a rainbow-like halo is visible around the Moon. This type of aura occurs when light is bent by ice crystals high in the atmosphere.

Raining cats and dogs
Occasionally, air currents keep hailstones in freezing clouds for so long that they grow to be several centimetres in diameter and cause considerable damage when they fall. There are also isolated cases of ice-blocks several metres wide hitting the Earth. Sometimes, very strange things have been known to have dropped from the sky, including beans, fish and frogs. The best explanation is that they were sucked up by tornadoes.

Thunder and lightning
During a thunderstorm, positive charges build up at the top of a storm cloud and negative charges collect at the base. Sometimes, the voltage is so high that the charge 'jumps' in a bolt of electric lightning, either to the next cloud, or to the ground. The heat of the lightning causes the air to expand so rapidly that it lets out a huge crack of thunder. The force of lightning can split trees, set fire to buildings and kill people.

▽ *Circles of flattened crops can seem mysterious, but many are hoaxes. Others may be caused by mini whirlwinds.*

AIR AND WATER

The Climate

Although the weather in a region may vary from day to day, and from season to season, there is almost always a cycle that is repeated each year. The average weather an area experiences, season by season, year by year, gives us a measure of its climate. Meteorologists take into account temperature, rainfall, air pressure, sunshine, humidity and many other factors. Places around the Earth with similar climates can be grouped into nine distinct climate zones. These range from cold polar lands, to warm, wet equatorial regions, to hot, dry desert areas.

△ *Tree rings can reveal much about the story of our climate. In a warm year the rings that are laid down around the trunk are broad. Other years, when frosts are severe, there is less growth and the rings are thin.*

▽ *Rock carvings found deep in the Sahara Desert suggest that 7,000 years ago this area had enough rainfall to support humans and animals.*

The warming Sun

Climate is largely dependent upon the amount of the Sun's heat that reaches the Earth's surface. The Earth's rotational axis, running between the North and South Poles, is tilted towards the Sun – it is this that gives us the seasons. Depending on the angle of the Earth to the Sun, the areas closest to the poles receive different amounts of sunlight – so there are cold, dark winters and warm, light summers. The equator receives nearly the same amount of heat all year round and as a result its temperature varies very little.

Ocean currents

The Earth's climate zones are also affected by the oceans. The sea absorbs much of the Sun's heat, and ocean currents spread this to other areas. This is why the winter climate of Britain, in the warm Gulf Stream, is milder than that of Newfoundland, Canada, even though they are on the same latitude. Away from the heat-storing oceans, the interiors of continents always have more extreme temperatures.

Global greenhouse

Although a lot of the Sun's heat is absorbed by the land and sea, some of it is reflected back into space. But gases in the Earth's atmosphere act like the glass in a greenhouse and stop much of the heat from escaping. This greenhouse effect is responsible for fears about global warming, but it is also essential to life. Without it, most of the Earth would be about −15°C. Ice would cover the planet and there would be no life.

AIR AND WATER

△ *The world can be divided into nine main climate zones. They are polar* (mauve), *subpolar* (light blue), *temperate* (light green), *subtropical* (orange), *desert* (yellow), *tropical* (dark green), *equatorial* (dark blue), *subpolar* (pink), *mediterranean* (red).

Sunspots

Sunspots, the dark patches on our star's surface, appear to have an effect on the Earth's climate. Between 1450 and 1800, sunspots were entirely absent. This coincided with a period that has been called the 'Little Ice Age' during which the River Thames in England froze over in winter and frost fairs were held on the ice.

◁ *Climate shapes our planet and determines the landscape, vegetation and wildlife of each region.*

△ *All three forms of water – ice, liquid and vapour – are found on the Earth. Together, they help provide a climate that is just right for life.*

Climate change

Alternating periods of hot and cold weather reach back through the history of our planet. Before the recent ice ages began 3.25 million years ago, for 250 million years it was consistently warmer than at present. Prior to this long period, there was a 100-million-year freeze. Changing carbon dioxide levels, volcanic activity or events beyond the Earth were all possible causes for these changes in climate.

49

AIR AND WATER

Climate Threat

Since 1958, scientists have been monitoring the amount of carbon dioxide in the atmosphere from an observatory high on a mountain in Hawaii. They have found that the concentration of the gas has been rising every year. It is now thought that this is primarily due to the burning of fossil fuels such as coal and oil. But extensive forest clearance also releases carbon dioxide and makes the problem worse by removing trees that would otherwise soak it up. Overall, human activity is adding about 8 billion tonnes of carbon to the atmosphere each year, together with lesser amounts of other greenhouse gases such as methane, nitrogen oxides and CFCs.

△ *This image of Ferrybridge power station in England has been coloured to highlight the sulphur dioxide in the smoke.*

▽ *An aerial shot of the Brazilian rainforest reveals the extent of human damage. The forest shows up pink; areas cleared for agriculture are blue and green. The orange patch is a rainstorm washing away soil where the vegetation has been cleared.*

A global trend

Although temperatures vary from year to year, on average the Earth has been getting increasingly warmer over the past century. There is mounting evidence that this is due to the large quantities of greenhouse gases in the atmosphere. If greenhouse gas emissions continue at the current rate, temperatures will probably continue to rise, and the consequence could be a dramatic change in climate.

Predictions for the future

To find out what might happen to the climate in the future, meteorologists build models in supercomputers, rather like those used to forecast the weather. Most of their findings indicate that the world's overall temperature is likely to warm by two-and-a-half degrees during this century.

Climate change

The effect of such a temperature rise may be profound. Deserts would probably become drier and coastal regions would grow stormier. The warm Atlantic Gulf Stream that brings heat from the Caribbean to western Europe would probably be disrupted too. Arctic water would not be cold enough to sink and return the flow south, like a conveyor belt. The circulation would stop and Europe would actually get colder.

AIR AND WATER

△ *During an El Niño event* (top), *warm waters* (shown in purple) *reach the coast of South America* (right) *and prevent the cold nutrient-rich waters* (shown in blue) *from rising. Normally* (bottom), *an upwelling of cold water occurs and the winds push the warm waters east, towards Australia* (left).

Facing the consequences

The world's climate has, of course, changed in the past. The difference now is that human activity probably is responsible for the change, and humans – not dinosaurs – must face the consequences.

◁ *Greenhouse gases in the atmosphere insulate the Earth and prevent heat from escaping, raising the planet's surface temperature.*

El Niño

There is one ocean current that is already causing chaos with the world's weather. El Niño occurs when westerly winds reverse an ocean current in the South Pacific. This causes an accumulation of warm water off South America, and prevents the arrival of the cold, nutrient-rich waters that are needed to sustain wildlife in the region. As a result of El Niño there are droughts and storms around the globe.

△ *When slash-and-burn farmers move into an area they do just that, clearing forests, burning the timber and releasing carbon dioxide into the atmosphere.*

AIR AND WATER

Water Power

The Earth is the only planet we know of where water exists in all three forms – ice, liquid and vapour. And in each of these states, water holds a tremendous power, both creative and destructive. Water is responsible for circulating the Sun's heat around the planet. Solar energy lifts vast quantities of water from the oceans to the mountains by vaporizing it, which causes it to rise. As it cools, the vapour condenses into the tiny droplets that make up clouds from where it falls to the ground as rain or snow. The rain becomes the rushing torrents of mountain streams and rivers. These are powerful forces which sculpt the landscape into hills, valleys and plains and carry rock particles back into the sea.

△ *Acidic rainwater has eroded limestone by dissolving it, leaving these towering rock formations in China.*

The great leveller

A downpour of rain can wash away huge quantities of sand and stone in one go. As the water races downhill, it chisels away at the rock, so eventually, over thousands of years, great V-shaped valleys are carved out. Once clear of the hills, the river slows and drops its sediment, creating a new path for itself. Some sediment is carried all the way to the sea, where it settles to form a wide, fan-shaped delta.

Dissolving rocks

It is not just the physical force of water that cuts into rock. As it falls through the air, rain dissolves carbon dioxide to become weakly acidic. This particularly effects limestone rock, which is dissolved by this type of rain. Over many years, whole networks of caverns and passages are carved out of hillsides. As the water flows, now saturated with dissolved calcium carbonate, it deposits this to form stalactites and stalagmites.

▽ *Clusters of stalactites slowly grow when water, saturated with dissolved limestone, drips from the cave roof. These may eventually reach to the floor.*

▷ *As it leaves the mountain, the speed and cutting power of the river decreases and it deposits soil across the plains, creating fertile lands in which to grow crops.*

52

AIR AND WATER

Wave power

The awesome power of water flowing down towards the sea is matched only by the power of the water in the sea itself. Each metre of an exposed coastline receives about 50 kilowatts of continuous power in the form of waves. Picking up stones, then dragging them back again, waves constantly erode coastlines. Although wave power generators exist, none has been able to survive the destructive force of the sea. So far, no one has yet managed to harness wave power economically.

▷ *Water, warmed by the Sun, evaporates and rises into the atmosphere. The water vapour cools, forms clouds and falls as rain or snow. The force of gravity makes the water flow downwards and over many years it shapes the landscape.*

▷ *The Grand Canyon was cut into the dry rocks of Arizona, US, by the Colorado River. The system of canyons stretches for over 300 km and reaches a depth of 1,600 m in places. It slices through rock, some of which is 500 million years old.*

AIR AND WATER

Floods and Droughts

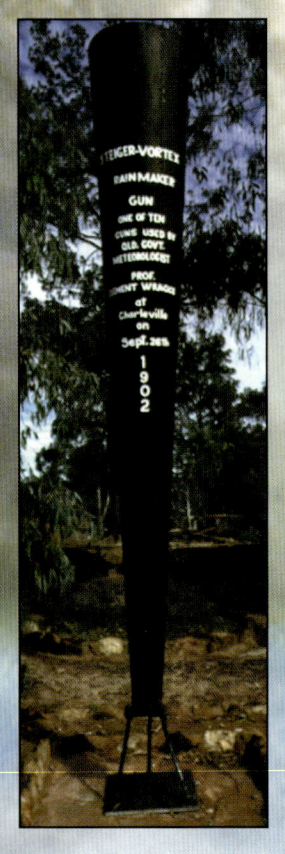

Human life is dependent on water. We need it to drink and to irrigate our crops, and we harness its power to generate electricity. But if we lose control of our water supplies, if we find that we have either too much water, or not enough, the effects can be devastating. The world's oceans contain over one billion cubic kilometres of water. All the rivers, lakes and clouds contain just 0.03 per cent of that. Yet, a river in flood or a dried up river can mean the difference between life and death. Floodwaters can come from any direction – from above in exceptional rainfall, from a burst dam or in a freak storm from the sea.

△ Huge guns were once used to fire dust into clouds, in a failed attempt to trigger rain over parched areas of Australia.

Upsetting nature

In the natural scheme of things, a river will meander across its broad flood-plain, depositing fine sediment to make rich, fertile soil. But humans prefer rivers that stay in one place and build banks to constrain them. Mud becomes deposited on the riverbed and the riverbanks have to be built higher. Eventually, the river is raised up above the towns and farmland on its flood-plain. If heavy rain occurs, the river may burst its banks, flooding great expanses of land.

△ Dams hold water to supply homes and fields, or to generate electricity. But a small crack in a dam wall can be catastrophic. The force of water behind it will turn a hairline crack into a giant hole in minutes. The result is a wall of water released into the valley below.

◁ A Sudanese farmer looks in despair at his parched land. The failure of the rains means that his family could starve.

Storm surge

On February 1, 1953, storm winds and high tides combined to drive a wedge of water down the North Sea onto the coasts of eastern England, Holland and Belgium. Coastal communities were devastated, Dutch dykes were breached and the sea swept 60 kilometres inland. For Europe, this was exceptional, but in Bangladesh such flooding is a regular occurrence, causing homelessness and disease on a massive scale.

Drought damage

Excessive rain in one place is often balanced by drought in another. Many semi-arid countries rely on tiny amounts of rainfall to sustain crops. Their lands can only support a small population and are already overcrowded. When the rains fail entirely for a year or more, the result can be famine.

Future sea levels

If global warming melts the ice caps and destabilizes the western Antarctic ice shelf, the oceans could rise by more than ten metres. Even a one-metre rise in sea level would threaten low-lying coral islands such as the Maldives, as well as countries like Bangladesh and Holland. A bigger rise in sea level could easily leave New York, Bombay, London and Sydney under water.

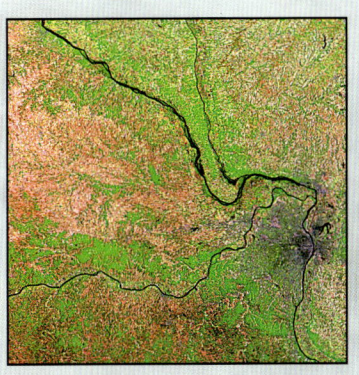

△ *Just north of St Louis, US,* (shown in pink and purple) *the Missouri and Illinois Rivers flow into the great Mississippi.*

△ *In July 1993, the Mississippi River burst its banks* (shown in blue and black), *flooding an extensive part of the city.*

AIR AND WATER

Lands of Ice

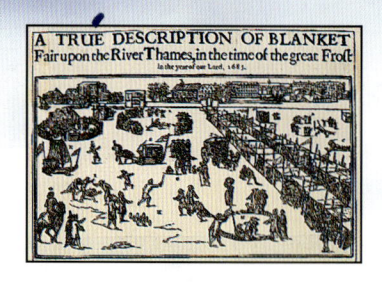

△ *Between 1645 and 1715, Europe experienced extreme winters in a period known as the 'Little Ice Age'. This engraving, from 1683, shows a frost fair held on the River Thames.*

One of the strangest features of the world that we inhabit is ice. No other substance has a solid form which is less dense than the liquid form. To put it another way, ice floats. So, when the temperature drops and the sea begins to freeze, the ice is on top of the ocean, not underneath it. That is good news for life, since the ice creates an insulating layer which prevents the rest of the sea from freezing. In past ice ages, notably one about 700 million years ago, when sea ice stretched to the equator, life would have died out had the oceans frozen solid. The effects of ice on land are different. As water expands to become ice, it can shatter a rocky landscape, and a large ice sheet can even push down a whole continent.

Waiting for an ice age?

Throughout the Earth's history, the temperature has fluctuated many times, perhaps due to changes in the Sun's activity or continental drift. The polar caps that exist today are a remnant of the last ice age, which began 3.25 million years ago. Since then, the northern ice sheet has advanced four times to cover large areas of North America and northern Europe. We may still be in an interglacial period today, waiting for the ice to advance once more.

Secrets in the ice

The polar ice caps carry clues to the past. By drilling out cores of ice, scientists can reconstruct the Earth's history. The thickness of the layers gives clues to the snowfall. Dust and chemicals in the ice keep a record of recent pollution and ancient volcanic eruptions. Trapped within the ice are tiny bubbles of the ancient atmosphere.

Rivers of ice

Although solid, ice can slowly deform and flow. Vast areas of the Antarctic ice sheet are in motion, carrying thick slabs of ice from regions of high snowfall downhill towards the sea. Once there, they eventually melt and are washed by the tides until giant icebergs break off, some of them as big as a small country. In mountainous regions, the snow packs harder and harder into ice, forming glaciers which flow down valleys, gouging out the rock as they go.

△ *Where a glacier meets the sea, there is a constant battle between ice and water. Sometimes avalanches of ice break off and crash into the sea, as has happened with this glacier in Alaska, US.*

△ When a glacier finally retreats from the landscape, it leaves deep U-shaped valleys, some so deep that they are flooded by the sea, creating fjords like this one in Norway.

▷ Like a frozen river, a glacier flows slowly through a rocky landscape shattered by ice. Lines of rocky debris build upon its surface as it gouges out a deep valley.

△ Air and water can sculpt icebergs into complex shapes. But 90 per cent of a berg is underwater, as ships such as the Titanic have found to their cost.

LIFE STORY

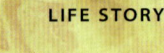

Changing Times

If the mighty continents are only the scum on the surface of our vast planet, sedimentary rocks seem even less substantial. They are literally the dust of ages, accumulated on the ocean floor then lifted up into mountain ranges. Yet, these rocks represent the history book of the planet, and within their pages, their layers, the story of life is told. The story is spelled out by fossils, but it is only in the last 100 years that we have started to understand them, and so have been able to read the story. Before then, our ancestors must have wondered what these strange shapes were. Perhaps they had grown inside the rock? Many Christians believed that they were the remains of creatures that had died in the Biblical flood.

△ *What events caused animals to either die out or alter dramatically? Was there a great flood after all?*

The fossil hunters

In the nineteenth century, William Smith, a surveyor, realized that similar layers of rock containing similar fossils occurred in different places, and that the sequence of layers was always the same. Sir Charles Lyell, now seen as the father of geology, argued that, because rocks formed at the same rate they do today, deep layers of sedimentary rock must be millions of years old.

Learning to read

As they looked closer, early geologists noticed that some of the fossil forms seemed to change subtly from layer to layer. If each layer was like a new page in the story of life, it appeared that the story was also divided into chapters. Between each chapter, there were clearly great changes in the creatures that inhabited the Earth. At last, they were able to recognize each chapter heading – the geological periods. The question remained as to what caused these changes.

▽ *By the time creatures such as this fish were swimming in the Earth's oceans, the planet was around four billion years old. Yet, the proliferation and diversification of life was only just beginning.*

Numbering the pages

For many years, people have tried to estimate the age of the Earth. In 1650, an Irish bishop decided that the Creation occurred in 4004BC. By examining rocks, Victorian geologists thought that it was 20 million years old, a sensational suggestion at the time. Now, using radioactivity readings, we can put a much more accurate date on the rock layers of our 4.5 billion-year-old planet.

Ancient clues

For a long time, geologists believed that fossils were animals that had been turned to stone. We now know that even if this is not true, quite often the original molecules of life are still preserved in rock. Although it is not yet possible to recreate these creatures in a real-life Jurassic Park, they do give us invaluable clues to evolution.

△ *Around one billion years ago, as the oxygen increased in the atmosphere, tiny animals started to evolve.*

◁ *During the Ordovician period, about 450 million years ago, the first animals were crawling onto the land to feed off the newly established plants.*

▽ *It was only about one million years ago that our human ancestors began to develop larger brains and the ability to use tools.*

LIFE STORY

The Dawn of Life

No one knows how life on the Earth began. Present-day life-forms seem far too complex and dependent on each other to have come into being spontaneously. But there are some new clues to suggest how and where life might have first arisen. Direct evidence in the fossil record is sparse, but research into chemical systems that can organize themselves, the discovery of new habitats where life can survive extreme conditions and studies of the genetic relationships of living organisms are all changing our understanding. In 1952, a chemist named Stanley Miller put methane, ammonia and hydrogen gases – thought to be components of the Earth's early atmosphere – into a flask containing some water. Through them, he sparked an electrical discharge to simulate lightning. By the next day, the flask contained amino acids, the building blocks of all life.

△ Charles Darwin's suggestion that humans had evolved from apes was greeted with a mixture of horror and ridicule.

▷ Darwin developed his theory of evolution as a result of observing finches on the Galapagos Islands. Their beaks had adapted to the type of food available on each island.

Building blocks

We now know that the early atmosphere was actually made up mostly of carbon dioxide and nitrogen, from which the chemicals of life form less easily. But they do form, and Stanley Miller's experiments began a whole new study into the chemical origins of life.

RNA world

There is a world of difference between a soup of organic chemicals and life itself. For life to get started, you need chemicals that can store information, reproduce and also have the ability to mutate. Today, most life-forms carry their information in genes made out of the chemical DNA. Although DNA would have had trouble reproducing on the young Earth, it may be possible for RNA, a simple version of DNA, to do so. Perhaps the start of life was an evolving chemical system based on RNA.

◁ *Stanley Miller used a flask to combine simple chemicals and electrical discharges in order to investigate the complex chemical origins of life.*

The early years

It is extremely difficult to read the history of life in rocks from the Precambrian, by far the longest period in the Earth's history. Nevertheless, microscopic traces of primitive bacteria and algae have been isolated. And, by the late Precambrian, there is evidence for much larger, multicellular organisms, which resemble jellyfish and worms.

▷ *Some of the chemical building blocks of life may have been seeded on the Earth in meteorites. This one is mostly made of iron, but others are rich in carbon – an essential component of all life.*

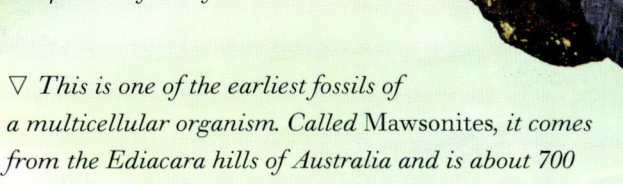

▽ *This is one of the earliest fossils of a multicellular organism. Called* Mawsonites, *it comes from the Ediacara hills of Australia and is about 700 million years old. It may have been a kind of jellyfish.*

Fire and ice

Four billion years ago, when life was beginning, the Sun was weak and the planet may have been icebound. If so, life may have begun around volcanic springs deep in the ocean, or in pockets under the ice. In places, cometary impacts may have melted the ice. Warm pools may have been life's birthplace, on a scaffolding of mineral grains.

Alien invaders

At the time that life was getting started, our planet was still under bombardment from space. So, life may have been destroyed and reborn many times. It is possible that life did not originate on the Earth at all, but came from space, carried on comets and meteorites.

LIFE STORY

Wonderful Life

Well-preserved sedimentary rocks older than 600 million years are seldom found, so fossils prior to this date are exceptionally rare. Because of this, little is known about life on the Earth before that period. After this time, however, the fossil record reveals that something quite spectacular happened on the planet. From the start of the Cambrian period, there is evidence that the Earth was suddenly teeming with multicellular life-forms. Most of the invertebrate groups in the world today also appear in fossils, alongside a wide variety of creatures that seem completely alien to us. This growth of new life was so rapid and diverse that it has been called the Cambrian explosion.

▷ *This small shellfish, a brachiopod called* Lingula, *is one of life's success stories. It has managed to survive almost unchanged for more than 500 million years. A present-day specimen is almost identical to those found fossilized within Cambrian rocks.*

A moment in time

Each of the many layers of shale and sandstone that survive from the Cambrian period is evidence of the past, recording what happened on the sea floor. We might see the ripple marks produced by currents of water, disrupted here and there by the tracks of soft-bodied creatures that have long since disappeared. By examining these tracks, we can determine the behaviours and lifestyles of these ancient animals.

△ *Trilobites were around for several hundred million years, swimming in shallow seas and burrowing in the mud. The trilobite's closest modern relative is the horseshoe crab.*

Meet the relatives

Much of our understanding of Cambrian life comes from the Burgess Shale in the Canadian Rockies. An amazing range of creatures has been found here and it is possible to recognize the relatives of crabs, insects, corals and worms that exist today. One creature, called *Pikaia*, looked like an animated anchovy fillet and could be our own ancestor.

Who's for dinner?

In one slab of rock, we can see the tracks of a trilobite, a predator that looked similar to an oversized woodlouse. The tracks lead up to the burrow of a small worm and you can still see where, one day 540 million years ago, the trilobite dug down into the burrow and had the unsuspecting worm for dinner.

Times of change

The fossil record shows that the course of evolution has been far from smooth and steady. Sometimes, there were great bursts of diversification, with hundreds of new species appearing over a short period. At other times, there were mass extinctions, probably caused by dramatic changes in the environment.

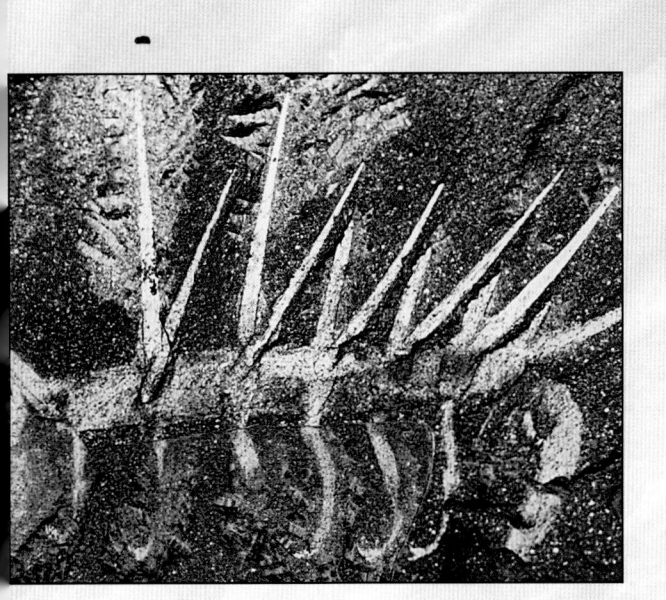

△ *This fossil creature from the Cambrian Burgess Shale seems so bizarre that it was named* Hallucigenia.

◁ *Many extraordinary creatures lived in the sea in the Cambrian period. Top left is* Opabina; *to its right,* Sanctocaris *and a jellyfish. Small arthropods feed off a dead trilobite on the left and along the bottom are sponges, corals and scaly creatures called* Wiwaxia. *Bottom right is the large crustacean* Canadaspis.

LIFE STORY

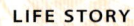

The Fossil Sky

For more than 500 million years, the Earth has been a generous host to life. But life has also changed the planet. Whether they are plants or animals, all living things are composed almost entirely of nutrients extracted from the earth and carbon from the atmosphere. Plants begin the process using sunshine to convert carbon dioxide and water into living matter. In consuming carbon, these organisms help keep the planet at a constant temperature. And when they die, they are re-absorbed into the earth to make new land and rock. Across the world, vast deposits of limestone and chalk are the end products of that process — they are, effectively, the ancient sky transformed into stone.

△ *Diatoms are tiny plant-like organisms that use carbon dioxide from the atmosphere for making food. The fossilized remains of these microscopic organisms form the rock diatomite.*

▷ *Carbon is the basis for all organic compounds including all living things and fossil fuels. Carbon is continuously recycled through the atmosphere, earth, plants and animals.*

△ *Deep-sea muds are often entirely formed from the tiny skeletons of microscopic organisms such as forams. They are also found in limestones and preserved in deep-water shales.*

Limestone

Many fossils are found in limestone, a sedimentary rock made from carbon, calcium and oxygen (calcium carbonate). There have been many periods in the world's history when thick deposits of limestone have formed. When there were no ice caps, higher sea levels and temperatures caused limestone to amass around the edges of continents and on flooded basins of land.

Carbon body-building

In these ancient shallow seas, the building materials of life were available in abundance. Vast quantities of calcium carbonate were used by microscopic organisms to build their intricate skeletons. The chalky White Cliffs of Dover, England, are made of the fossils of these creatures.

LIFE STORY

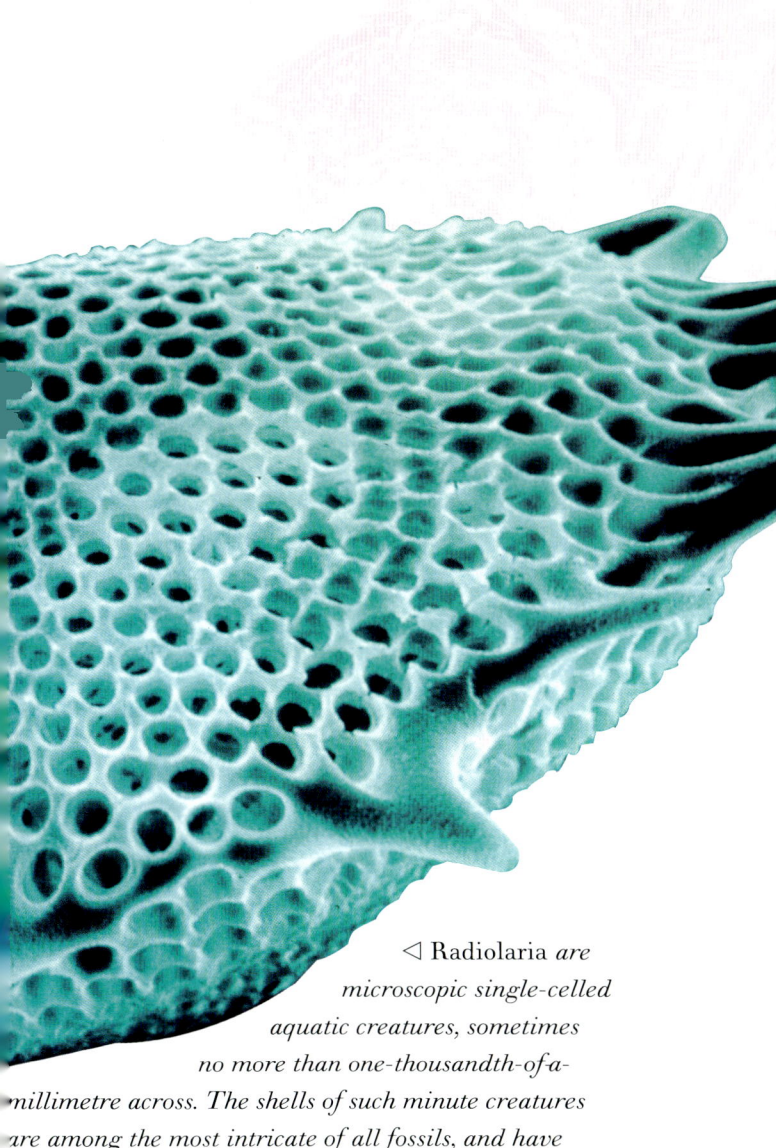

△ The shells of these fossil brachiopods are made of calcium carbonate, which originally derived from carbon in the atmosphere. Fossilization happens when an organism is buried and its bodily structures are slowly hardened by minerals such as silica and calcite.

◁ Radiolaria *are microscopic single-celled aquatic creatures, sometimes no more than one-thousandth-of-a-millimetre across. The shells of such minute creatures are among the most intricate of all fossils, and have complex structures of spikes, spindles and crevices.*

Climate control

If life did not consume carbon dioxide from the atmosphere, our climate might be more like that of Venus. There, a thick blanket of carbon dioxide traps the planet's heat and the surface temperature reaches 480°C. On the Earth, vast chalk cliffs and limestone mountains are reminders of just how much carbon has been turned into stone, ensuring that life has thrived.

Consumers of carbon

Larger organisms, such as corals and shellfish, make use of calcium carbonate to build themselves protective shields. Tiny plants, which feed on carbon dioxide, are eaten by copepods. These tiny animals then excreted the carbon into the sea.

Fossil formation

When an organism is buried in sediment, the soft parts start to decay, but the hard parts, like bones and shells, are often preserved. Compressed by layers of rock, other minerals penetrate the cracks and crevices and harden. The calcium carbonate structures that protected these creatures in life have helped them to survive as fossils.

▽ *In the past, people often identified fossils with mythical creatures. The curved shells of the oyster-like bivalve* Gryphaea, *found in many parts of Europe, were called 'devil's toenails'.*

LIFE STORY

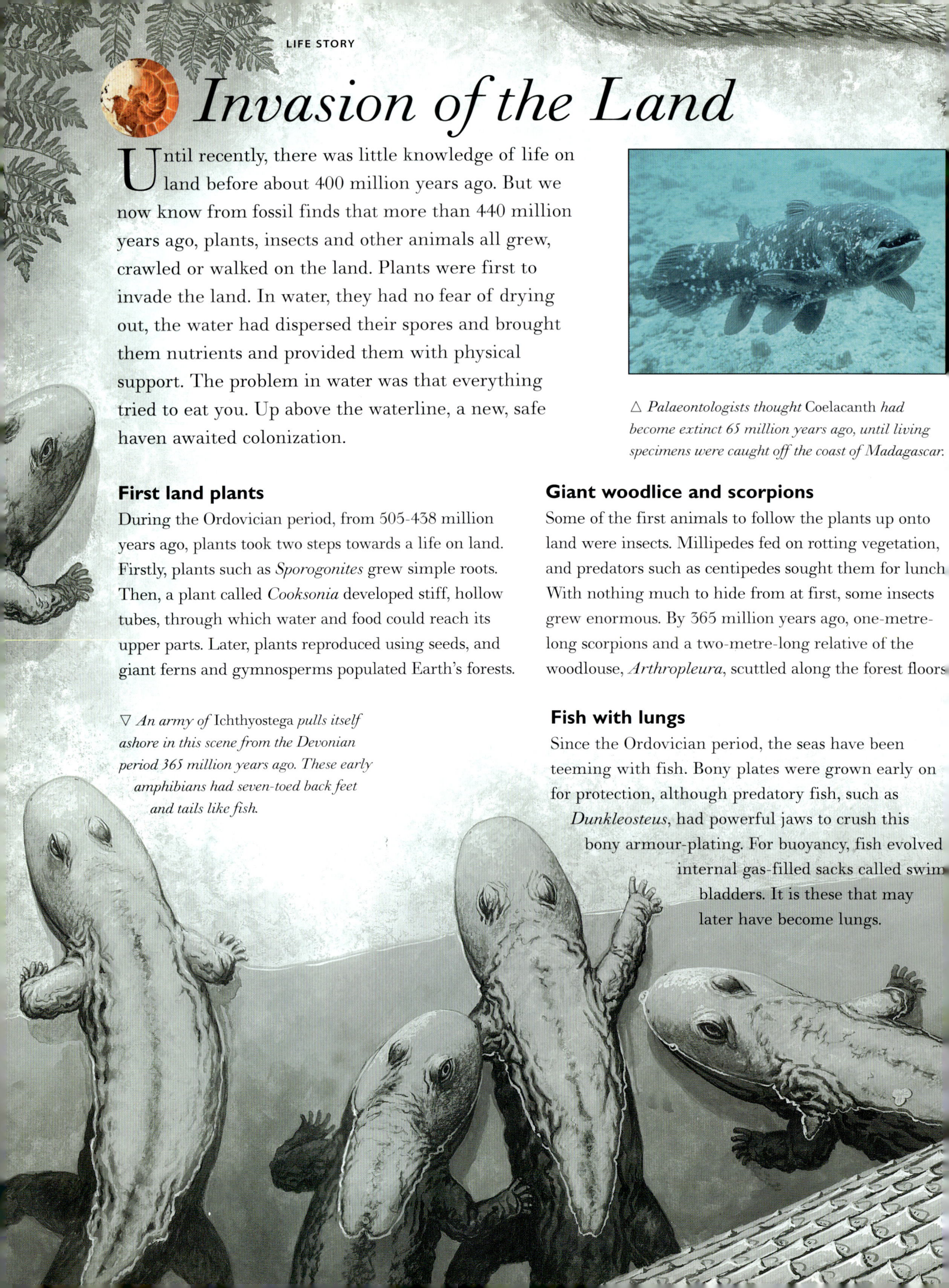

Invasion of the Land

Until recently, there was little knowledge of life on land before about 400 million years ago. But we now know from fossil finds that more than 440 million years ago, plants, insects and other animals all grew, crawled or walked on the land. Plants were first to invade the land. In water, they had no fear of drying out, the water had dispersed their spores and brought them nutrients and provided them with physical support. The problem in water was that everything tried to eat you. Up above the waterline, a new, safe haven awaited colonization.

△ *Palaeontologists thought* Coelacanth *had become extinct 65 million years ago, until living specimens were caught off the coast of Madagascar.*

First land plants

During the Ordovician period, from 505-438 million years ago, plants took two steps towards a life on land. Firstly, plants such as *Sporogonites* grew simple roots. Then, a plant called *Cooksonia* developed stiff, hollow tubes, through which water and food could reach its upper parts. Later, plants reproduced using seeds, and giant ferns and gymnosperms populated Earth's forests.

▽ *An army of* Ichthyostega *pulls itself ashore in this scene from the Devonian period 365 million years ago. These early amphibians had seven-toed back feet and tails like fish.*

Giant woodlice and scorpions

Some of the first animals to follow the plants up onto land were insects. Millipedes fed on rotting vegetation, and predators such as centipedes sought them for lunch. With nothing much to hide from at first, some insects grew enormous. By 365 million years ago, one-metre-long scorpions and a two-metre-long relative of the woodlouse, *Arthropleura*, scuttled along the forest floors.

Fish with lungs

Since the Ordovician period, the seas have been teeming with fish. Bony plates were grown early on for protection, although predatory fish, such as *Dunkleosteus*, had powerful jaws to crush this bony armour-plating. For buoyancy, fish evolved internal gas-filled sacks called swim bladders. It is these that may later have become lungs.

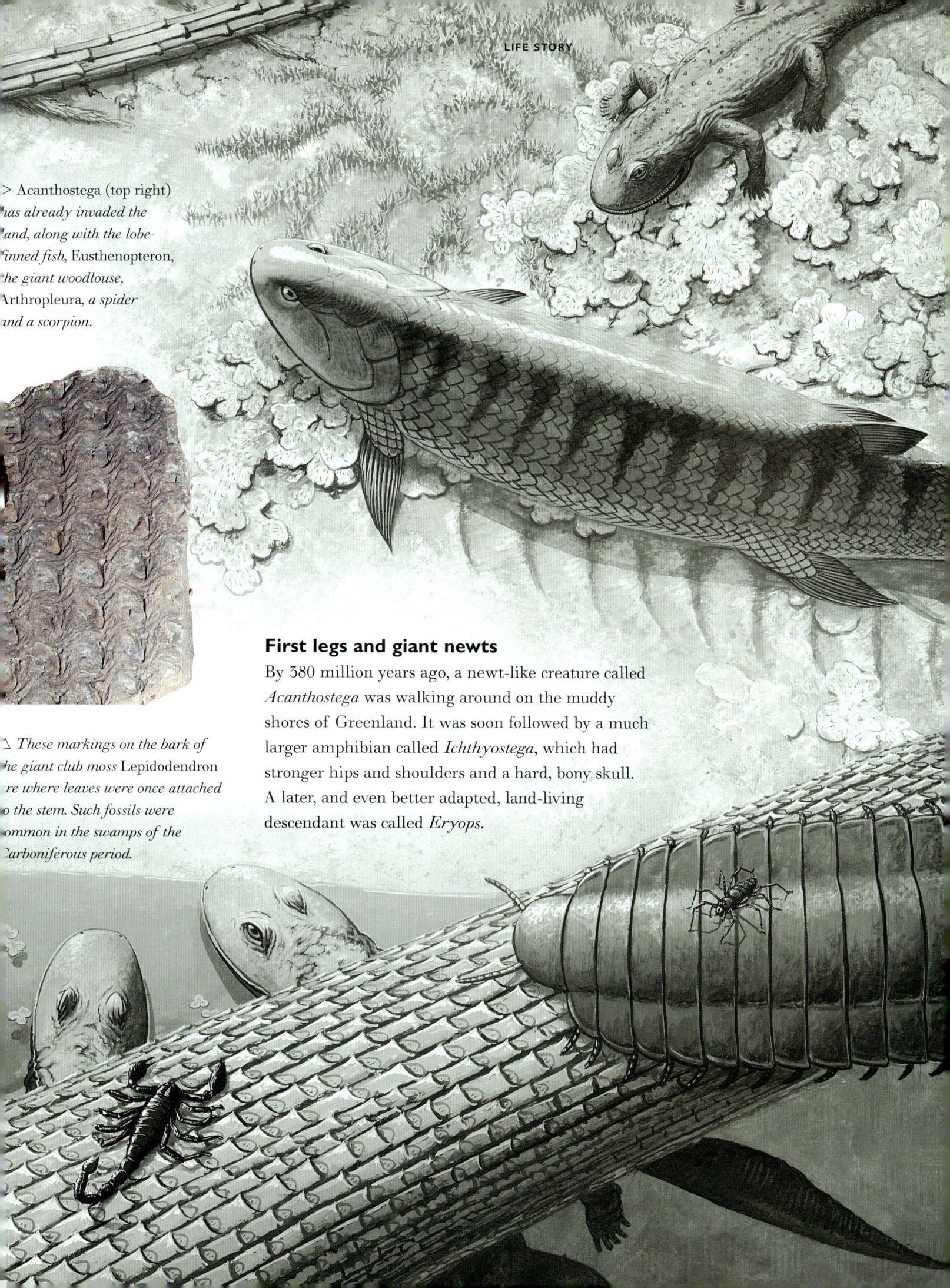

> Acanthostega (top right) has already invaded the land, along with the lobe-finned fish, Eusthenopteron, the giant woodlouse, Arthropleura, a spider and a scorpion.

△ These markings on the bark of the giant club moss Lepidodendron are where leaves were once attached to the stem. Such fossils were common in the swamps of the Carboniferous period.

First legs and giant newts

By 380 million years ago, a newt-like creature called *Acanthostega* was walking around on the muddy shores of Greenland. It was soon followed by a much larger amphibian called *Ichthyostega*, which had stronger hips and shoulders and a hard, bony skull. A later, and even better adapted, land-living descendant was called *Eryops*.

LIFE STORY

The Real Jurassic Park

By 205 million years ago, the great supercontinent of Pangaea had begun to break up. Between the continents of Laurasia to the north and Gondwanaland to the south, there was a new sea of warm, shallow water, the Tethys. There were no polar ice caps and the global climate was warm. This was the start of one of the most successful geological periods for life, and a period when dinosaurs became dominant. It was the real Jurassic Park.

△ *During the early 1800s, Mary Anning was frequently to be seen with her hammer along the Dorset cliffs near Lyme Regis, in England. She is said to have found her first ichthyosaur fossil at the age of 11.*

△ *These fossil bones make up one of the paddles or flippers of an ichthyosaur. The top (left) is made of fused limb bones, while the flexible part has evolved from the bones of the feet.*

Life in the sea

The Jurassic seas must have been thriving. A warm, tropical climate, plenty of nutrients, great blooms of plankton – all these provided rich pickings for larger life-forms. Jurassic limestones and shales lain down in those seas are full of fossil corals, sponges and shellfish – bivalves, gastropods and ammonites – as well as rarer fossils of reptiles and fish.

Sea monsters

Ichthyosaurs must have been the dominant predators in the sea. Although streamlined and similar to dolphins, they were not mammals, but reptiles. As were the long-necked plesiosaurs, with their powerful paddles and sharp teeth. Could it be that the legend of the Loch Ness monster is based on sightings of a living plesiosaur?

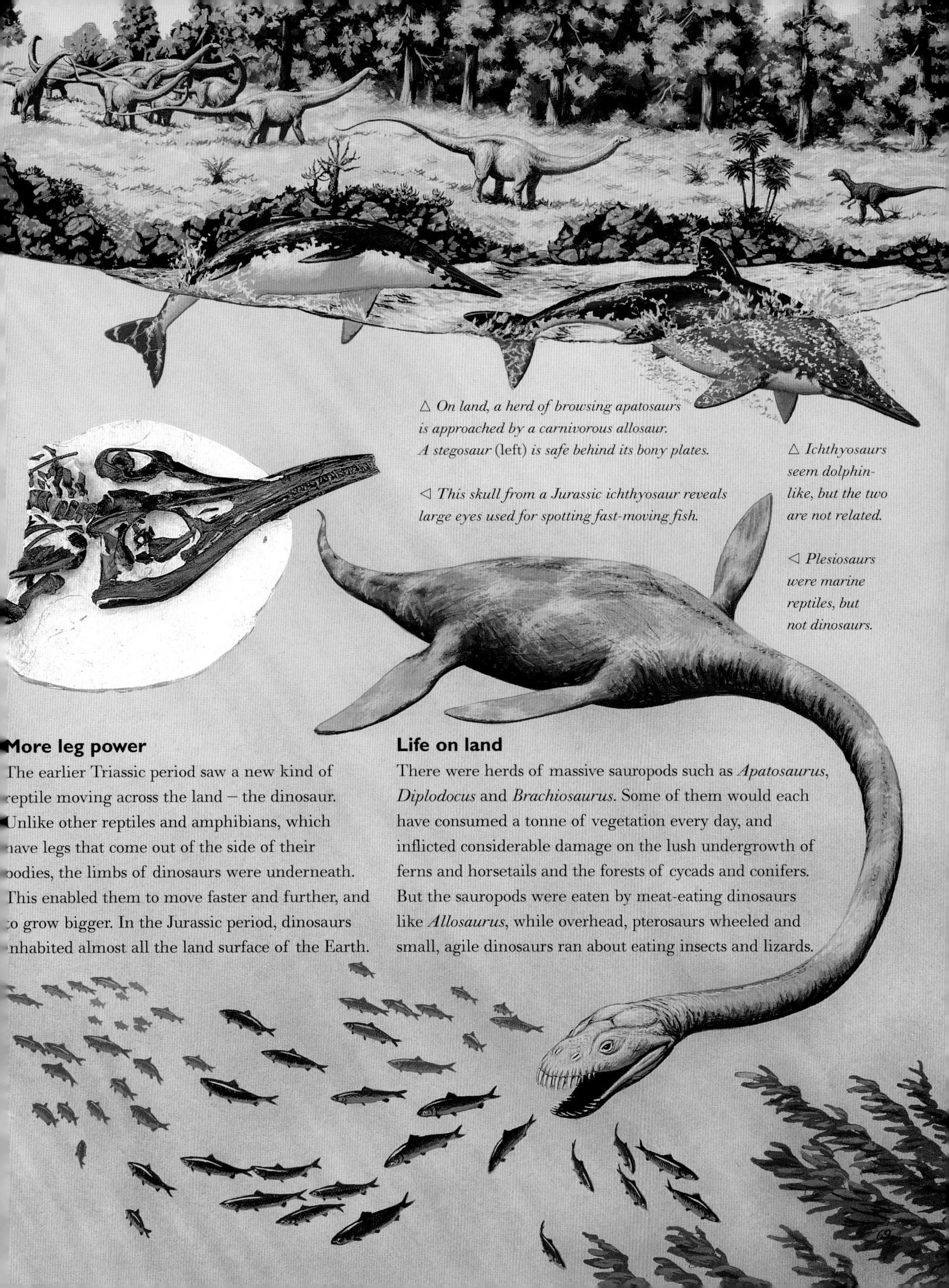

△ On land, a herd of browsing apatosaurs is approached by a carnivorous allosaur. A stegosaur (left) is safe behind its bony plates.

◁ This skull from a Jurassic ichthyosaur reveals large eyes used for spotting fast-moving fish.

△ Ichthyosaurs seem dolphin-like, but the two are not related.

◁ Plesiosaurs were marine reptiles, but not dinosaurs.

More leg power

The earlier Triassic period saw a new kind of reptile moving across the land – the dinosaur. Unlike other reptiles and amphibians, which have legs that come out of the side of their bodies, the limbs of dinosaurs were underneath. This enabled them to move faster and further, and to grow bigger. In the Jurassic period, dinosaurs inhabited almost all the land surface of the Earth.

Life on land

There were herds of massive sauropods such as *Apatosaurus*, *Diplodocus* and *Brachiosaurus*. Some of them would each have consumed a tonne of vegetation every day, and inflicted considerable damage on the lush undergrowth of ferns and horsetails and the forests of cycads and conifers. But the sauropods were eaten by meat-eating dinosaurs like *Allosaurus*, while overhead, pterosaurs wheeled and small, agile dinosaurs ran about eating insects and lizards.

LIFE STORY

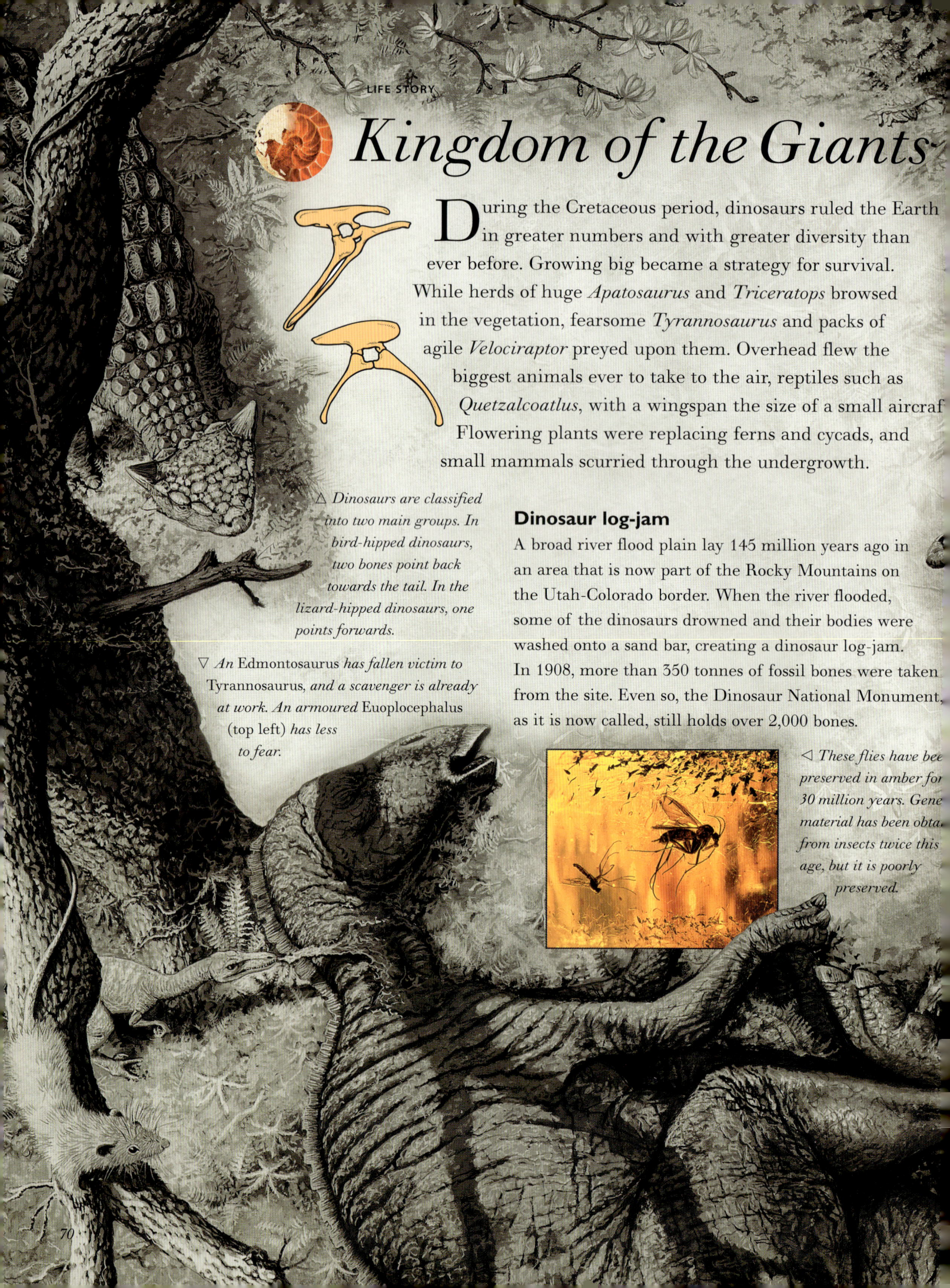

Kingdom of the Giants

During the Cretaceous period, dinosaurs ruled the Earth in greater numbers and with greater diversity than ever before. Growing big became a strategy for survival. While herds of huge *Apatosaurus* and *Triceratops* browsed in the vegetation, fearsome *Tyrannosaurus* and packs of agile *Velociraptor* preyed upon them. Overhead flew the biggest animals ever to take to the air, reptiles such as *Quetzalcoatlus*, with a wingspan the size of a small aircraft. Flowering plants were replacing ferns and cycads, and small mammals scurried through the undergrowth.

△ *Dinosaurs are classified into two main groups. In bird-hipped dinosaurs, two bones point back towards the tail. In the lizard-hipped dinosaurs, one points forwards.*

▽ *An* Edmontosaurus *has fallen victim to* Tyrannosaurus, *and a scavenger is already at work. An armoured* Euoplocephalus *(top left) has less to fear.*

Dinosaur log-jam

A broad river flood plain lay 145 million years ago in an area that is now part of the Rocky Mountains on the Utah-Colorado border. When the river flooded, some of the dinosaurs drowned and their bodies were washed onto a sand bar, creating a dinosaur log-jam. In 1908, more than 350 tonnes of fossil bones were taken from the site. Even so, the Dinosaur National Monument, as it is now called, still holds over 2,000 bones.

◁ *These flies have been preserved in amber for 30 million years. Gene material has been obtained from insects twice this age, but it is poorly preserved.*

△ In this scene from the film Jurassic Park, *a baby dinosaur, supposedly reconstructed from fossilized genes, hatches from an egg.*

Warm-blooded?

One of the biggest arguments among dinosaur experts is whether dinosaurs were warm-blooded or not. Microscopic structures in some dinosaur bones are similar to those of warm-blooded birds and mammals today. This suggests that they could control their own body temperature. So perhaps some dinosaurs were not the cold-blooded monsters they are often portrayed to be.

Cretaceous Park

The film *Jurassic Park* implied that genetic material taken from blood-sucking insects preserved in amber could be used to reconstruct a living dinosaur. DNA has been recovered from Cretaceous insects found in amber, but it is likely to be damaged. Even with a limitless supply of perfect DNA from a living organism, mapping all its genes is a major task. For the time being, *Jurassic Park* remains fiction.

◁ This claw bone from a dinosaur called Baryonyx *was found in Surrey in 1983. Its outer curve is 31 cm long. The claw would have enabled* Baryonyx *to hold onto wriggling prey such as fish.*

LIFE STORY

Extinction

The age of the dinosaurs came to an abrupt end 65 million years ago. Although individual species of dinosaur seldom survived more than a few million years, the group as a whole had persisted for 160 million years, showing a remarkable ability to specialize for many different ways of life. At the same time as the demise of the dinosaurs, 12 per cent of all families of marine organisms became extinct, as did many land plants. Clearly, something dramatic must have happened to affect so many forms of life so severely.

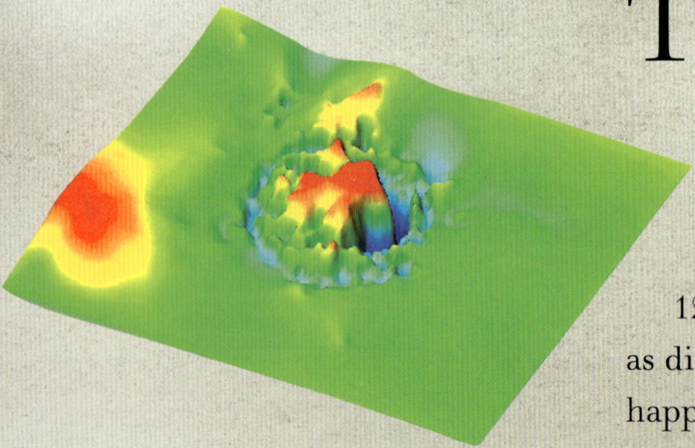

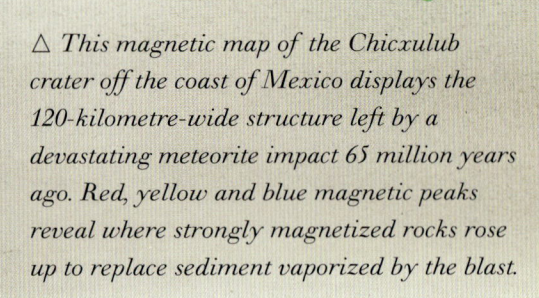

A controversial theory

During the 1970s, Walter and Luis Alvarez were studying clay that dated back to the end of the Cretaceous period and found that it was rich in the rare metal iridium. The best-known source of iridium is outer space, leading them to suggest that a giant meteorite colliding with the Earth had caused the extinction of the dinosaurs.

△ *This magnetic map of the Chicxulub crater off the coast of Mexico displays the 120-kilometre-wide structure left by a devastating meteorite impact 65 million years ago. Red, yellow and blue magnetic peaks reveal where strongly magnetized rocks rose up to replace sediment vaporized by the blast.*

Cosmic impact

The Alvarez theory had little to support it – until, in 1991, a giant crater was found under the sea off Mexico. To cause such a crater, a meteorite several kilometres across, travelling at great speed, must have hit the planet. The impact would have released more energy than one thousand nuclear weapons, causing tidal waves and global fires, and been followed by semi-darkness for several years. It would have been a bad time to be a dinosaur.

▽ *Radar on the Space Shuttle reveals this 17-kilometre-wide crater beneath the sands of the Sahara Desert. It was formed several hundred million years ago and is one of many impact craters now identified.*

LIFE STORY

Threats and opportunities

Many rival theories have attempted to explain mass extinctions – but we can never know which one is correct. What we do know for certain is that the extinction of one group of animals is the evolutionary opportunity for another. It seems that the largest and most specialized organisms suffer most, as was the case with the dinosaurs. And 65 million years ago, the small, adaptable animals that were waiting for their big chance were the mammals. Today, another mass extinction appears to be in progress, but this time it is caused by human activity. Global warming and the destruction of habitats are set to send thousands of living species the way of the dinosaurs.

▽ *Grazing in what is now Mexico, herds of late Cretaceous dinosaurs look on in bewilderment at the flash of the giant meteorite. Their days are numbered – destruction and extinction will soon follow.*

◁ *Rock samples from the Caribbean act as a record of the meteorite's collision with the Earth. At the moment of impact, thousands of tonnes of seawater and rock rose into the air. This fallout eventually dropped to the Earth to form a distinctive white layer in the rock.*

LIFE STORY

The Birds and the Bees

In the late Jurassic period, 150 million years ago, in part of southern Germany that now lies just north of Munich, there was a warm, salty lagoon. Fish swept in by storms perished in its stagnant waters and sank to the bottom. A horseshoe crab staggered around, leaving spiral tracks, before dying. Anything that entered the lagoon perished, and the remains were preserved in the fine layers of muddy limestone. The fossils that have been found there are not only of creatures that crawled or were washed into the lagoon. Some must have been blown in by the winds, or even flown there.

First flight

In 1860, a single feather was found preserved in the rocks of what had once been the lagoon. It was the same shape as the flight feather of a modern bird. A year later, the complete skeleton of a feathered creature was found. It was named *Archaeopteryx*, meaning ancient wing. It had teeth rather than a beak, but it was winged, with a feathered tail, and clearly could have flown.

▷ *Creatures of all sorts have taken to the air, including mammals, reptiles (pterosaurs) and birds, the only group to develop feathers. Here, a flock of* Archaeopteryx *looks down on a late Jurassic scene.*

Chinese flocks

A remarkable find in China in 1996 may shed some light on the evolution of *Archaeopteryx*. *Sinosauropteryx* was found in rocks that are 120 million years old. It was slightly smaller than a chicken and had distinct traces of downy filaments up to 4 cm long all over its body. These proto-feathers may have originally evolved for insulation.

△ This Archaeopteryx fossil is from Solnhofen, Germany. Around its tail and front limbs are the well-preserved traces of feathers. But Archaeopteryx also still had claws on its fingers and teeth in its jaw.

△ This spectacular dragonfly, from the late Jurassic, was also preserved in the silts of Solnhofen.

Getting launched

So how did the first birds take to the air? They may have run fast along the ground, jumping up to catch insects. Or perhaps they ran up trees to launch themselves like gliders. And once up, how did they stay there? As well as feathers and wings, early birds needed thick muscles around the breastbone, and lightweight, hollow bones.

A change in the landscape

The warm lagoon saw the demise of many early insects, including large dragonflies, mayflies, locusts and cockroaches. During the Cretaceous and the great extinction, wasps, butterflies and, in particular, bees began to appear. Their presence indicates that a dramatic change from ferns and conifers to broad-leafed, flowering plants was taking place.

LIFE STORY

Creatures of the Ice

Any creature that survived the cataclysmic events at the end of the Cretaceous lived in a time of great opportunity. All the large predators and herbivores had been wiped off the face of the Earth. The remaining reptiles — lizards, snakes, turtles and small crocodiles — carried on much as they had before. However, small, adaptable creatures that had until then spent much of their lives in hiding were suddenly presented with the opportunity to inherit the Earth. This Tertiary era, the third age of life on the Earth, has been the age of the mammals and the birds.

△ *This frozen baby mammoth was recovered in 1977 from the permafrost of Siberia. Though shrunken, its internal organs and reddish hair had been preserved for more than 9,000 years. Flesh like this is so well preserved that, in the past, such finds were fed to dogs. Today, they are kept for genetic analysis.*

▽ *Woolly mammoths, woolly rhinoceroses, bears and buffalo roamed over the ice age tundra. These large creatures were well adapted for life at low temperatures, but they proved less adaptable than smaller mammals once the ice retreated.*

Survival of the fittest

Whereas birds had developed insulating feathers from the hard scales of their dinosaur ancestors, mammals grew fur from soft, porous skin. This was just as well because the world's climate grew progressively cooler over the next 50 million years. Mammalian evolution also saw experiments with size and ferocity. There were giant rhinos measuring 4 m at the shoulder and weighing 15 tonnes, and huge deer, such as the Irish elk. Sabre-tooth tigers and their marsupial equivalents lived alongside a host of other mammalian monsters, such as the woolly mammoths of Europe and the mastodons of North America.

LIFE STORY

The great freeze
Following the break-up of the supercontinent Pangaea, mammals evolved differently on each landmass. Then, 15 million years ago, an ice cap began to form on Antarctica and sea levels fell. This allowed animals to migrate between the different continents. It continued to get colder until, about 3.25 million years ago, variations in the Earth's orbit were large enough to trigger the first of a series of ice ages.

Adapt or die
As the polar regions froze, the ice reflected sunlight back into space and the Earth cooled further. When the higher latitudes cooled, equatorial regions became drier, forming the basis for the savannah grasslands and deserts of today. Though some mammals developed thick layers of fat or fur to keep warm, the changing climate led to the extinction of many species. But one group used its ingenuity to keep warm, clothing itself in the skins of others and lighting fires. These mammals were our own ancestors.

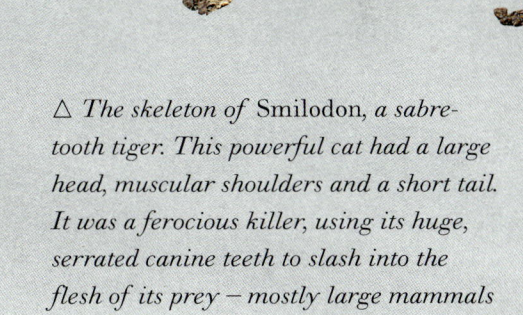

◁ *Part of the skull and the spectacular tusks of an adult woolly mammoth that roamed the tundra of England during the last ice age. This one was found in what is now part of the suburbs of London, England.*

△ *The skeleton of* Smilodon, *a sabre-tooth tiger. This powerful cat had a large head, muscular shoulders and a short tail. It was a ferocious killer, using its huge, serrated canine teeth to slash into the flesh of its prey – mostly large mammals such as mammoths and bison.*

LIFE STORY

Our Ancestors

In 1974, a group of anthropologists found fragments of bone near Hadar in Ethiopia. Before long, they had built up much of the skeleton of a young hominid (human ancestor) called *Australopithecus*, meaning southern ape. Naming her Lucy, they established that she was about three million years old. She had an ape-like skull and a small brain, but her arms were short and she could walk upright on her long legs. Since then, bones of a different *Australopithecus* have been found. These belong to a more ape-like species which had a developed skull, but longer arms and short legs.

△ These ancient handprints were found in an Argentinian cave, along with many paintings of animals.

△ Flint hand axes like this were used by early hum This one was foun Britain and is abo 250,000 years old.

Footprints in the sand

One day, about 3.6 million years ago, on what is now the Laetoli Plain of northern Tanzania, a layer of fresh ash from a nearby volcano was softened by a shower of rain. Three creatures wandered across it, walking upright on two legs. Two may have been holding hands, the third, smaller and younger, walked behind. Were they our ancestors?

▷ A group of *Homo erectus*, about 1.5 million years ago, plans a hunt across the African savannah. These intelligent, early people walked upright, leaving their hands free to use tools.

The toolmakers

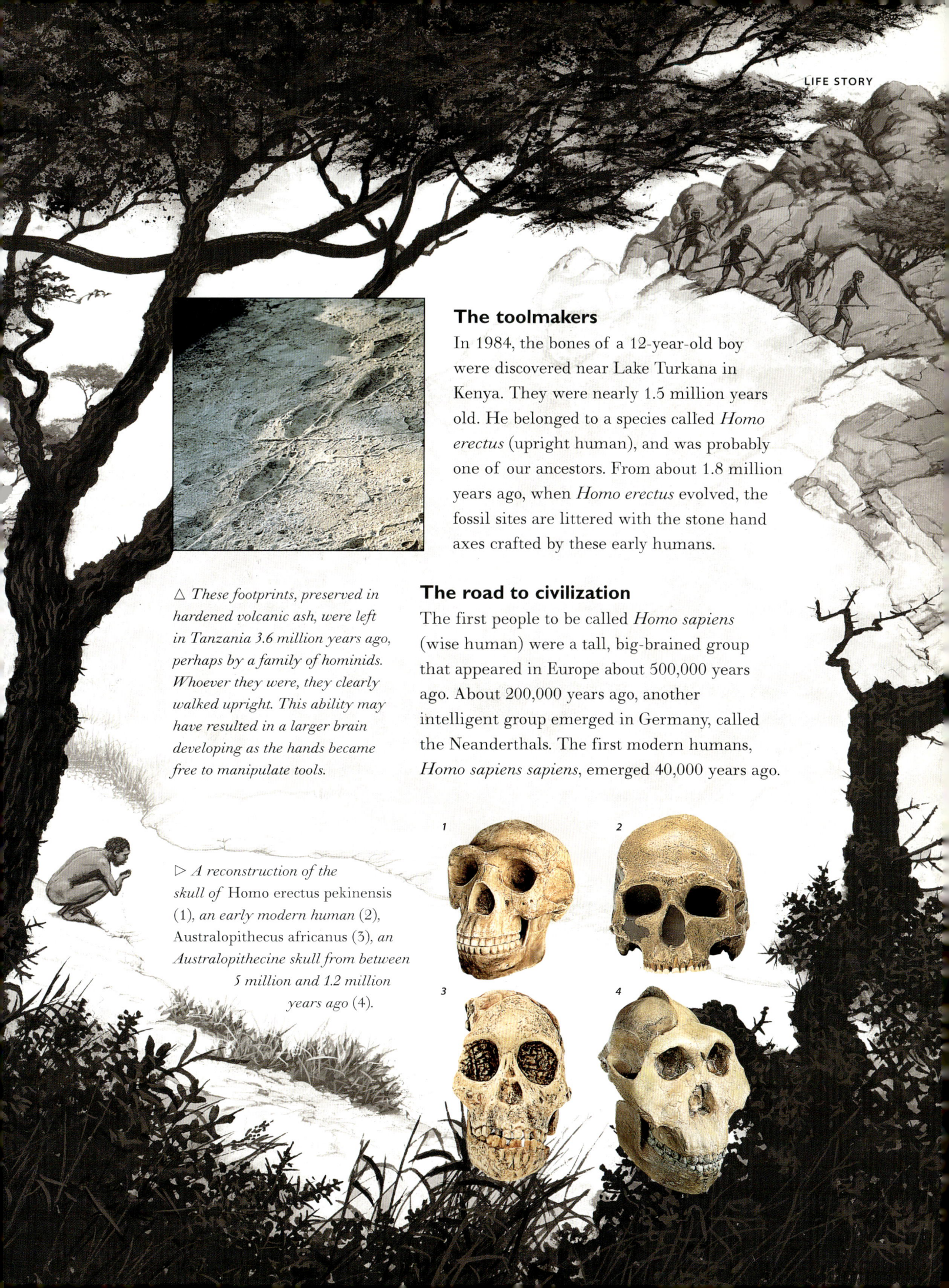

In 1984, the bones of a 12-year-old boy were discovered near Lake Turkana in Kenya. They were nearly 1.5 million years old. He belonged to a species called *Homo erectus* (upright human), and was probably one of our ancestors. From about 1.8 million years ago, when *Homo erectus* evolved, the fossil sites are littered with the stone hand axes crafted by these early humans.

△ *These footprints, preserved in hardened volcanic ash, were left in Tanzania 3.6 million years ago, perhaps by a family of hominids. Whoever they were, they clearly walked upright. This ability may have resulted in a larger brain developing as the hands became free to manipulate tools.*

The road to civilization

The first people to be called *Homo sapiens* (wise human) were a tall, big-brained group that appeared in Europe about 500,000 years ago. About 200,000 years ago, another intelligent group emerged in Germany, called the Neanderthals. The first modern humans, *Homo sapiens sapiens*, emerged 40,000 years ago.

▷ *A reconstruction of the skull of* Homo erectus pekinensis *(1), an early modern human (2), Australopithecus africanus (3), an Australopithecine skull from between 5 million and 1.2 million years ago (4).*

PEOPLE AND THE PLANET

Fuel from the Earth

△ *Coal is usually mined by sinking shafts underground. Galleries are then cut along the lines of the coal seams. Since oil is liquid, an offshore oil production platform (far right) needs only narrow bore holes to pump it out.*

△ *Oil is not always found where it is needed. The trans-Alaskan pipeline carries oil 1,284 km across the Arctic.*

▽ *This nuclear power station at Sizewell in Suffolk, England, is powered by uranium. Only a tiny quantity of fuel is required, but the radioactive waste it produces is difficult and expensive to handle safely.*

For more than one billion years, planet Earth has teemed with life. During that time, living organisms have trapped the Sun's energy and stored it in the chemicals of their bodies. Much of that chemical energy is now stored underground as fossil fuels – coal, gas and oil. Today, we are releasing that trapped solar energy by burning the fuels, and putting the carbon they contain back into the atmosphere as carbon dioxide. The fuels provide us with energy to fire our power stations and generate electricity. They give us fuel for cars and aircraft, and they provide most of the raw materials for making plastics, artificial fibres and a host of other chemicals.

Fossil forests

During the Carboniferous period 300 million years ago, vast forests covered much of the Earth's land surface. Giant tree ferns and cycads grew, died and decomposed. Where they fell in swampy ground, there was not enough oxygen for them to rot and they turned into thick layers of peat. Sometimes, sea levels rose and covered the remains with layers of sand or shale. As it was buried deeper and deeper, the peat was compressed into coal.

Oil and gas

Many of the great multitude of creatures that live in the oceans are eaten or decomposed by bacteria. However, some sink into oxygen-poor waters and become buried in the sediments. The abundant bacteria that live hundreds of metres beneath the sea floor survive off these organic remains and slowly convert them into oil and methane gas.

△ These wind turbines in California provide an alternative source of energy to coal and oil. It has been estimated that by 2025, wind power could provide one quarter of the electricity needed by many countries.

Finding oilfields

Oil and gas are much less dense than rock. Once formed, they tend to rise up through porous rocks until they can go no further. Oil prospectors searching for the 'black gold' begin by looking for the sort of geological formations that will trap it. The oil and gas themselves fill the tiny spaces within rocks such as sandstone. Where rocks of the right age are overlaid by domes of impervious rocks such as clay or salt, huge reservoirs of oil and gas may collect.

Oil strike!

One hundred years ago, shallow oil wells would often produce a gush of oil under natural pressure. Today, the technology to extract oil has become complex and expensive. Pumping out the oil only extracts a fraction of what is there. Seawater and chemical solvents help extract more. Even so, at the present rate, the oil will only last a few decades; the coal and gas a little longer.

△ Sometime in the future, the coal and oil will run out, but the Sun will continue to shine. Banks of reflecting dishes such as these in Australia are already used to concentrate the Sun's energy and generate electrical power.

81

PEOPLE AND THE PLANET

Metals from the Earth

The Earth was formed from raw ingredients originally cooked up inside stars and spewed out into space. Processes inside the planet have concentrated these elements, such as metals, in quantities useful to humans. The minerals that contain these concentrated elements are called ores. Some minerals are carried along cracks and fissures in rock when molten igneous rocks rise through the crust. Other minerals are deposited in crystalline veins as heat drives off water containing dissolved minerals. Some of the richest mines of copper, lead, zinc and gold are formed in this way.

△ *When hot fluids containing dissolved minerals fill a cavity in a rock, they form a geode. First, silica is deposited, then as the cavity fills, larger quartz crystals grow, often coloured by trace metals.*

Extracting metals

Few metals occur in their pure form in nature. Gold is a notable exception. Most metallic minerals are chemical compounds with very different properties to the metals they contain. The process of smelting is used to extract the metal from the ore. Both heat and a reducing agent, such as carbon in the form of charcoal, are used to pull the metal's chemical companions away from it.

▽ *Useful minerals are often deposited around hot, igneous rock. Water, saturated in dissolved minerals, is driven outwards by the heat.*

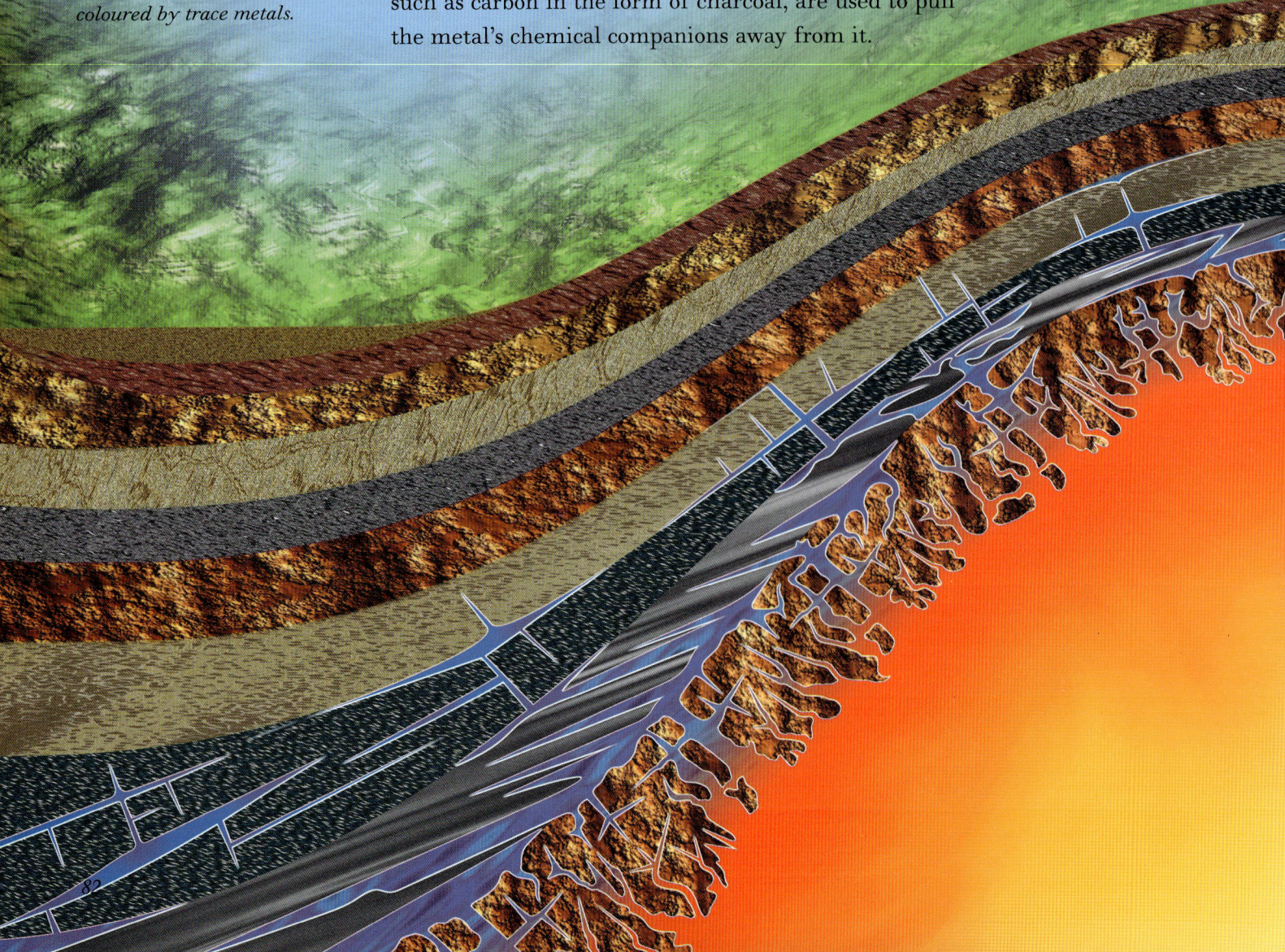

PEOPLE AND THE PLANET

◁ *Protected by heat resistant clothes, a worker takes a sample of molten iron from a blast furnace. Inside the furnace, hot air fans the flames through a mixture of iron ore, coke and limestone. Once the waste, or slag, is skimmed off, the molten iron is cast into ingots.*

The other side

Despite the value of the metals they produce, mines have also left a legacy of pollution and damage. For every tonne of ore extracted, there can be thousands of tonnes of waste rock spilled across the hillside. Sometimes, the waste rocks contain poisons that kill the surrounding trees. Artificial dams burst, mines flood and tanks leak, washing mud, debris and toxic chemicals down rivers. In some cases, the mines are located in environmentally sensitive areas or in populated territories.

Holes in the ground

Mining techniques depend on the concentration of the ore, its depth and its value. Where ore lies in a thick vein underground, tunnels and shafts can be sunk. Sometimes there is a large body of less concentrated ore near the surface and it can be dug out from an opencast pit. Sometimes nature has already done the digging. Deposits of gold, for example, are concentrated in river gravels.

Future prospects

As mines on the land become exhausted, we will need to look elsewhere. There are potentially rich sources in the ocean. Some areas of the ocean floor are littered with manganese nodules and other rare metals. However, they lie at great depths and are in international waters. One day, mining might happen in space. A single small asteroid, towed back to the Earth, could provide many of the valuable metals that the world needs for centuries.

▽ *Once the rock cools, the minerals are left in cracks and fissures, forming metal-rich veins. Miners cut shafts and galleries underground to reach the veins.*

▽ *This great opencast mine in New Mexico, US, is one of the largest artificial holes on the planet.*

83

◁ *Lapis lazuli is a complex sodium aluminium silicate. This semi-precious stone is formed in igneous and metamorphic rocks that are rich in carbonate.*

PEOPLE AND THE PLANET

Gems from the Deep

▽ *For centuries, the prospect of great wealth led alchemists to try to convert base materials into gold and gems. We know now that they could never have succeeded.*

Any stone or crystal worn as jewellery can be regarded as a gem. Some are organic in origin, such as amber (fossilized tree resin), jet (hard, black coal), opal (silicified wood) and pearl (shell). Many other semi-precious stones are silicate minerals such as quartz (rock crystal), amethyst, jade, garnet and topaz. The most precious stones are also the rarest and the most durable – ruby, sapphire, emerald and diamond. These mineral gems are formed under particular conditions of pressure and temperature, deep in the Earth's mantle. It is only later that they are thrown up to the surface.

△ *Natural diamond crystal is found embedded in volcanic kimberlite rock. This type of rock is named after the area in which it is found – Kimberley, South Africa.*

▽ *Carbon is dragged down from the Earth's surface to the upper mantle, where the pressure transforms it into diamond.*

Humble beginnings

The tightly packed crystal structure of diamond makes it the hardest natural substance on the Earth. Yet, it is made of carbon, the same element that makes pencil lead or soot. Where this carbon came from is uncertain. Perhaps it was once limestone, coal or even a carbon-rich meteorite (*see below, illustration 1*) and was then pulled into the Earth's mantle on a slab of old ocean crust (*2*).

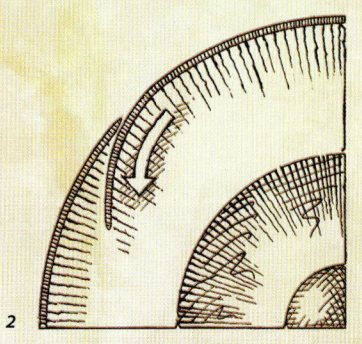

◁ Quartz is a form of silica. This quartz crystal was photographed using coloured light. Flaws in the quartz catch the light, making it shimmer.

△ Rutilated quartz contains needle-like crystals of rutile, an ore of titanium.

The birth of a diamond

Over millions of years and at about 600 kilometres beneath the Earth's surface, the carbon was slowly transformed into a diamond. However, its rise to the surface would have been much more rapid. This is because it must have been ejected in the type of volcano, now mercifully extinct, which erupted at supersonic speeds (*3*).

Many facets

A rough natural diamond has eight sides (*4*). To give it its sparkle, the surface must be carefully cut so that it has many facets (*5*). The best-known diamond cut is called a brilliant and has 58 facets, making it especially sparkly. As well as adorning jewellery, diamonds can also be used in the blades of delicate saws or in drill bits.

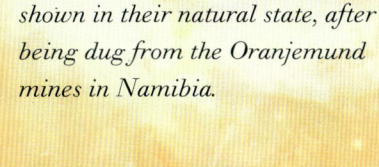

△ These two uncut diamonds are shown in their natural state, after being dug from the Oranjemund mines in Namibia.

△ A cut, polished diamond may be worth several thousand dollars per carat. One carat is 0.2 grammes.

Emerald alchemy

Emeralds usually form in hot granite when scaldingly hot fluids containing beryllium and chromium react with carborundum or aluminium oxide. However, some of the most beautiful emeralds are from Colombia and seem to have formed when highly pressurized hot water dissolved salt and gypsum from sedimentary rocks which then reacted with clay minerals in the surrounding shale.

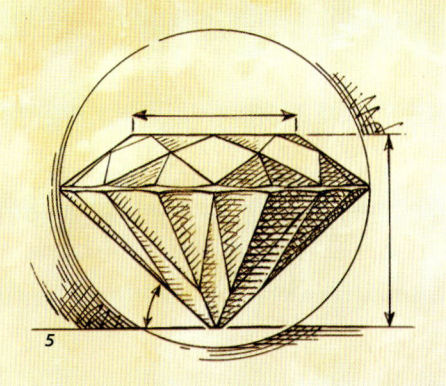

85

PEOPLE AND THE PLANET

Human Creators

In the four billion years since the heavy bombardment of the Earth ceased, continents have split and collided, oceans have opened and vanished, mountain ranges have grown, then eroded away. But never has change been faster or more spectacular than over the past few thousand years. The recent transformation of the planet is mostly due to the activities of a single species, *Homo sapiens sapiens* – ourselves. It is hard to imagine what the world would be like without human beings. Since ancient times, we have built and burrowed, chopped and changed – taming the landscape to suit our needs. The concrete jungles and cultivated landscapes are clear evidence that we have become the rulers of the surface of the Earth and all the species upon it. We are the creators and the destroyers of wonders.

△ *Though now surrounded by jungle, the great Mayan pyramids of Tikal in Guatemala are impressive examples of human creativity.*

A new garden of Eden

Look down at the surface of the Earth from a plane, or even from space, and the patterns are striking. For hundreds of kilometres, parts of the Earth are a patchwork of fields, outlined by the unnaturally straight lines of roads and fences. It is even possible to see political and economic boundaries, as different agricultural policies meet along lines that seem to be drawn with a ruler.

◁ *Powerful people of every era have tried to leave enduring monuments to their life and times. These giant faces of American presidents are carved out of the natural rock of Mount Rushmore in South Dakota, US.*

Protecting and preserving

Many regions of wilderness do still remain on the planet, complete with a rich biodiversity of plants and animals. Work is in progress to preserve these areas and to prevent further pollution and destruction. We have also taken it upon ourselves to try to protect individual species, or at least the ones we have identified. Huge efforts are going into the preservation of rare animals such as the giant panda of China or the California condor.

The wonders of the world

Not all human industry is destructive – we have created some works of great beauty and benefit too. Which ones qualify as the wonders of our civilization is a matter of individual taste. Maybe they are the great buildings of our modern age. Perhaps they are products of science, such as space rockets and suspension bridges. They could even be on a smaller scale – a painting, a piece of music, a book or a garden in full bloom.

PEOPLE AND THE PLANET

A web of knowledge

One of the greatest human achievements is the quest for knowledge and understanding. We have explored our planet's surface and journeyed into space. We are discovering the secrets of science and the mysteries of our own bodies. No one person can contain all this knowledge, but through our libraries and communications networks, we have spun a web of knowledge around the planet that people can access. It brings a potential far greater than that of any individual.

△ *Great buildings, ingenious structures and powerful machines keep our economies thriving and our lives moving. But some human creations are designed to fulfil our spiritual needs, while others are simply for pleasure or amazement.*

PEOPLE AND THE PLANET

Human Destroyers

Life on the Earth may be facing an even greater crisis than the mass extinctions of the past. For the last three hundred years, vertebrate species have been disappearing at an average of one per year, and today more than 3,500 animal species are under threat. Plants, fungi and micro-organisms are also vanishing. If the present trend continues, it has been estimated that at least one quarter of all living creatures will disappear before the human population levels out in about 50 years' time. The reasons for current losses are hunting, competition from introduced species and, in particular, loss of habitats.

△ *Untreated waste pours into the sea from an outflow pipe on the English coast. Untreated sewage can cause blooms of algae which use up oxygen from the water. Chemicals can poison life directly.*

◁ *Despite improved techniques for dealing with oil spills, it can take many years for an area to recover from a major spill.*

Lost worlds

Humans have been changing the landscape since the ice ages. With the invention of the flint hand-axe, the systematic felling of the forests of much of northern Europe began. In Australia, the telltale signs of charcoal show that the first human settlers arrived 40,000 to 50,000 years ago, and this coincides with the extinction of large birds and marsupials on that continent. Today, about 1% of the world's 17 million square kilometres of tropical rainforest is cleared every year. This also releases huge quantities of carbon dioxide into the atmosphere.

Polluted planet

Six billion people produce a lot of waste, much of which is dumped with little or no treatment. We live in an industrialized world that requires the manufacture, use and transport of concentrated chemicals and even radioactive materials. It is often the case that laws are broken, not enforced or non-existent, and the land, rivers and seas suffer as a result.

PEOPLE AND THE PLANET

▷ *A stricken oil tanker floats helplessly in the sea, its precious cargo spilling out to clog beaches and poison wildlife.*

Danger for humankind

What about the idea of Gaia (named after the Earth goddess), that our planet acts like a single organism to keep conditions favourable for life? Does that mean that we can leave nature to clean up the mess? Professor James Lovelock, who introduced the concept of Gaia, does not doubt that this theory is correct — but he has never claimed that it will operate in favour of one species, least of all humankind.

Islands of hope

In the sea of destruction, there are islands of hope. In the 1870s, with the Industrial Revolution well underway, the world's first national park was established — Yellowstone, in Wyoming, US. Today, there are more than 3,000 national parks and wildlife reserves, covering more than four million square kilometres of the world. And perhaps the invention of space flight has come just in time. Not for us to evacuate, but for us to recognize the need to protect our planet. From space, polluted rivers, forest fires and deserts are clearly visible, national boundaries fade away.

△ *After the oil tanker* Sea Empress *ran aground off the coast of South Wales in 1996, trawlers towed floating booms to try to contain the oil slicks and prevent them from drifting onto beaches.*

◁ *During the Gulf War in 1991, many Kuwaiti oil wells were left blazing. The thick palls of smoke travelled hundreds of kilometres and were clearly visible from space.*

◁▽ *Several billion years into the future and the Earth and Moon have been scorched to cinders. The Sun is expanding into a red giant and has boiled away the oceans and atmosphere. Planet Earth is no longer the blue and green jewel that we once called home.*

PEOPLE AND THE PLANET

The End of the Earth

The Earth has been our home for about half a million years, and home to life in some form for most of its 4.5 billion years. But as we have discovered, the Earth is a dynamic and active planet. Volcanoes erupt, continents split in two, mountains rise up, even rock is not steady. One day, the radioactive heat sources that fuel such changes will decay, the molten outer core will freeze and the Earth will be nothing more than a dead ember floating in space. However, more immediately, our planet is under constant threat from outside and even from ourselves.

▷ *Whatever the cause, we can be sure that one day the Earth will not be as hospitable as it is now. If human life is to survive, we will have to find ourselves a new home elsewhere in the Universe.*

Heavy artillery

The Earth has been under more or less regular bombardment since its birth. The early impacts were huge, probably melting the entire surface. Though their size and frequency have lessened, they have not stopped. Comets and asteroids have caused mass extinctions in the past, and unless we can deflect them, they will almost certainly do so again. But even if there is a major impact, past evidence suggests that life will not only survive but make the most of a catastrophe.

Cosmic roasting

Space is a dangerous place for a small planet. Old massive stars, our Sun's neighbours, could explode as supernovae in a thermonucleur fireball. This would damage the Earth's ozone layer and affect life, but probably not destroy it altogether. Similarly, the gamma ray burst released in a collision between two neutron stars would blast the Earth with radiation, roasting it as it turns, like a chicken on a spit. But again, the damage would probably not be terminal.

The human threat

Could we destroy our planet by our own actions? With the powers that we have today, the answer is, probably not. For all the devastation they cause, nuclear weapons are no match for explosive volcanoes and asteroid impacts. Maybe our activities will change the climate, damage the ozone layer or release dangerous new organisms and chemicals into the environment. The results would indeed be terrible, but life is resilient. Somehow the world would survive, with or without us.

The end of the Sun

When time does run out for the Earth, it will probably be because the hydrogen at the heart of our Sun has been exhausted. As the Sun dies, it will begin to swell into a bloated red giant. Then, over a few thousand years, it will engulf the Earth and scorch away the atmosphere, oceans and, eventually, all life. But there is no need to worry quite yet. It will be another four or five billion years before this catastrophic event happens, and by then, we should be well on our way to the stars.

△ *The last of a series of giant spacecraft pulls away from Earth orbit and leaves to colonize new worlds. Constructed out of an asteroid, the craft, named* Utopia, *carries a complete sample of life on the Earth – land, sea, plants and animals, as well as the last 1,000 human descendants. Our planet is dead, but life goes on.*

THE CHANGING OCEANS

Planet Ocean

Oceans cover more than two-thirds of our planet's surface. A ship could sail around the world without touching land and, if it sank, would probably plunge more than 3,000 metres before reaching the seabed.

These vast, hidden depths are home to millions of different plants and animals. Oceans also gave rise to life on dry land. All land plants' and animals' ancestors lived in ancient seas. Even today, we could not survive without the oceans. They act like huge radiators, spreading the Sun's warmth around the globe. These vast reservoirs of water also recycle rain, preventing continents from turning to deserts. They supply us with seafood and their colossal stores of oil, gas and minerals help to fuel today's civilization.

Continents split the deep into four connected basins, containing the Pacific, Atlantic, Indian and Arctic oceans. The Pacific Ocean, the largest and deepest, could hold every continent, or the water of the other three oceans. The Arctic is the smallest, shallowest and coldest ocean of all.

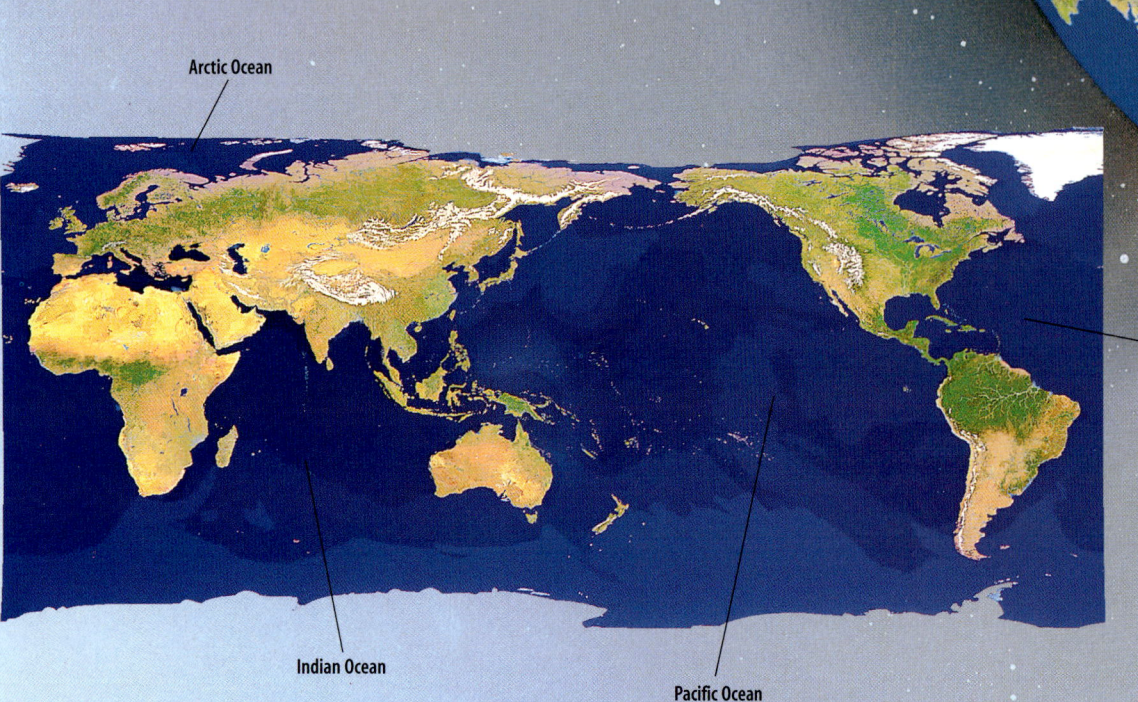

Arctic Ocean

Atlantic Ocean

◁ *There are four main oceans – the Pacific, the Atlantic, the Arctic and the Indian oceans. Together they cover more than two-thirds of the Earth's surface.*

Indian Ocean

Pacific Ocean

THE CHANGING OCEANS

▽ From above the Pacific, an astronaut's view of the Earth and Moon suggests our planet is almost all water. In fact, the Pacific Ocean covers just over one-third of the globe.

◁ About 97 per cent of the world's water lies in oceans. Just over two per cent is ice, and less than one percent is fresh water and water vapour.

Oceans
Ice
Vapour

Arctic Ocean
14,090,000 sq km

Indian Ocean
74,929,000 sq km

Pacific Ocean
179,680,000 sq km

Atlantic Ocean
106,460,000 sq km

Arctic Indian Atlantic Pacific

1,300 m
3,897 m
3,300 m
4,280 m

5,450 m
7,450 m
9,144 m
10,911 m

△ This chart shows the total area of water that is covered by each ocean. The Pacific is nearly 13 times larger than the Arctic Ocean.

◁ The average and maximum depths of the oceans vary greatly. The Arctic has the shallowest average and maximum depths, while the Pacific has the greatest. The Atlantic and the Indian fall between these two.

▷ Mount Everest, the Earth's tallest peak (8,848 metres), could be sunk without a trace in the deepest part of the ocean.

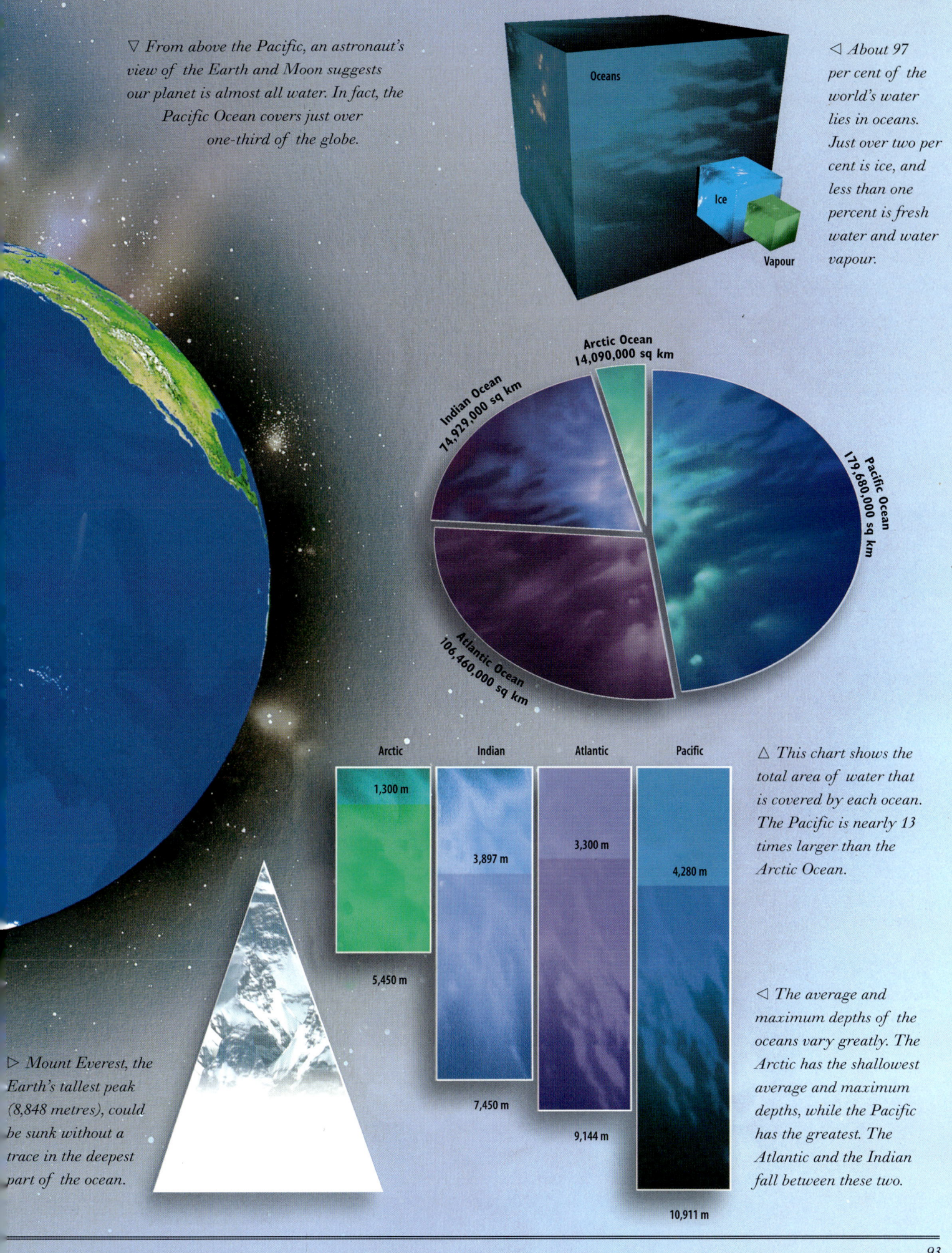

THE CHANGING OCEANS

The Invisible Landscape

The sea floor, or ocean basin, is a landscape as mountainous as any on dry land. The rim of this basin, known as the continental shelf, is submerged up to 180 metres deep. From the shelf's outer edge, the continental slope slants down at least 3,000 metres to form a colossal boundary wall. Deep canyons scar this slope. Sediments settling at the foot of the slope form the continental rise.

This gentle slope ends on the sea floor. Here the abyssal plains are found. These are coated with a smooth layer of sediments. Next come ridges of abyssal hills, occupying nearly one-third of the sea floor. Beyond these rears a mid-ocean mountain range flanked by a central rift valley. Up to 2,000 metres high, these ranges run through all the oceans, creating Earth's greatest mountain chain.

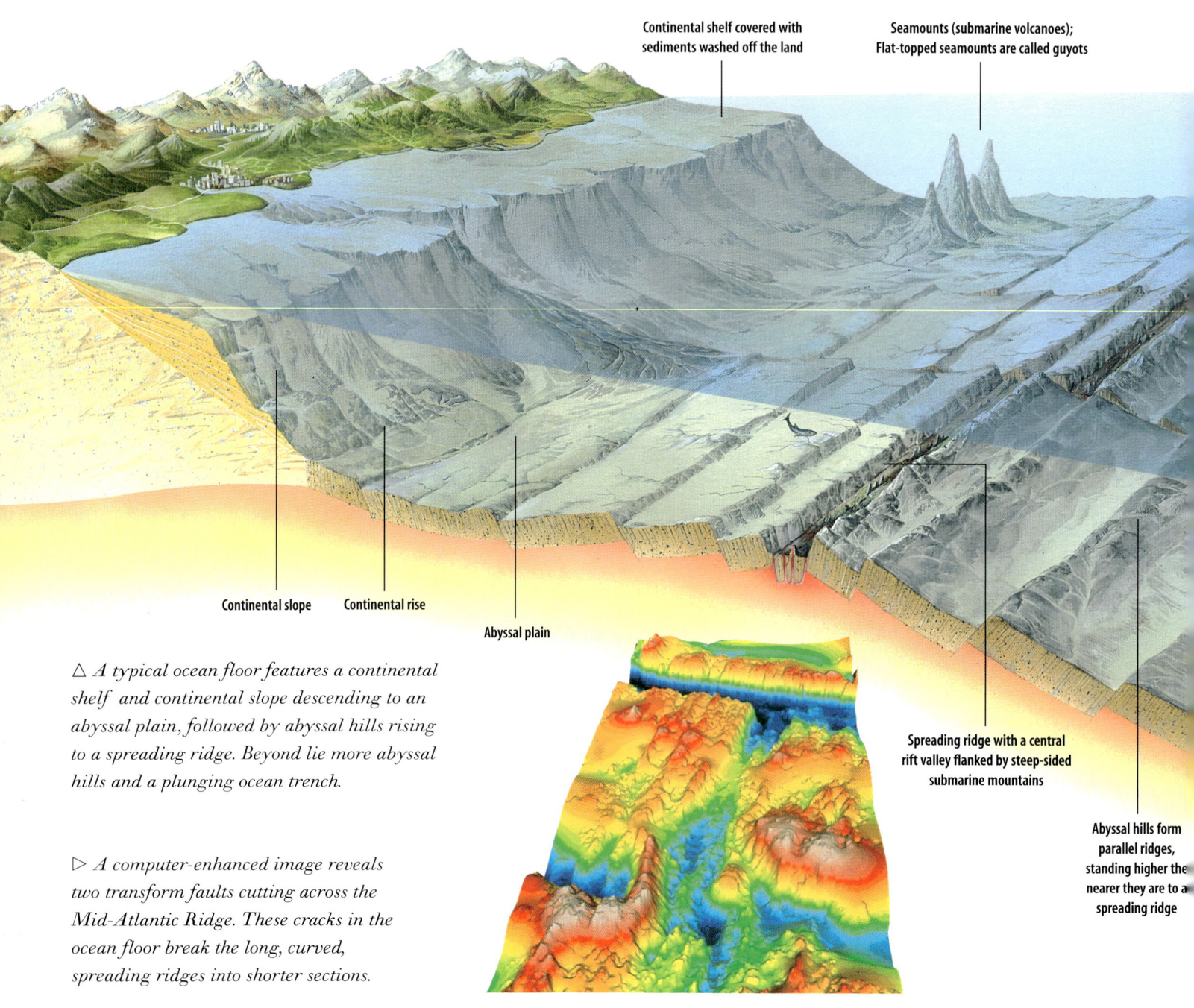

Continental shelf covered with sediments washed off the land

Seamounts (submarine volcanoes); Flat-topped seamounts are called guyots

Continental slope **Continental rise**

Abyssal plain

Spreading ridge with a central rift valley flanked by steep-sided submarine mountains

Abyssal hills form parallel ridges, standing higher the nearer they are to a spreading ridge

△ *A typical ocean floor features a continental shelf and continental slope descending to an abyssal plain, followed by abyssal hills rising to a spreading ridge. Beyond lie more abyssal hills and a plunging ocean trench.*

▷ *A computer-enhanced image reveals two transform faults cutting across the Mid-Atlantic Ridge. These cracks in the ocean floor break the long, curved, spreading ridges into shorter sections.*

THE CHANGING OCEANS

▷ *Ocean floor sediments include mud and sand washed off the land (terrigenous deposits), dust from volcanoes (red clay), chalky planktonic shells (calcareous ooze) and tiny skeletons (radiolarian and diatom ooze).*

- Terrigenous deposits
- Calcareous ooze
- Red clay
- Radiolarian ooze
- Diatom ooze

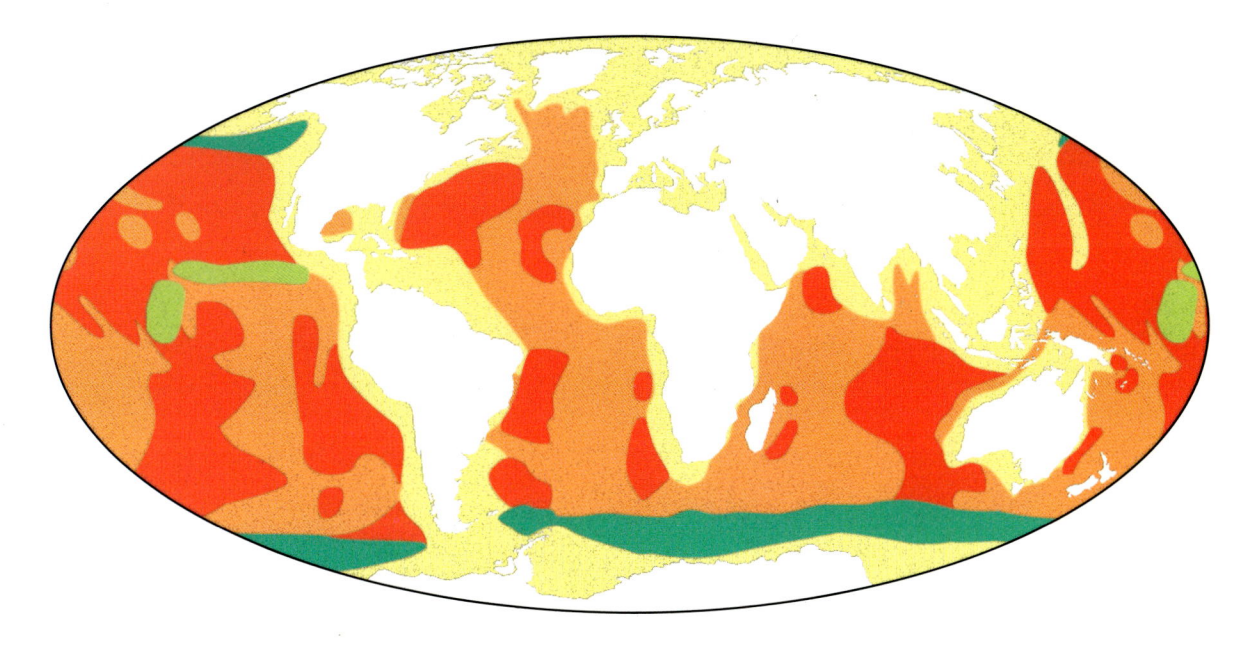

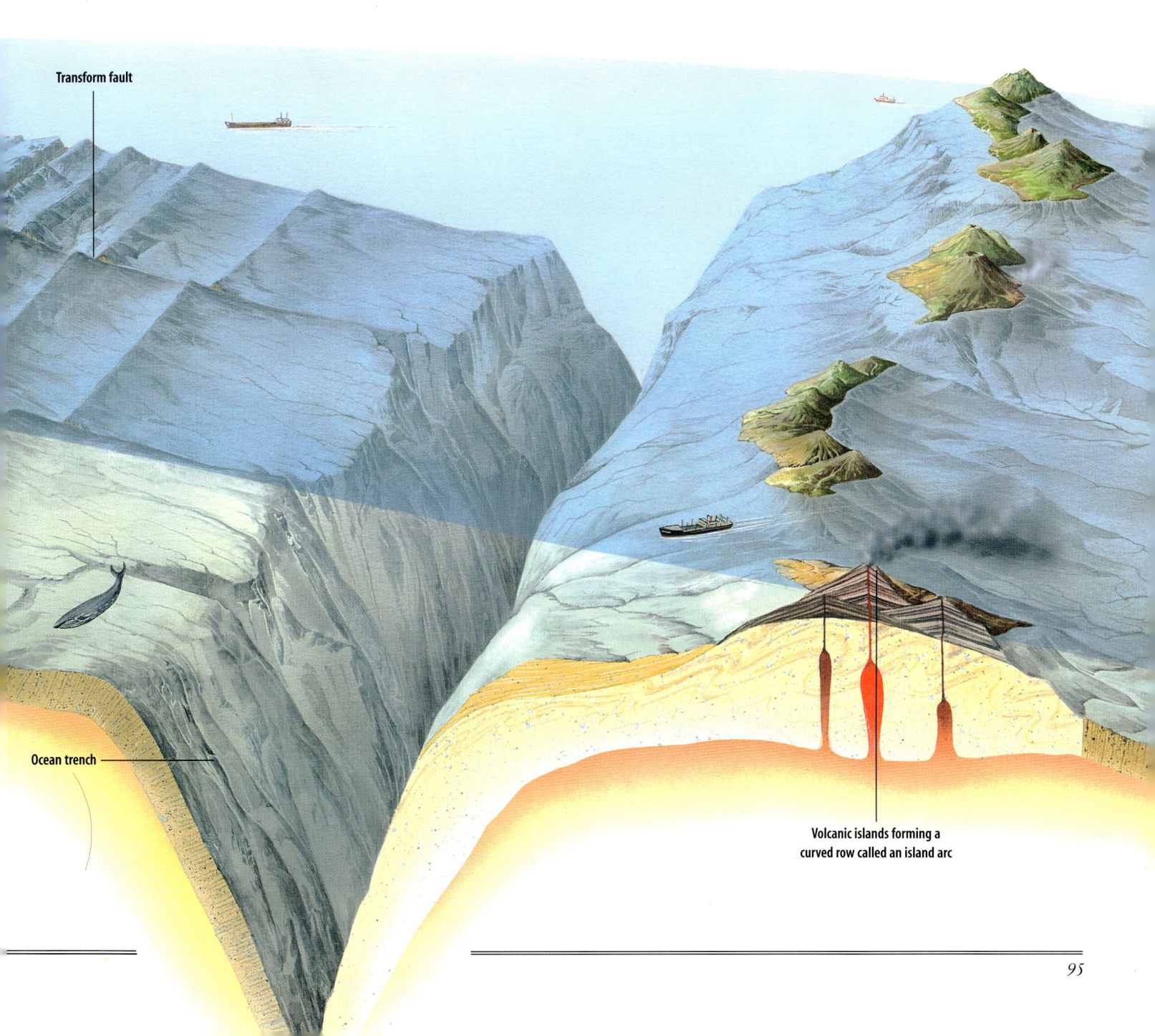

Transform fault

Ocean trench

Volcanic islands forming a curved row called an island arc

95

THE CHANGING OCEANS

Tides

On most coasts, sea level rises and falls twice a day. The main cause of these tides is the pulling force of the Moon. Its gravitational attraction lifts the ocean surface on the side of the Earth facing the Moon. At the same time, the Earth's spin tries to throw off water on the side of the Earth furthest from the Moon. These water bulges travel around the Earth at the same pace as the orbiting Moon, bringing high tides. In between are the troughs that cause low tides.

About twice a month, the combined pull of the Moon and the Sun creates the highest high tides and lowest low tides called spring tides. In certain narrow bays these tides can rise higher than a house. Neap tides, with the smallest tidal range, occur between spring tides.

There are several factors that affect the behaviour of tides. The Earth's spin steers them to one side and slows them down, while coasts and seafloor ridges deflect or block them. Oceans are also divided into tidal units. These units have a point at their centre where there is no tide at all. The tidal range is greatest where waves move into shallow coastal water.

▷ Traditionally, fishermen in the Bay of Fundy, Nova Scotia, waited for low tide to collect fish that had been swept into staked nets by the high tide. The Bay of Fundy has the greatest tidal range on Earth.

△ Seawater pours through the barrage across the Rance estuary, France. The rush of water spins turbine blades to generate electricity. Built in 1966, this was the world's first major tidal power station.

▷ Spring tides (the highest high tides and lowest low tides) occur when the Moon and Sun line up, combining their gravitational pull. Weaker neap tides (the lowest high tides and the highest low tides) occur when the Moon and Sun pull at right angles. Spring tides happen at new and full moon. Neap tides coincide with the Moon's first and last quarters.

Spring tides

THE CHANGING OCEANS

◁▽ At low tide (left), a vast sandy beach links Mont St Michel to mainland France. At high tide, the sea turns the rock into an islet.

◁▽ The Severn Bore is a wave that travels far up the River Severn, England. A bore occurs where a high spring tide moves up a shallow estuary against river water flowing downstream.

Neap tides

Incoming tide   Tidal crest   River flow

97

THE CHANGING OCEANS

Waves

Waves are raised by winds. A wave's size and speed depends upon the wind's strength and its fetch – how far across the sea it blows. Strong steady winds that blow across a great expanse of ocean can build huge smooth-topped waves called swells. The length between one crest and the next (the wavelength) can be one kilometre with speeds up to 55 kilometres per hour.

In 1933, during a North Pacific storm, a ship's officer measured one towering wave 34.2 metres high. More than 60 years later this was still a wave height record for a storm wave. Its wavelength was nearly 400 metres.

Waves form rows of ridges and valleys moving through the water. Sometimes waves from two storms cross each other's path. If crest meets crest, the waves increase in size. If crest meets trough (the bottom of the wave), the waves grow smaller. Waves meeting at right angles create a choppy sea.

The biggest waves to strike a shore are seismic sea waves or tsunamis, set off by earthquakes, landslips or volcanoes. Nearly 7,000 years ago, a tsunami wave 360 metres high swamped the Shetland Islands. In 1755, seismic sea waves hit the Portuguese capital Lisbon, killing about 60,000 people.

△ Floating objects in the open ocean often bob up and down on a passing wave without being carried along. Instead, the wave lifts the water particles that support the floating objects in a circular motion – up, forward, down and back again.

▷ A huge ocean wave breaks inshore. As its crest rears up, the mass of water overbalances and starts to topple forward on to the shore.

▷ Fierce winds generate storm waves out at sea (far right). Hurricane-force winds can blow up to 170 kilometres per hour and they may form waves more than 13 metres high.

THE CHANGING OCEANS

▽ *A device installed on a windy coast is used to harness wave power. Firstly, a wave drives air out of the chamber, spinning the turbine blades that generate electricity. Then the wave recedes, letting in more air for the next wave to force out. This air trap system has been put to effective use in Ireland and Norway.*

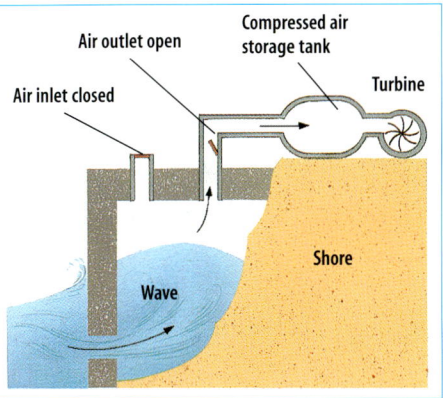

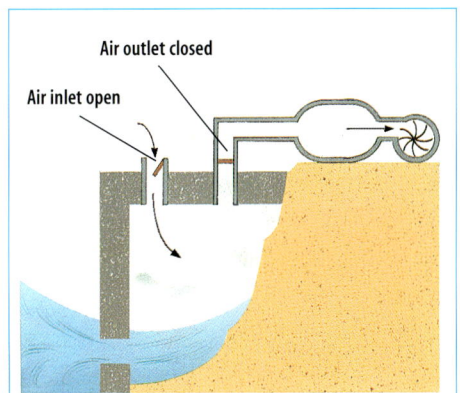

▷ *Wind-driven waves dragging on a shallow seabed slow, steepen, rise and break. The water that then rushes up the beach is called the swash. The backwash is the return flow.*

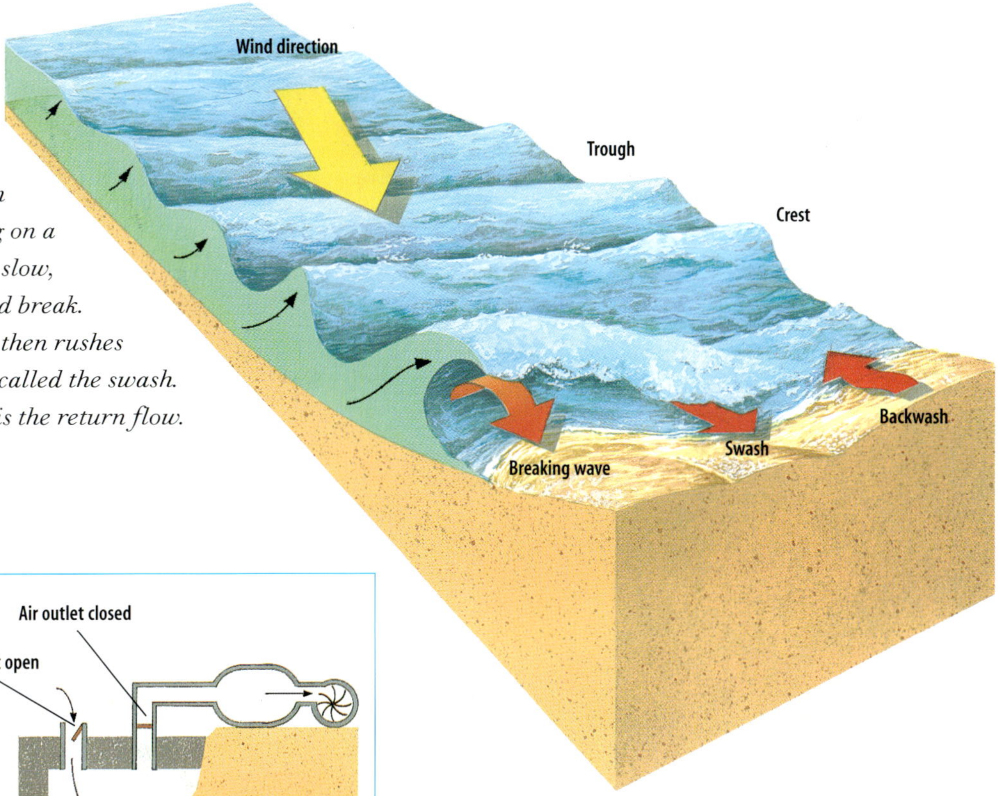

Fish

Sea fish are superbly adapted to life in the oceans. Their gills breathe oxygen dissolved in water. Most swim with powerful sweeps of the tail, steering and braking with fins. Nostrils, eyes, and vibration-sensitive cells on their flanks warn them of prey and predators.

Prey fish use various methods to avoid being eaten. Sardines swim in shoals for protection, their dark backs and pale bellies providing camouflage when viewed from above or below. If chased, flying fish leap from the sea and glide on wing-like fins.

The great majority of the 20,000 different species of fish are bony fish. They have special bladders controlling the level at which they swim. Bony fish include tuna, sardines, flatfish such as plaice and sole, and sailfish – the world's fastest fish which can reach speeds of up to 100 kilometres per hour.

The 600 cartilaginous, or gristly, kinds of fish include torpedo-shaped sharks and flat rays. Gristly fish tend to sink unless they keep swimming.

△ The great white shark, the largest carnivorous fish, can weigh more than 1.5 tonnes. Some may grow to more than six metres in length.

Herring

Pike

Flying fish

Piranha

Catfish

△ The distinctively-shaped ocean sunfish, or mola mola, appears to have more head than body. Weighing two tonnes or more, this weak swimmer is the heaviest of all bony fish.

△ A spiny 'mane' gives the lionfish of the Indian and Pacific oceans its name. Its hollow spines are poisonous.

▷ Only the eyes and mouth of this stargazer peep from the sandy sea floor. Stargazers hide, then stun their prey with an electric shock.

▷ A tiny cleaner wrasse removes parasites from inside the mouth of a much larger grouper fish. This big predator, found mostly around rocky shores and coral reefs, leaves the cleaner wrasse unharmed.

◁ The silvery sides of horse mackerel make them clearly visible in the water. However, by swimming in dense shoals mackerel can confuse any would-be attackers.

◁ A whale shark can grow up to 13 metres in length and weigh up to 20 tonnes. Although it is the world's largest fish, it is also a harmless giant, guzzling nothing larger than plankton.

▷ The hammerhead shark, carpet shark and stingray belong to the Chondrichthyes class (fish that have a gristly skeleton). All other fish in the side panels, including marine and freshwater species, are Osteichthyes (fish that have a bony skeleton).

Archerfish

Sailfish

Red mullet

Flounder

Pufferfish

Stingray

Hammerhead shark

Carpet shark

Sturgeon

Alligator gar

OCEAN LIFE

Sea Mammals

Mammals are warm-blooded creatures that cannot breathe under water, yet millions of years ago some took to the sea to find food. Their descendants developed into expert swimmers, with flipper-shaped limbs and thick body fat to protect them against the deadly cold of the water.

Seals, sea lions and walruses are graceful swimmers in water but clumsy movers on land. Most come ashore only to breed or rest. Other sea mammals, such as sea cows and whales, cannot leave the sea at all, although their ancestors could. In 1994, scientists discovered the 50 million year old fossil of *Ambulocetus*, a small whale with hind legs.

Whales either have teeth or whalebone (baleen) plates. Toothed whales mainly hunt fish or squid, although killer whales seize penguins, seals and even other whales. A baleen whale's plates trap tiny fish or plankton when it squirts out a mouthful of water. Baleens include the blue whale – the largest of all animals.

△ *Male northern elephant seals fight for control of a beach. A victorious male mates with the females on the beach he controls.*

▽ *Manatees are distantly related to elephants. Their paddle-shaped forelimbs and flat tails makes them powerful swimmers. Manatees never come ashore. They eat plants growing in warm, shallow Atlantic waters and rivers.*

▽ *Walruses use their snouts rather than their tusks to dig clams from the seabed. Males can grow to over three metres in length and weigh around 1,200 kilogrammes.*

OCEAN LIFE

△ Sperm whales are toothed whales up to 20 metres in length and weighing up to 70 tonnes. Males can dive 3,000 metres to hunt squid on the seabed, and stay down for nearly two hours.

△ The largest creatures on Earth, blue whales can grow up to 33 metres in length and weigh more than 170 tonnes. Until their slaughter was banned, they were hunted almost to extinction.

▽ Sea otters eat and sleep on their backs. They swim off North Pacific coasts and feed on crabs, clams, fish and mussels. A sea otter often uses its front paws to grasp a shellfish and smash it open against a rock balanced on its belly.

◁ Bottle-nosed dolphins are small, fast, toothed whales with fish-like fins and flippers. These graceful creatures hunt fish in warm or tropical waters around the world.

△ The streamlined bodies of California sea lions make them very agile in the water. They hunt for fish among the kelp forests off the west coast of North America.

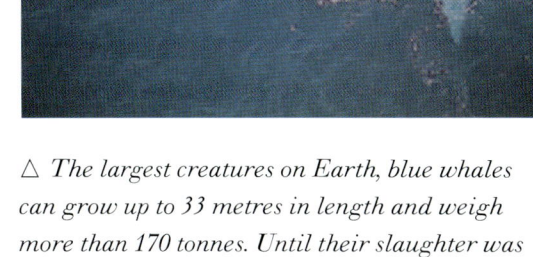

OCEAN LIFE

Coral Reefs

Coral reefs stand in warm, shallow seas and oceans. A reef is made up from billions of little stony cups, most no bigger than a thumbnail. Each cup once hid a tiny coral polyp, a creature related to sea anemones and jellyfish. When the polyp dies it leaves behind a hard, outer skeleton over which new polyps begin to grow. Colonies of living polyps create green, purple, orange and yellow corals shaped like crusts, brains, branches, fans or stags' horns.

Coral reefs support a huge variety of life. Sponges, sea anemones, lionfish, sea slugs, and predators such as sea snakes, groupers and barracudas are just a few of the reef's many inhabitants. In fact one third of all fish species can be found on coral reefs.

The reef provides each creature with a plentiful food supply. Sponges suck in tiny organisms and sea anemones paralyse and eat small fish. Butterflyfish probe coral heads for crustaceans and molluscs. Certain creatures, such as the crown-of-thorns starfish, feed on the coral itself.

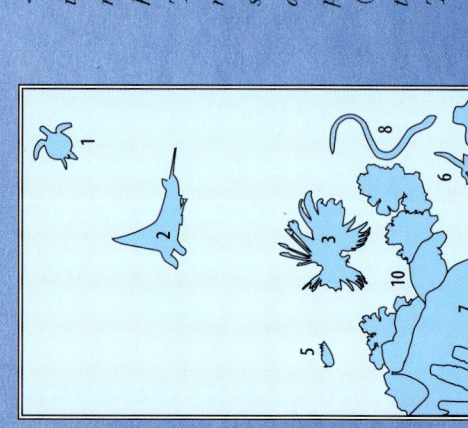

▽ Coral reefs are found in clear, shallow water where the temperature is never less than 20°C. Coral polyps – the tiny creatures that build the reef – thrive in these light and warm conditions.

▷ A single coral colony can support hundreds of different animal and plant species. Although reef-forming coral grows only a few centimetres each year, many reefs started developing over 10,000 years ago. This long period has given reef-dwellers the opportunity to evolve a vast array of

▽ Creatures of this coral reef include a sea turtle (1), a manta ray (2) and a lionfish (3) which has deadly poisonous spines. The brilliant colours of two nudibranchs (4 and 5) and a starfish (6) make them stand out against other species. Top predators such as the grouper (7) and sea snake (8) live among the sponges (9) and corals (10). The coral-eating crown-of-thorns starfish (11) lurks at the bottom.

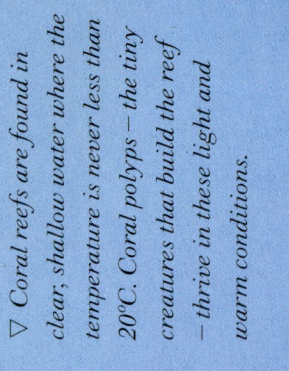

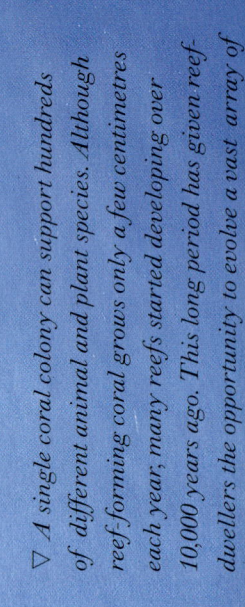

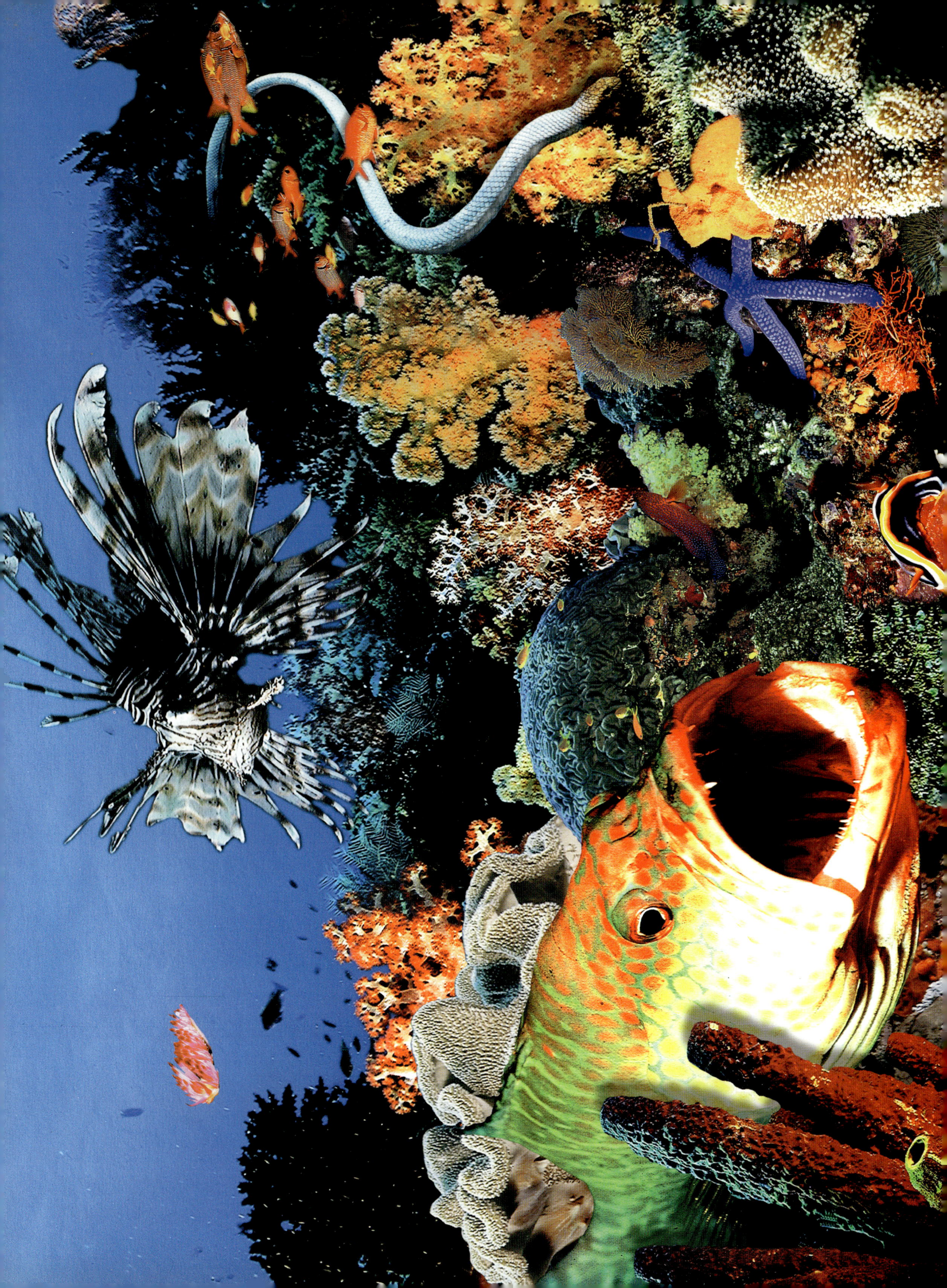

OCEAN LIFE

Life in the Depths

Most sea creatures depend on plant-like phytoplankton for their food supply, but not much of this can flourish in the dim light below 180 metres. Creatures of the twilight zone (150–1,000 metres deep) eat one another, or survive on dead animals and algae that rain down from above. Some swim up to feed at night, camouflaged by darkness. Down here, sharks find prey by scent or vibrations set off by their victims' bodies. Other inhabitants include swarms of squid, shrimps, prawns and billions of deep-sea copepods.

Black bodies conceal some fish from their enemies at these levels. Lanternfish and hatchet fish, however, glow with little lights or shine with silvery, reflective sides to confuse their predators.

No light penetrates below 1,000 metres. Small, flabby fish live here, such as viperfish and gulper eels with fanged jaws and elastic stomachs for the rare big meals that come their way. Few of these ferocious-looking deep-sea fish are more than 30 centimetres long – a larger fish would not find enough food to survive.

△ An expandable stomach and hinged mouth allows the deep-sea swallower to devour prey larger than itself.

▽ The razor-sharp fangs of the viperfish make it an effective predator. Like many deep-sea fish, the viperfish swims open-jawed, catching any prey between its sharp teeth before swallowing.

▽ The various species that survive in the depths of the ocean are rarely more than 30 centimetres long. Some live deeper than others, and several swim to the surface at night. Many have developed special adaptations to survive in this extreme environment. The viperfish (1) and lanternfish (2) have light organs on their bodies to confuse their enemies. Others such as this anglerfish (3) and stomiatoid (4) use luminous lures to attract prey. Male anglerfish sometimes attach themselves to a much larger female anglerfish (5) and live there permanently. The vicious teeth of the fangtooth (6) earn this hunter its name, while the pelican-like mouth of the gulper eel (7) is almost a quarter the length of its body.

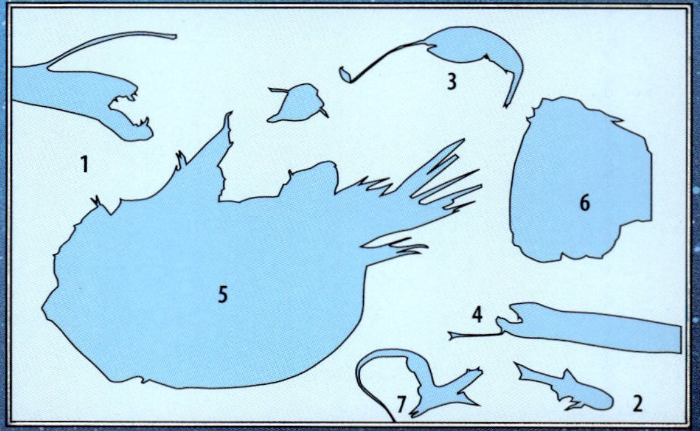

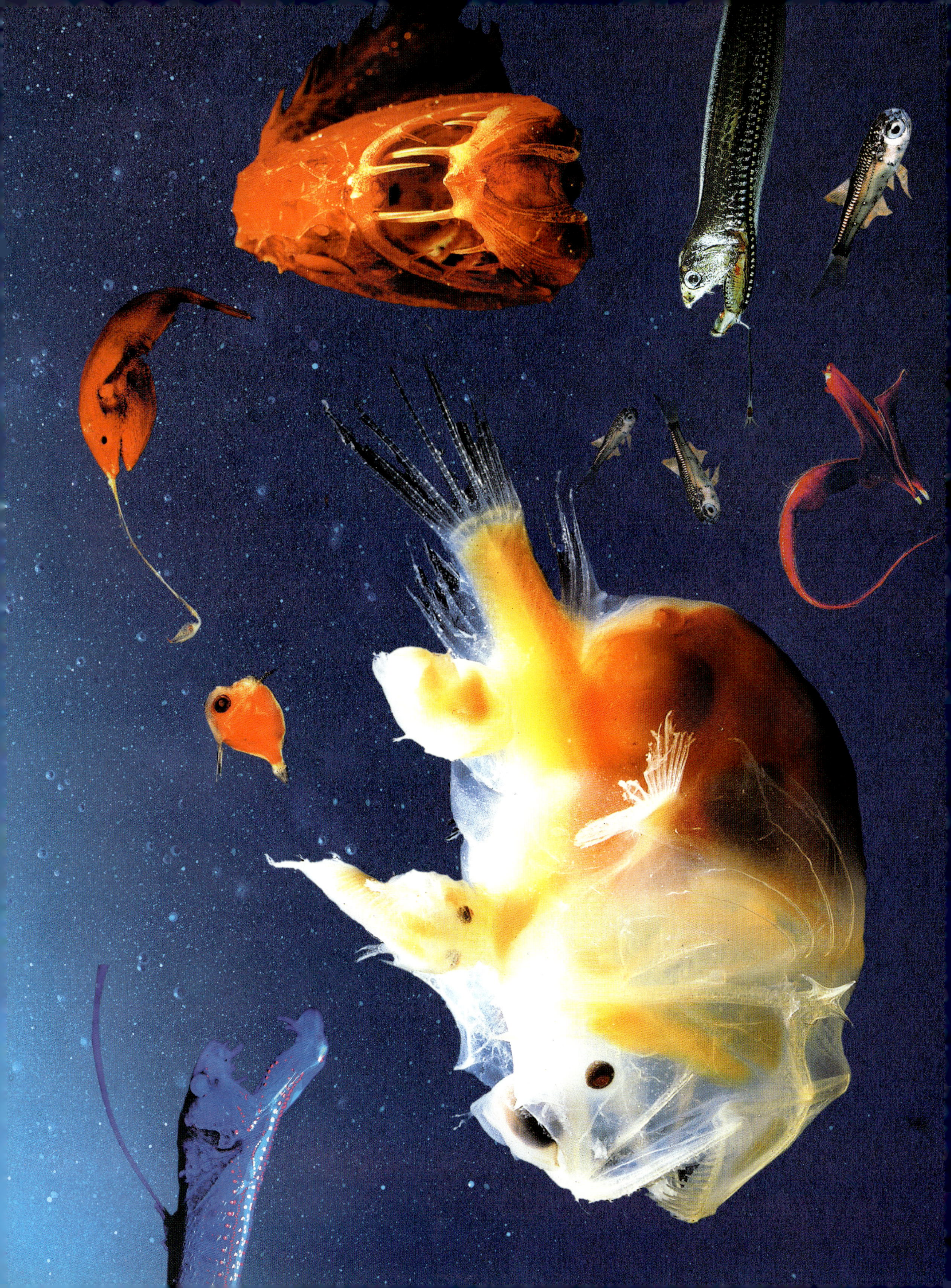

OCEAN LIFE

Rocky Shores

Where the sea meets the land either might gain the upper hand. In some places the land thrusts out into the sea. Elsewhere the sea eats into the land. Storm waves can undermine a sloping coast until its top tumbles and it becomes a wave-washed boulder beach backed by a retreating sea cliff.

Rocky shores are battered by storm waves and drowned by high tides. They bake in the heat and almost freeze during cold spells. Organisms found on rocky shores have evolved to survive and make the most of the conditions.

Water buoys up the fronds of seaweeds, while their root-like holdfasts prevent waves from wrenching them off the rocks. Sea squirts, sponges, sea anemones, acorn barnacles and mussels also attach themselves to rocks. They eat scraps of food washed in with the tide. Limpets and topshells graze algae growing on the boulders, while dog whelks bore holes in fellow molluscs' shells and eat their flesh. At low tide, the shells of acorn barnacles and limpets keep them safe from predators and ensure their insides remain moist.

Rockpools hold water even at low tide. Crustaceans, such as shrimps and crabs, ferocious ragworms, starfish, and small fish all find food and hiding places here.

△ *Some rockpools have sandy floors. Marine creatures such as this common shrimp can burrow into the sand to avoid predators.*

◁ *Over time, the endless pounding of waves has cut an arch through Gaada Stack in the Shetland Islands, north of Scotland's mainland. The sea is the main cause of coastal erosion.*

△ *Toppled boulders litter the shore around a rocky beach at Pondfield Cove in Dorset, England. Rockpools, along with cracks and crevices in rocks and caves, provide a home for a large variety of creatures.*

OCEAN LIFE

◁ A pencil urchin has long, broad spines with sharp ends. Slender tube feet, with strong suckers, drag it along or hold it in place. Like a starfish, this sea urchin has a mouth below the middle of its body.

◁ Sea cucumbers are related to starfish and sea urchins. They can grow to 30 centimetres long. At low tide some wedge themselves into rock crevices. When a sea cucumber is threatened, it squirts out sticky threads to entangle an attacker.

▽ Root-like holdfasts anchor this brown seaweed to a rock. The flexible fronds extending from the holdfasts prevent the seaweed from being ripped apart by the waves.

▽ A beadlet anemone's sticky base keeps it firmly attached to hard surfaces. Stinging cells in its tentacles stun small prey. At low tide, or when threatened, anemones withdraw their tentacles back into their bodies.

◁ Shells protect common limpets against enemies and drying out. At high tide they search for seaweed on rocks. After feeding, limpets always return to the same spot.

OCEAN LIFE

Sand and Pebbles

Pebbly and sandy beaches often form gently shelving shores. Pebbles are stones that have broken off a rocky coast and been rubbed smooth against one another by waves. Most sand grains are scraps of ground-down pebbles. Waves coming ashore at an angle drive pebbles and sand along a coast, sort them into sizes, and then drop them in sheltered waters where they accumulate and form beaches. Bay-head beaches develop between headlands (cliffs jutting out into the sea). Others include lowland beaches backed by dunes, bars (offshore beaches) and spits (beaches growing out into the sea).

Few organisms can survive the crushing force of stones rolled up and down a pebble beach by waves. A sandy beach also poses problems.

▷ *This gently sloping beach in California, USA, was built from eroded sea cliff ground down by the sea. Wind-driven waves have carried and piled up pebbles along the water's edge.*

△ *Cockles are heart-shaped bivalves — molluscs with a shell of two hinged halves. Cockles burrow and move around using a muscular foot.*

▽ *Razor shells are long, narrow bivalves that bury themselves in the sand. At high tide their feeding tubes poke above the sand to suck in plankton carried in by the water.*

◁ *Winds have shifted sand and built up dunes behind this beach in Scotland. Marram grass, rooted in the loose sand, helps to fix the dunes in place.*

OCEAN LIFE

The sand dries out in the sun, shifts in storms and lacks rocks for animals to grip or hide beneath. Even so, millions of burrowing creatures find safety a few centimetres underneath the surface of a sandy beach.

At low tide, tiny pits and bumps betray an invisible army of worms, molluscs, crabs, shrimps and echinoderms, such as heart urchins and sand stars. At high tide, some burrowers climb out and swim or crawl in search of food. Others stay put and suck in plankton through feeding tubes, or poke out tentacles to capture passing morsels. Lugworms remain buried, extracting nourishment from muddy sand.

Even burrowing does not always give protection to small inhabitants of sandy shores. At high tide, fish swim inshore to snap up the unwary. At low tide, wading birds with long, sensitive beaks pry molluscs from their crumbly caves.

◁ *Grunions lay their eggs on the beaches of southern California between February and September. These small fish wait until night, when very high tides sweep them up onto the sandy shores.*

▽ *A lugworm (left) sucks in sand containing scraps of food and squirts out waste in coils. At low tide, a hole betrays its burrow on the beach.*

▷ *When a masked crab burrows in the sand, it draws water through its long tube antennae. At high tide it crawls out of the sand to feed.*

PEOPLE AND THE OCEANS

Early Ocean Explorers

Tens of thousands of years ago, people were making sea-crossings by canoe or raft to settle empty continents. The Old Stone Age ancestors of Aboriginal Australians arrived by sea from Southeast Asia at least 60,000 years ago.

From about 3000BC Micronesian, Melanesian and Polynesian seafarers began to discover the islands of the South Pacific. By AD1000 the Polynesians, the greatest of these early ocean explorers, had settled all the major islands lying in the area bounded by Hawaii, New Zealand and Easter Island. These islands form the tips of a vast triangle covering 20 million square kilometres.

Further west, Bronze Age traders and explorers were making daring voyages in fragile sailing ships. Reed ships probably traded across the Arabian Sea 4,300 years ago. A thousand years later, wooden cargo ships sailed the Mediterranean carrying precious goods such as gold, ostrich eggs and ivory.

Experts disagree about which navigator first reached North America. Vikings had sailed to Newfoundland from Greenland by AD1000. However, it is also possible that Chinese sailors, ancient Egyptians or an Irish monk might have set foot in North America much earlier.

△ *Brendan, an ox-hide boat, was sailed from Ireland to Newfoundland by the British adventurer Tim Severin in 1976. Old Irish writings hint that an Irish monk reached North America in a boat made from animal skins about AD570. Severin's expedition proved it was possible to make this voyage in a similar boat.*

◁ *Norsemen were Europe's greatest seafarers during the early Middle Ages. From about AD800–1000, their oared sailing ships carried Viking sea raiders and traders from Scandinavia around Europe and far up its rivers. Norse settlers also crossed the Atlantic, reaching Greenland, Iceland and Newfoundland.*

◁ The Pacific islands lying in the vast Polynesian triangle formed by Hawaii, New Zealand and Easter Island were settled by voyagers from about 1500 BC. They used two canoes, fixed together with a platform, to carry passengers, animals and plants.

▷ In 1970, Norwegian explorer Thor Heyerdahl sailed from Morocco to the Caribbean in a reed boat. He believed that this journey showed that ancient Egyptians from North Africa used similar boats to reach the Americas thousands of years ago.

△ Thor Heyerdahl holding a model reed boat. His 1947 voyage in the raft Kon-Tiki showed that ancient seafarers from South America may have reached the Polynesian islands before settlers from the west.

PEOPLE AND THE OCEANS

The Age of Exploration

▽ *These modern replicas of Christopher Columbus' ships* Santa María, Niña *and* Pinta *set sail from Spain in 1992. Five hundred years earlier, Columbus' fleet of three ships, sponsored by Queen Isabella of Spain, crossed the Atlantic and reached the Bahamas.*

Five centuries ago, sailors from Europe began criss-crossing the oceans and exploring the world. In the 1400s, improved navigation aids and new sailing ships, called caravels and carracks, gave European navigators confidence to sail far out of sight of land. First, Portugal sent caravels down the west coast of Africa to bypass hostile Mediterranean powers and find a new sea route to the spice-rich lands of India and Southeast Asia. By 1488, Bartholomew Dias had rounded the tip of southern Africa and by 1499, Vasco da Gama had sailed to India and back.

△ *Henry the Navigator (1394–1460) played a major part in starting off the great age of ocean exploration by European seafarers. This Portuguese prince organized and sent out 50 naval expeditions. Many explored the west coast of Africa as far south as Sierra Leone.*

Soon Spain was competing with Portugal for Asian trade. In 1492, Christopher Columbus sailed west to seek a transatlantic route to Asia on behalf of the Spanish crown. Instead he found the islands of the Caribbean, marking the start of Spain's conquest of the Americas. In 1519, Ferdinand Magellan led a three-year Spanish expedition which became the first to circumnavigate the world and prove it is round. But war, disease and shipwreck took its toll — of the five ships and 241 men who set out, only the *Victoria* and 19 men returned.

Little by little such journeys helped cartographers to map the edges of the oceans. Major discoveries were still being made in the 1700s. Between 1768 and 1779, Captain James Cook led three British voyages of exploration probing the Pacific and visiting Australia, New Zealand and Hawaii.

△ The Victoria was the only surviving ship from a fleet of five that set out to circle the globe in 1519. Its return to Spain three years later proved to Europeans that the world is round.

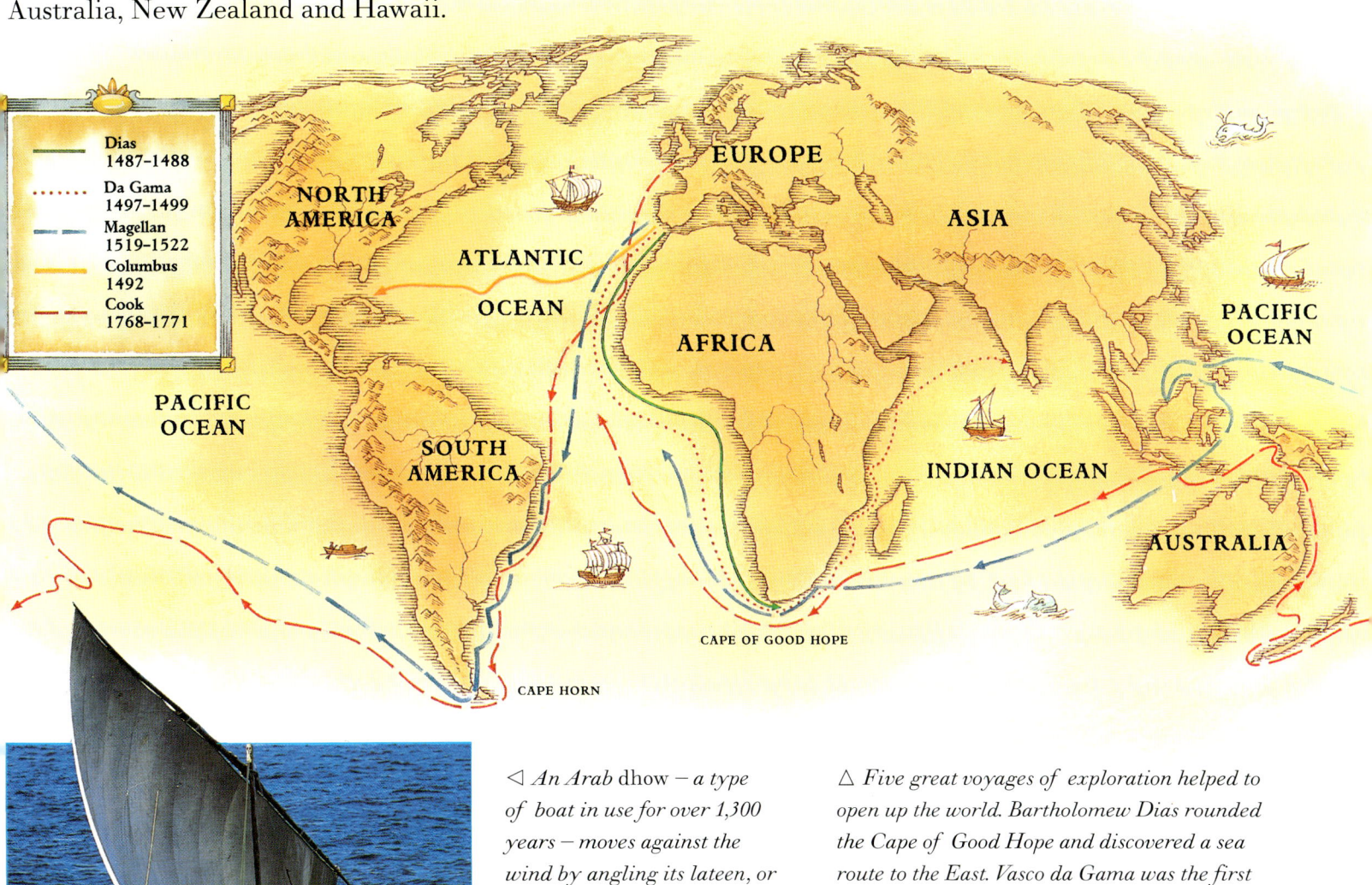

◁ *An Arab* dhow — a type of boat in use for over 1,300 years — moves against the wind by angling its lateen, or triangular, sail. Spanish and Portuguese ship designers in the 1400s copied this type of sail to make their vessels faster and more manoeuvrable.

△ Five great voyages of exploration helped to open up the world. Bartholomew Dias rounded the Cape of Good Hope and discovered a sea route to the East. Vasco da Gama was the first European to reach India by sea. Christopher Columbus crossed the Atlantic, reaching the Americas. Ferdinand Magellan's expedition circled the world and James Cook's voyages charted the coasts and islands of the Pacific.

115

PEOPLE AND THE OCEANS

Advances in Navigation

Without navigation equipment it is easy to become lost in the open ocean. Most early sailors kept within sight of land, but bolder mariners steered by steady winds or currents, or by following migrating birds. Even so, many lost their way before more accurate navigation aids were invented.

By 1200, the magnetic compass was being used by European sailors to plot direction. Later, the astrolabe and cross staff enabled them to find their latitude (north/south position) by measuring the Sun's midday height or the Pole Star's height at night.

By the 1500s, latitude could be measured with some accuracy. Longitude (east/west position) remained a problem for another two centuries. Measuring longitude, which relied on precise timekeeping, was finally made possible in the 1760s with the development of accurate clocks called chronometers.

The twentieth century saw many advances in navigation. Gyroscopic compasses, which are unaffected by magnetic forces, always give exact readings. Loran (long-range navigation) allows a ship to determine its position by radio signals beamed from a pair of transmitters. Radar helps a navigator locate obstructions, while ships' computers receiving signals from satellites can plot positions to within 30 metres.

△ In the 1500s, navigators used the astrolabe to calculate latitude by observing the Sun at midday.

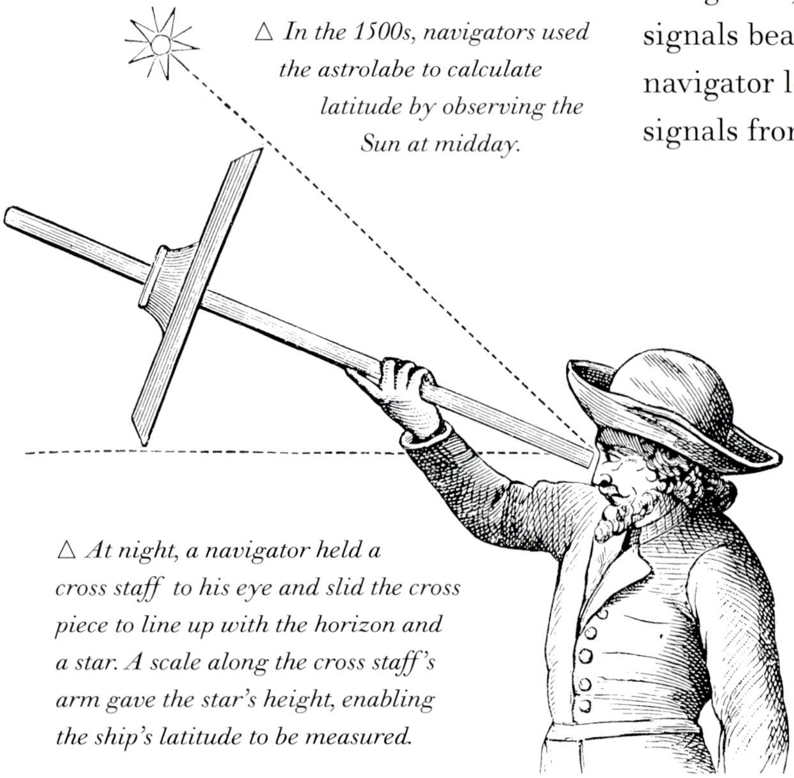

△ At night, a navigator held a cross staff to his eye and slid the cross piece to line up with the horizon and a star. A scale along the cross staff's arm gave the star's height, enabling the ship's latitude to be measured.

▽ In the late 1500s, the maps of Gerardus Mercator introduced a new way of showing the globe on a flat piece of paper. His system, which used lines of latitude and longitude, helped navigators plot more accurate routes.

◁ The English naturalist Charles Darwin used this sextant on his voyage around the world betwen 1831 and 1836. Sextants are still used today to determine latitude.

▷ In this Micronesian stick map, curved sticks stand for ocean swells and the shells represent islands. Micronesian seafarers used such maps to chart parts of the Pacific.

△ A sextant usually includes an arm, a graduated arc and mirrors. The navigator looks through the eye-piece and swings the arm until a reflected image of a star or the Sun appears. The arc shows its height, from which the latitude is calculated.

△ A radar screen helps a navigator to plot a course. Radar bounces radio signals off a target. The returning signals indicate the position of obstructions and other vessels even in thick fog.

▷ Harrison's chronometer of 1760 allowed longitude to be measured by comparing the time in London with the local midday time. This enabled navigators to calculate their east/west position accurately.

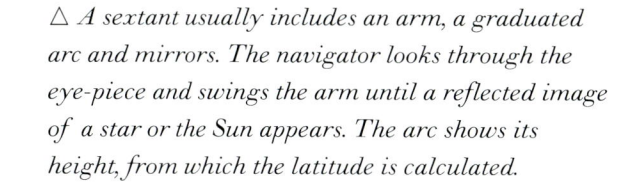

117

PEOPLE AND THE OCEANS

The Sea and the Arts

Over the last 250 years, the sea has inspired many composers, writers and painters. But the sea has not always been a subject in its own right. In paintings of the 1400s and 1500s, for example, it was used as a background for gods and goddesses, or historical events.

From the late 1700s, however, the sea began to loom large in poems, paintings and music. Some artists saw it as a world of terror and mystery, others as a place of gently changing moods or as a setting for pleasure.

Artists such as William Hodges and J.M.W. Turner painted the sea to show nature at its most powerful. Their pictures show the helplessness of people in the face of an overwhelming sea storm or waterspout. The terrifying dangers of the open sea are brilliantly caught in the shipwreck paintings of Winslow Homer. Mystery and terror also feature in works of literature and music, such as Herman Melville's novel *Moby Dick* and Richard Wagner's opera *The Flying Dutchman*.

The sea's changing moods fascinated French impressionist painters of the late 1800s, as well as composers from Felix Mendelssohn to Benjamin Britten. The opera *Peter Grimes*, written by Britten in 1945, shows the sea raging in a storm, glinting in the sun and sulking in the fog.

△ *Winds that blow across the sea are given human form in this detail from the* Birth of Venus *(see bottom right).*

◁ *A boat is dwarfed by the raging sea in* The Breaking Wave off Kanagawa. *This print was made by the great Japanese artist Hokusai (1760–1849).*

△ *A whale snatches up a boat in a poster for a film based on* Moby Dick, *the novel by the American writer Herman Melville (1819–1891). This adventure tells the story of Captain Ahab's fanatical hunt to catch a fierce white whale that eventually kills him.*

PEOPLE AND THE OCEANS

◁ *A lone man drifts helplessly on a battered boat circled by sharks.* The Gulf Stream, *by the American artist Winslow Homer (1836–1910), captures human powerlessness when faced by one of the ocean's many dangers.*

△ *A visit to the Scottish island of Staffa inspired the German composer Felix Mendelssohn (1809–1847) to compose* The Hebrides (Fingal's Cave).

▷ *The sea provided little more than a background for Renaissance paintings, such as the* Birth of Venus. *This picture by the Italian artist Sandro Botticelli (1445–1510) is based on a Greek myth. It tells the story of how Venus – the goddess of love – was born in the sea and blown ashore in a seashell by the winds.*

△ *A sandy beach crowded with bathers features in* The Beach in Front of the Casino Café, *by the American artist Martha Walter (1875–1976). By the mid-1800s railways had put coasts within easy reach of city-dwellers. Artists began to paint the seaside as a popular playground for holidaymakers.*

PEOPLE AND THE OCEANS

Food from the Sea

Fish provide much of the world's protein food supply. Every year, about 75 million tonnes of fish are caught. The richest fishing grounds lie where seawater contains plenty of nutrients for the plankton on which fish depend. Mackerel, pollack, herring and tuna are important pelagic, or surface-living, fish. Demersal, or bottom-living, species include cod, flounder, plaice, haddock, and shellfish such as crabs, lobsters and shrimps.

Inshore, nets are thrown and traps set by hand to catch fish, crabs and octopuses. Out at sea, sonar devices help fishing boats to track down large shoals, and special nets or hooks catch fish living at different depths. Trawlers hunt demersal species by dragging trawl nets over the seabed. Purse seine nets are pulled shut to trap mid-water species. Pelagic fish are either snared on long curtain-like drift nets hung from buoys, or caught on baited hooks attached to long lines.

Small craft may supply one big factory ship, where fish are gutted, frozen and stored for several weeks. A factory trawler may catch and process up to 600 tonnes a day. However, intensive fishing can also threaten ocean resources. Overfishing has dramatically reduced the stocks of some species.

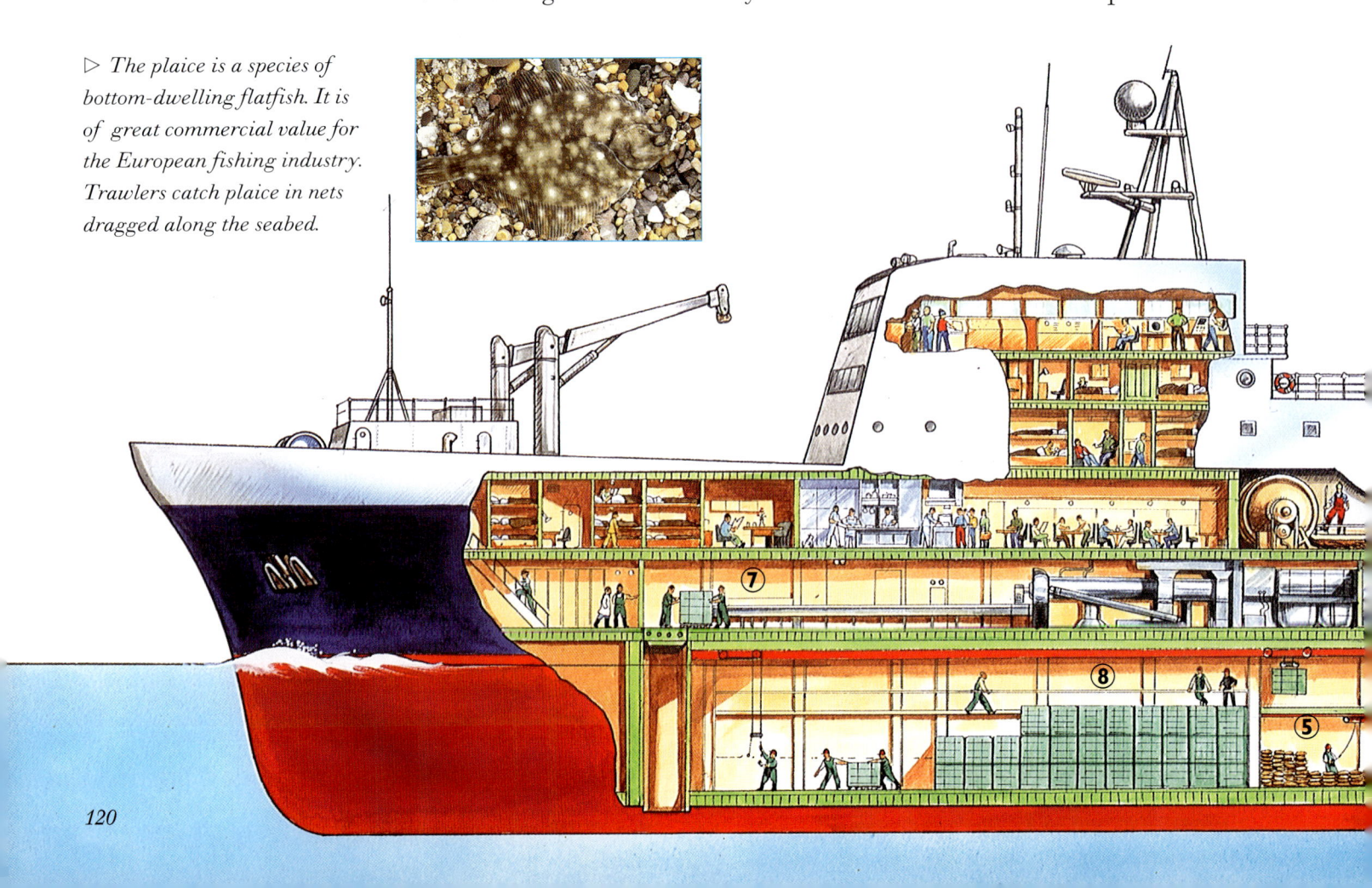

△ A wood and wire cage, filled with lobsters caught off the coast of Brazil, is raised from the sea. Lobster pots, or traps, are baited with fish or fish offal and lowered to the seabed.

▷ The plaice is a species of bottom-dwelling flatfish. It is of great commercial value for the European fishing industry. Trawlers catch plaice in nets dragged along the seabed.

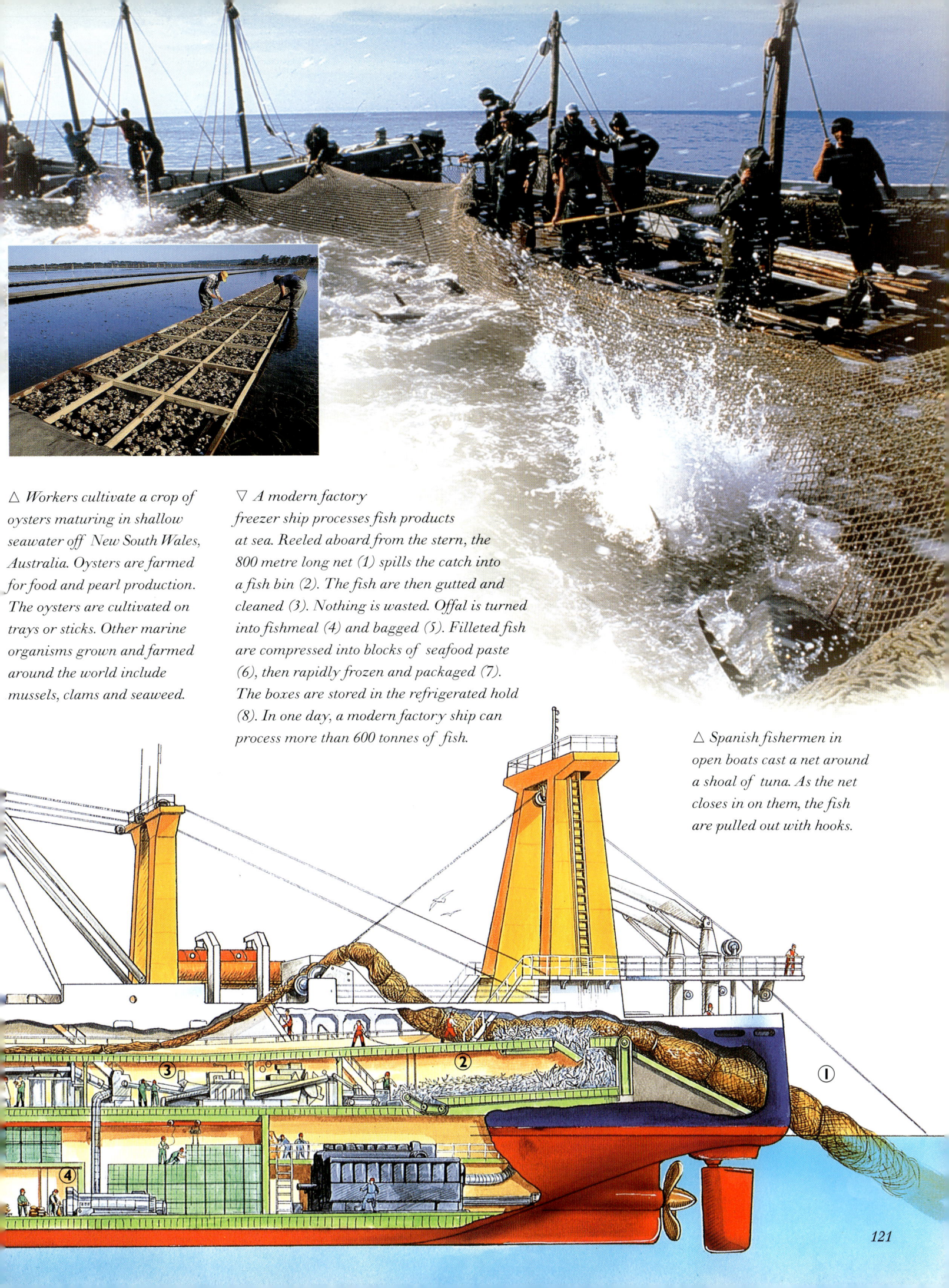

△ Workers cultivate a crop of oysters maturing in shallow seawater off New South Wales, Australia. Oysters are farmed for food and pearl production. The oysters are cultivated on trays or sticks. Other marine organisms grown and farmed around the world include mussels, clams and seaweed.

▽ A modern factory freezer ship processes fish products at sea. Reeled aboard from the stern, the 800 metre long net (1) spills the catch into a fish bin (2). The fish are then gutted and cleaned (3). Nothing is wasted. Offal is turned into fishmeal (4) and bagged (5). Filleted fish are compressed into blocks of seafood paste (6), then rapidly frozen and packaged (7). The boxes are stored in the refrigerated hold (8). In one day, a modern factory ship can process more than 600 tonnes of fish.

△ Spanish fishermen in open boats cast a net around a shoal of tuna. As the net closes in on them, the fish are pulled out with hooks.

121

PEOPLE AND THE OCEANS

Hidden Dangers

Ships face many dangers at sea. One of the most feared of naturally-occurring hazards are icebergs that have drifted from polar regions into shipping lanes. In 1912, just over 1,500 people drowned when the liner *Titanic* hit an iceberg. After this disaster, ice patrols began to keep watch for dangerous, drifting icebergs in the North Atlantic.

Underwater rocks and reefs have also been a risk since ships first put to sea. Shifting sandbanks are another invisible menace. Since 1500, more than 5,000 ships have foundered on the Goodwin Sands off southeast England. In recent years, several supertankers have run aground off Alaska, France and England.

Disasters have also been caused by human errors such as faulty ship design, overloading, navigational mistakes and even the failure to close a car ferry's sea doors. Poor maintenance killed 167 people in 1988 when a fire at sea gutted the *Piper Alpha* platform, a North Sea oil rig. However, the greatest of all sea catastrophes occurred during World War II when a Soviet submarine sank the German liner *Wilhelm Gustloff* and 7,700 passengers lost their lives.

△ Even in clear weather, icebergs can be a danger to ships that sail too near — 88 percent of a castle berg lurks invisibly under the sea.

▽ An aerial photograph shows salvage work on the wrecked and still smoking Piper Alpha oil platform. The explosion, in 1988, sparked off by a gas leak, caused the North Sea's worst-ever oil rig disaster.

PEOPLE AND THE OCEANS

◁ *In 1912, newspaper headlines around the world reported the sinking of the ocean liner* Titanic. *On her maiden transatlantic voyage from England to New York City, the world's largest ship struck an iceberg in the freezing waters of the North Atlantic. Believed to be unsinkable, the double-hulled liner sank in about two and a half hours with the loss of over 1,500 lives.*

△ *In 1993, the tanker* Braer *leaked oil and sank after grounding on rocks off the Shetland Islands. Even worse oil spills have occurred when supertankers have snagged on hidden reefs.*

▷ *Modern-day pirates in fast, small boats pose a major threat to cargo ships sailing off Indonesia. Crews fend them off with razor-wire fencing and jets of water squirted from hoses.*

123

PEOPLE AND THE OCEANS

Future Prospects

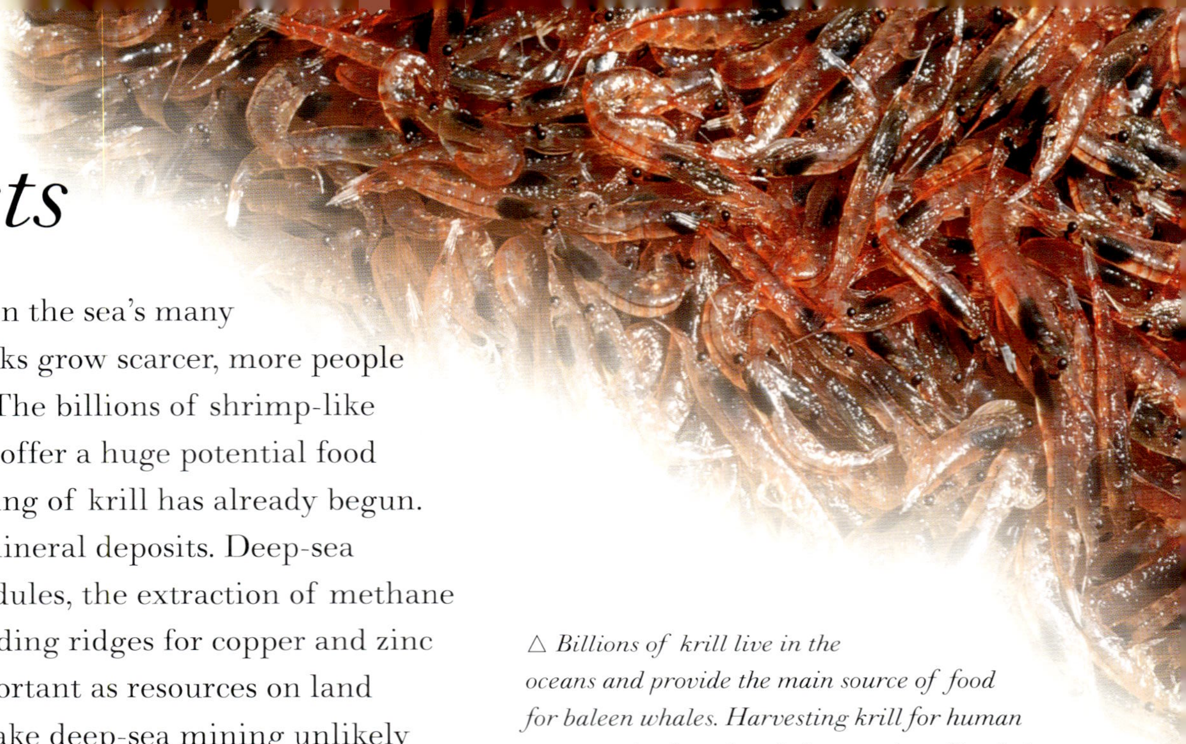

People will always depend on the sea's many resources. As wild fish stocks grow scarcer, more people are turning to fish farming. The billions of shrimp-like crustaceans called krill also offer a huge potential food supply. Small-scale harvesting of krill has already begun.

The seabed holds vast mineral deposits. Deep-sea trawling for manganese nodules, the extraction of methane gas and the mining of spreading ridges for copper and zinc will become increasingly important as resources on land dwindle. However, high costs make deep-sea mining unlikely until well into the twenty-first century.

Scientists are learning more about the crucial part that oceans play in the Earth's climate. If global warming continues, people will have to cope with melting ice sheets that raise ocean levels worldwide, drowning atolls and low-lying coasts. Planting mangroves could protect tropical deltas better than building high sea walls, but large tracts of low coast would have to be abandoned. Climatic change could also switch off the North Atlantic Drift that warms western Europe. If that happens, London might become as cold as the icy Labrador coast in the North Atlantic.

One way or another, the future of the Earth and its inhabitants is closely bound up with the oceans.

△ Billions of krill live in the oceans and provide the main source of food for baleen whales. Harvesting krill for human consumption has already begun. As well as being rich in protein, they contain chitin, a substance of great value for the medical industry.

△ If certain ocean currents are disrupted by changes in climate, London could one day have winters as cold and icy as this one in Labrador, Canada. Although on the same latitude as Labrador, the British Isles are kept warm by the North Atlantic Drift.

△ Billions of manganese nodules litter the seabed. These metallic lumps are rich in manganese, iron, copper, nickel and cobalt. However, until less expensive ways are found to mine them, manganese nodules remain a vast, untapped resource.

▽ The oceans would rise some 60 metres and drown cities if the ice caps suddenly melted. Some scientist believe that an increase of about 30 centimetres by the year 2050 is more likely, as a result of global warming. Even so, this would cause severe flooding in low-lying areas.

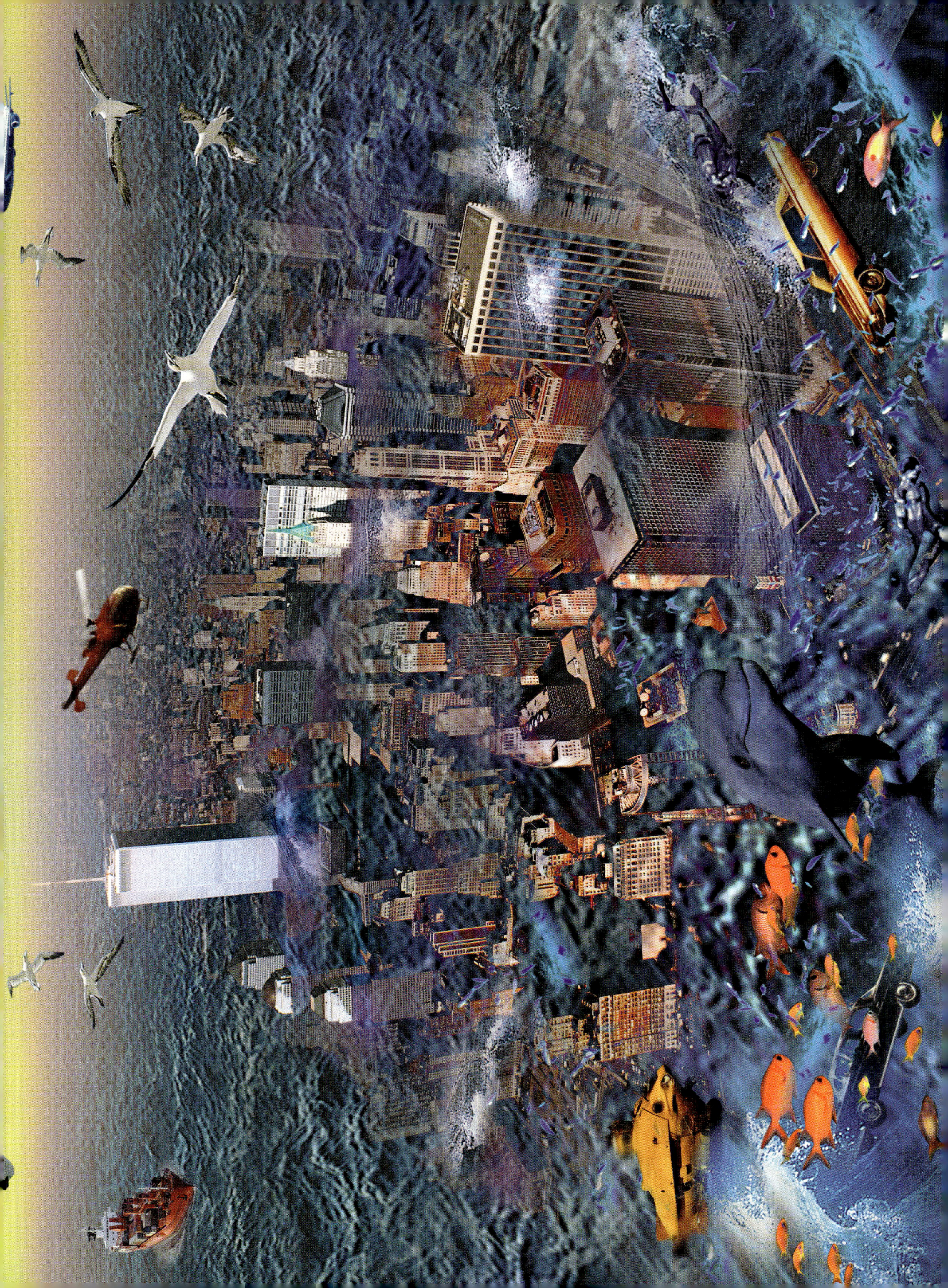

EXPLORING SPACE

A Place in the Cosmos

Our ancestors once believed that the Earth must be the centre of the Universe. Every morning they watched the Sun rise in the east and move across the sky. At night the Moon, stars, and planets filled the darkness and all appeared to revolve around the Earth. For almost a thousand years the Church encouraged this view because it placed humans, God's special creation, at the centre. By the 1500s, some astronomers began to argue that the Earth went around the Sun and, in the end, their evidence was overwhelming. Since then we have discovered that the Universe has no real centre. We inhabit one of nine planets orbiting a medium-sized star in a galaxy containing billions of other stars. This galaxy itself is just one among billions of other galaxies. The search for our place in the Universe must be played out on an altogether bigger stage than ever imagined by our ancestors. And that search is the story of this book.

△ *Great stone calendars such as Stonehenge, built over 4,000 years ago, helped people keep track of the Sun's daily and yearly movements.*

△ *Over 1,800 years ago, Ptolemy set out the Greek scholars' view of an Earth-centred Universe. This Christian version was painted in 1493.*

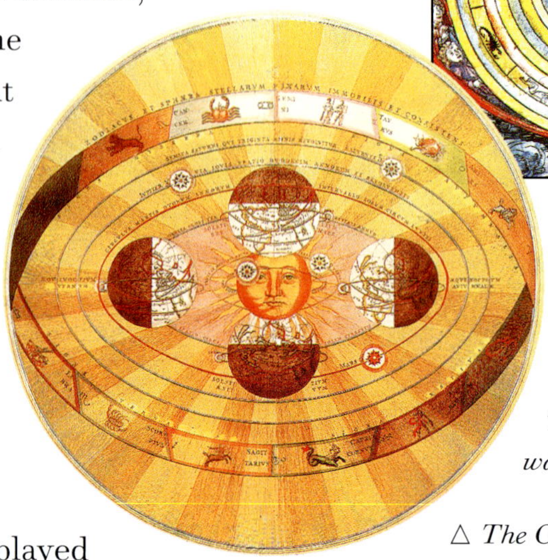

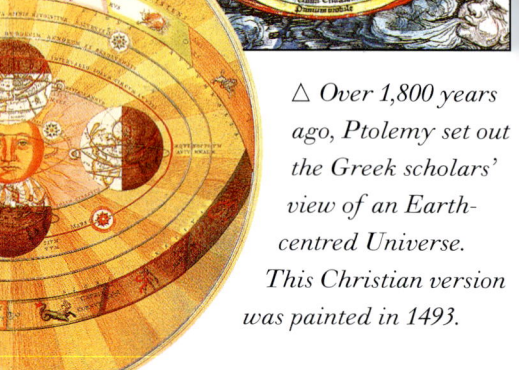

△ *The Copernican model of the Universe has the Sun at the centre. Copernicus first published his ideas in 1543.*

The view from Greece

In 270BC, a Greek philosopher called Anaxagoras suggested that the Earth went round the Sun. His ideas seemed so ridiculous to the people of Athens that he was thrown out of the city! Aristotle's theory, developed by Ptolemy in about AD120, put the Earth at the centre of the Universe with the planets revolving around it in simple circles.

Heavenly revolutions

Nicolaus Copernicus and Galileo Galilei suggested that calculations explaining the motions of planets only made sense if the Earth went around the Sun. Aristotle's model of a Sun-centred Universe was finally overturned in 1610 when Galileo, using his newly invented telescope, discovered that Jupiter had moons orbiting it.

True scale of the Universe

Our galaxy (*right*) lies in a tiny corner of the Universe. The Sun, around which we orbit at an average distance of 150 million kilometres, is no more than a dot in one of the Galaxy's spiral arms. Light takes 100,000 years to reach the Earth from the other side of the Galaxy and ten billion years from the furthest galaxies.

▽ *Albert Einstein provided the framework for our modern understanding of the Universe. In 1915, he proved that space and time cannot be clearly separated and space itself is curved.*

△ *Edwin Hubble was the first person to prove that there are galaxies other than our own. In the late 1920s, he showed that the galaxies are rushing apart from each other and that the Universe is expanding.*

EXPLORING SPACE

Looking Up

In 1609, news reached Italy that a Dutch instrument-maker had used two curved pieces of glass in a tube to magnify a distant object. The first lens focused the object into an image, the second magnified it. The Italian astronomer, Galileo, realized that this 'telescope' could be used to observe the sky, and the heavens became open to serious astronomical study. With this new scientific instrument, Galileo revealed four moons orbiting Jupiter, evidence for the idea that the planets might in turn orbit the Sun. The first telescopes used lenses. Reflecting telescopes, invented in the 1660s, have a concave mirror instead of a lens to focus and catch starlight. The mirror only needs to be curved on one side, so it can be made bigger and detect fainter objects in greater detail.

△ *Galileo's detailed sketches of the Moon were made using the telescope he constructed in 1609.*

▽ *William Herschel's telescope, completed in 178 was used to study and calculate the distribution of thousands of stars through space.*

▷ *The 100-inch (2.5 m) Hooker Telescop Mount Wilson, California, remained the biggest and most powerful telescope in the world until 1948.*

EXPLORING SPACE

◁ *The* Very Large Array *is a series of 27 radio telescopes in the New Mexico desert. Together they have the resolution of an instrument 27 km across, and provide detailed maps of distant galaxies.*

◁ *The 4.2 metre William Herschel Telescope is built on a high, dry mountain peak on La Palma in the Canary Islands. The lines in the sky are the trails of stars.*

Mirror power

A reflecting telescope's power depends on the size of its mirror. The latest generation of telescopes have mirrors over eight metres in diameter. Computers keep the mirrors in alignment. The *Very Large Telescope* in Chile, when it is completed in 2002, will have the power to spot a firefly 10,000 km away.

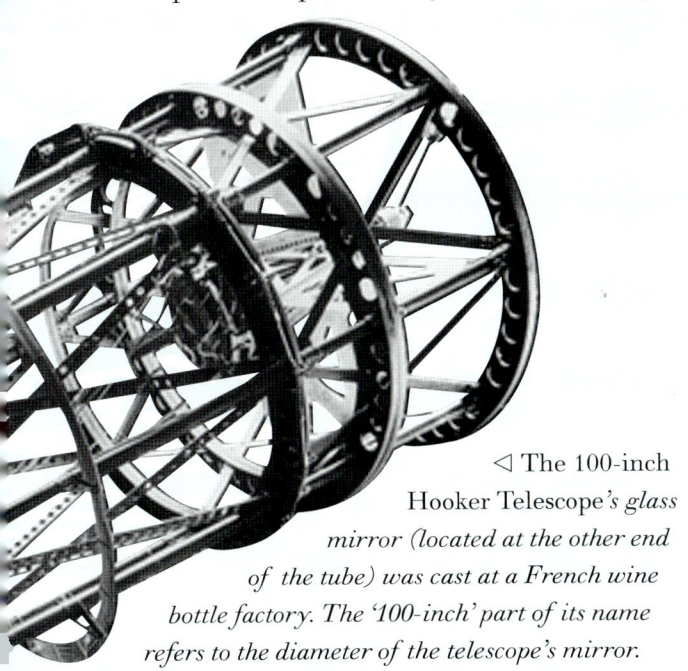

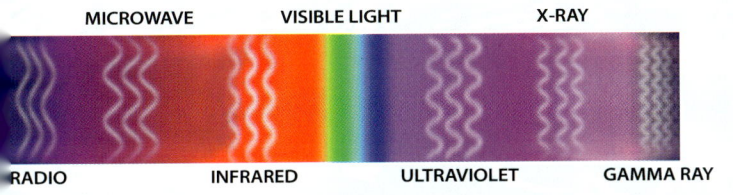

High and dry

Even on a clear night, the Earth is not a perfect place to put a telescope. Water vapour and turbulence in the atmosphere blur the images and make the stars seem to dance around. In order to avoid this, optical telescopes are usually built on mountains. But even here the window of the Universe is not fully open to astronomers.

Radio waves

Objects in the Universe emit radiation at all wavelengths, from gamma rays to radio waves. Visible light, from red to violet, is just one part of this electromagnetic spectrum. Apart from light, only radio waves can properly penetrate the Earth's atmosphere. Today, individual radio telescopes on different continents are linked by computer to give the equivalent of a single dish thousands of kilometres wide.

◁ *The 100-inch Hooker Telescope's glass mirror (located at the other end of the tube) was cast at a French wine bottle factory. The '100-inch' part of its name refers to the diameter of the telescope's mirror.*

▽ *Light is only one octave of the great keyboard of the electromagnetic spectrum. Only visible light and part of the radio spectrum penetrate far through the Earth's atmosphere.*

RADIO — MICROWAVE — INFRARED — VISIBLE LIGHT — ULTRAVIOLET — X-RAY — GAMMA RAY

△ *High, dry mountain peaks provide the best location for observing the sky. This radio telescope (left) and optical telescope (right) are found at Cerro La Silla in the Andes mountains of Chile.*

△ *The* Hubble Space Telescope, *launched from the space shuttle in 1990, has been a phenomenal success. Although its 2.4 m curved mirror was polished to the wrong shape, correcting lenses were fitted in 1993. The* Hubble Space Telescope *can also 'see' in the ultraviolet and infrared wavelengths.*

EXPLORING SPACE

Looking Out

▽ *The* Infrared Space Observatory *detected heat radiation with a curved mirror. Liquid helium kept the sensors cool.*

△ *Images from the* Hubble Space Telescope, *such as this one of a dying star, are radioed back to the Earth.*

A journey just a few kilometres up above the atmosphere opens a whole new window on the Universe. There is no reflected glare of city lights to dazzle an observer and there is nothing to blur the stars or make them twinkle. As a result, it is possible to see objects in far greater detail than from the ground. The *Hubble Space Telescope* is the first big optical telescope to be put into orbit. It has allowed astronomers to peer into the hearts of galaxies and out to the furthest reaches of the Universe. Astronomy satellites also make it possible to explore the full rainbow of radiation, from microwaves and infrared, to ultraviolet, x-rays and gamma rays. The only drawback is that you have to launch your telescope into space!

EXPLORING SPACE

Ultraviolet

Ultraviolet light comes from hot gas and stars. It carries the fingerprints of the atoms that emitted it and the gas clouds through which it has travelled. The *International Ultraviolet Explorer* (*IUE*) was one of the most successful astronomy satellites to date. Launched in 1978 with a planned life of three years, *IUE* focused the light with a 0.5 metre mirror. Instead of taking a picture, it spread the light out into the spectrum of wavelengths, revealing the atomic fingerprints. It was finally switched off in 1997 after nearly nineteen years in service.

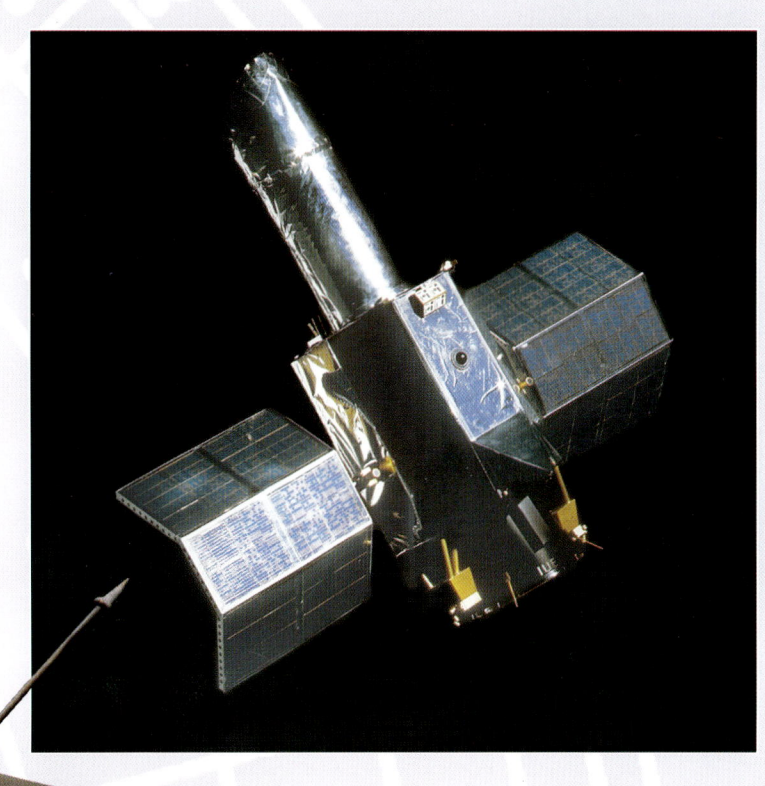

△ *Launched from the space shuttle* Atlantis, *the* Compton Gamma Ray Observatory *is named after Arthur Holly Compton, an American scientist who pioneered the study of gamma rays.*

Heat detection

Infrared, or heat radiation, comes from warm objects that are not as hot as the stars we see. These include planets and comets, regions where new stars are forming, and distant galaxies ablaze with young stars. Although telescopes located on high mountains can see some infrared radiation, the first comprehensive study came with the *Infrared Astronomy Satellite* (*IRAS*) in 1983. In 1995, Europe's *Infrared Space Observatory* (*ISO*) was launched to look in even greater detail.

Gamma rays

Gamma rays are released by the most energetic processes in the Universe. These include matter falling into a black hole, matter and antimatter annihilating each other and explosions in the cores of galaxies. Launched in 1991, the *Compton Gamma Ray Observatory* is an orbiting laboratory which has detected sudden bursts of gamma rays coming from huge distances.

△ *The* International Ultraviolet Explorer *was the only ultraviolet observatory in space until the launch of the* Hubble Space Telescope *in 1990.*

▷ Exosat *was designed to study x-ray sources. Between 1983 and 1986 it made and sent back over 2,000 observations.*

131

EXPLORING SPACE

Rise of the Rocket

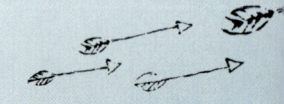

Gravity keeps us earthbound. To escape its pull and leave our planet far behind we need to travel at an incredible 11 kilometres per second (about 40,000 km per hour). To reach such speeds calls for the power of a rocket. The first rockets were more like fireworks and followed the invention of gunpowder by the Chinese in about AD 1000. They used rocket-propelled flaming arrows, launched from a basket, against their enemies (*see picture above left*). Warfare continued to be the driving force in the development of rocketry. During World War II, the V2 rockets of Nazi Germany terrorized British cities. Captured V2s were sent to the United States, and their successors, the intercontinental ballistic missiles, helped to launch the space age.

△ *Robert Goddard designed the first successful liquid-fuel rocket. Its maiden flight in March 1926 lasted 2.5 seconds.*

△ *After World War II, captured German V2 rockets, together with their inventor Wernher von Braun, played a key role in the American space programme.*

The pioneers

After the end of World War II, the pace of rocket research accelerated, with Wernher von Braun in the United States and Sergei Korolev in Russia leading the way. A race soon developed between the two superpowers – if a rocket could send a payload into Earth orbit, it could also deliver a bomb to the other side of the world.

Winners and losers

On October 4, 1957, the Soviet Union demonstrated that they had the edge when they put *Sputnik 1*, a 58-cm aluminium sphere with a radio transmitter, into orbit. Meanwhile, the US Navy *Vanguard* rocket blew up on the launch pad. Wernher von Braun was called in with his army team and, on January 31, 1958, his *Jupiter-C* rocket put *Explorer 1*, America's first satellite, into orbit.

◁ *The mighty* Saturn V *rocket lifts off from Cape Canaveral, Florida, on July 16, 1969 to put the first men on the Moon.*

◁ *Rockets often have several stages, each carrying its own oxygen with which to burn the fuel. The first stage of* Saturn V *had five great engines, burning 15 tonnes of kerosene and liquid oxygen every second. It produced a thrust of 3,500 tonnes and lasted for less than three minutes before falling back to the Earth.*

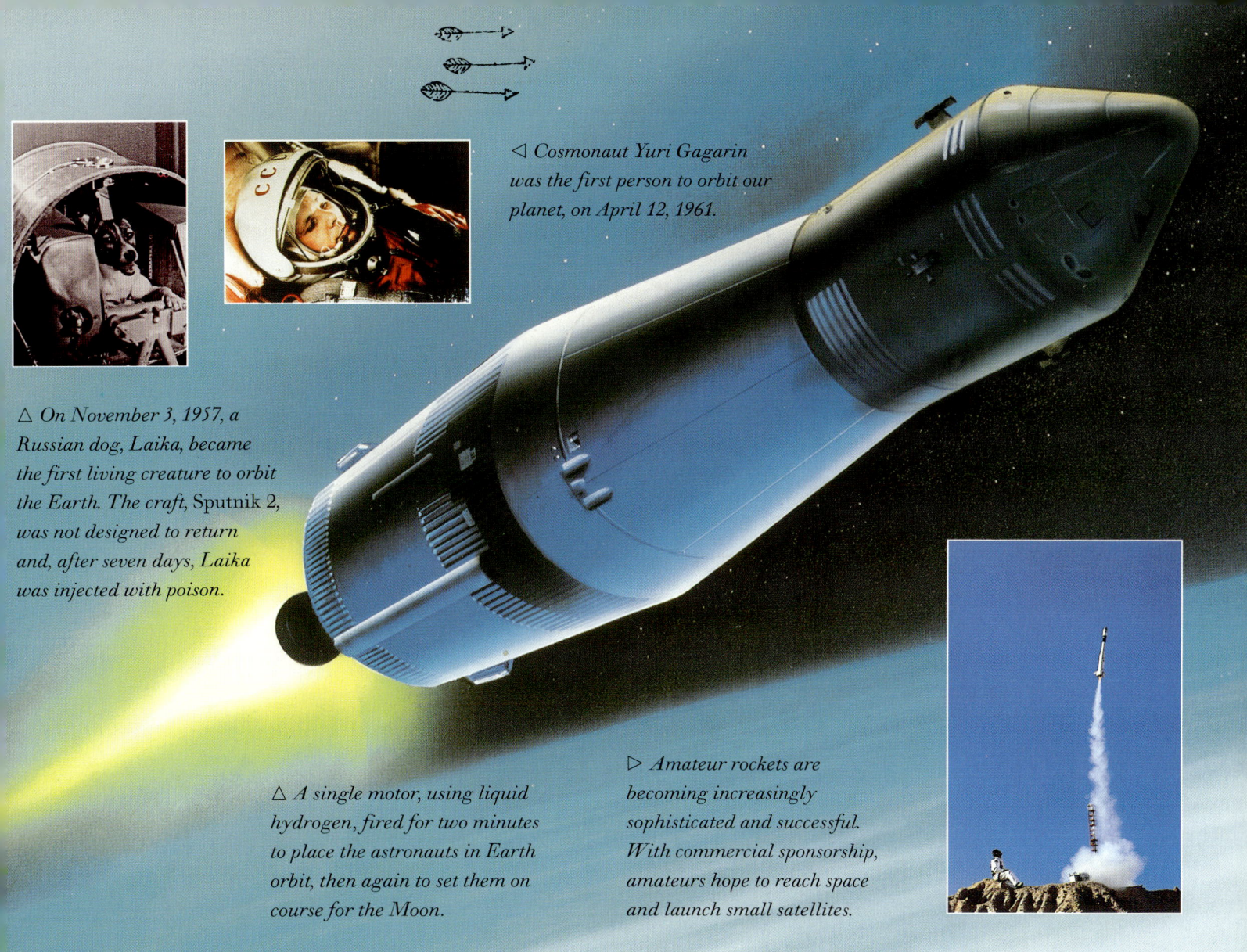

◁ Cosmonaut Yuri Gagarin was the first person to orbit our planet, on April 12, 1961.

△ On November 3, 1957, a Russian dog, Laika, became the first living creature to orbit the Earth. The craft, Sputnik 2, was not designed to return and, after seven days, Laika was injected with poison.

△ A single motor, using liquid hydrogen, fired for two minutes to place the astronauts in Earth orbit, then again to set them on course for the Moon.

▷ Amateur rockets are becoming increasingly sophisticated and successful. With commercial sponsorship, amateurs hope to reach space and launch small satellites.

Spacemen

The first man in space followed shortly after the first satellite. Again, Russia won the race, launching Yuri Gagarin into a single Earth orbit on April 12, 1961. Three weeks later, Alan Shepard became the first American to be blasted into space, though not into orbit, landing 15 minutes later in the Atlantic. Finally, on February 20, 1962, the American John Glenn made three Earth orbits.

△ Two seconds after the first stage broke away, the five rocket motors on the second stage fired, burning liquid hydrogen and liquid oxygen. This stage lasted for six minutes, during which time the escape tower (for use in a launch pad emergency) was jettisoned.

Popular destination

Since the late 1950s, thousands of rockets have been launched and hundreds of people have visited space. But it has never become routine. The dangers are such that each mission involves thousands of people on the ground, checking and re-checking the complex systems of spaceflight.

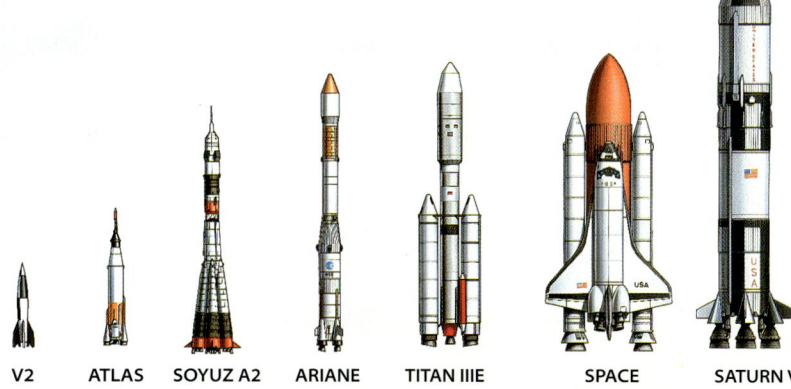

V2   ATLAS   SOYUZ A2   ARIANE   TITAN IIIE   SPACE SHUTTLE   SATURN V

△ At 110 metres high, Saturn V towers over other rockets. These include the German V2, first used in 1944, and Atlas and Soyuz, which took astronauts into space. The Titan and Ariane rockets launch satellites.

EXPLORING SPACE

Race to the Moon

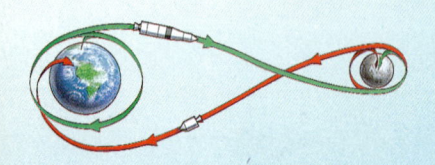

As soon as rockets could break away from the Earth's gravity, the next goal became the Moon. It was a whole new world waiting to be explored – and claimed! The Russians again took the lead, landing the first craft on the Moon and photographing the dark, or far, side in 1959. Meanwhile, the United States launched 11 unmanned Moon missions, without one completing its objective. Then, on May 25, 1961, President Kennedy committed the United States to putting a person on the Moon by 1970. The Apollo programme began, and on July 21, 1969, *Apollo 11* landed the first astronauts on the Moon.

△ From its Earth orbit, the final stage of the Saturn V rocket boosts the Command and Service Module (CSM) on its 400,000 km journey (green) to the Moon. The CSM stays in orbit around the Moon while the lunar lander visits the surface. The lander rejoins the CSM for the journey back home (red).

▷ Their mission completed, the lunar lander blasts off from the Moon, leaving the bottom half of the lander and a remote camera behind.

△▷ One astronaut stays orbiting the Moon in the CSM while the other two enter the lunar lander. The lander makes a vertical descent to the surface, using its single rocket to slow down the craft.

△ James Irwin salutes the US flag in front of Apollo 15's lander, after returning with a collection of rocks on the lunar rover (right).

134

EXPLORING SPACE

▷ Once the astronauts have rejoined the CSM, their lander ascent stage is jettisoned. It crashes back to the Moon's surface, sending shock waves to sensors already in place. These provide information about the structure of the Moon. The rocket on the CSM fires to return back home. Finally, the rocket is jettisoned and all that returns to the Earth is the command module.

Failure rate

From 1959 to 1976 there were 48 Russian and 31 American unmanned Moon missions. Of these, about half failed, but the pressure to get to the Moon was so great that both sides kept on trying. Slowly, reliability improved. Even so, there were a number of casualties. Three US astronauts died when fire broke out in the *Apollo 1* command module and four Russian cosmonauts died during re-entry.

△ Parachutes slow the command module before splashdown into the ocean. Airbags inflate to keep it upright and the astronauts disembark.

A change of direction

To land people on the Moon and return them to the Earth required a very powerful and reliable rocket. While the US's *Saturn V* fitted the bill, Russia's *N1* rocket suffered four failures. In 1974, Russia cancelled its programme and concentrated on establishing a permanent presence above the Earth with its space stations.

Houston, we have a problem

On April 13, 1970, *Apollo 13* was 56 hours into its flight when command module pilot Jack Swigert reported, "We have a problem". An oxygen tank had exploded, and the crew had to conserve power, air and water for four tense days before they could return to the Earth.

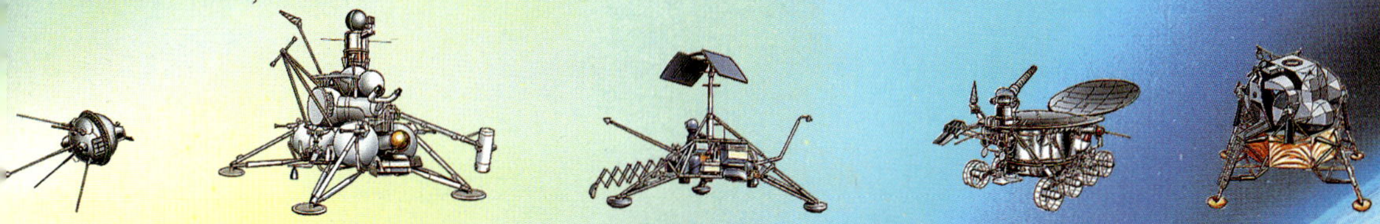

LUNA 2   LUNA 16   SURVEYOR   LUNOKHOD   APOLLO

△ In 1959, Russia's Luna 2 became the first space probe to reach the Moon. In 1970, the unmanned Luna 16 sent back a capsule with Moon rocks.

Five US Surveyor craft landed in the 1960s. In 1970, Russia's Lunokhod 1 travelled 10.5 km on the surface. Six Apollo craft landed on the Moon.

△ As the command module meets the Earth's atmosphere, friction makes it glow red-hot.

135

EXPLORING SPACE

The Space Shuttle

After the Apollo programme, the United States set out to create a cheaper alternative to maintain its presence in space. They needed a craft that could go into orbit and return to the Earth again and again. The obvious solution was to design a space shuttle, but it was not a simple task. A single stage craft could not carry enough fuel to reach orbit. Instead, two solid-fuel rocket boosters and a giant, external fuel tank filled with liquid oxygen and hydrogen, power the shuttle almost into orbit. The shuttle orbiter is covered with 32,000 heat-resistant tiles, each shaped and attached by hand, which protect it on re-entry to the atmosphere. *Columbia*, the first operational orbiter, made its maiden flight in April 1981.

△ Using a Manned Manoeuvring Unit (MMU) like a sort of jet-propelled armchair, an astronaut can fly freely from the shuttle's cargo bay. The MMU is used to help retrieve faulty satellites, take photographs, or just to admire the view.

▽ A space shuttle blasts off from the Kennedy Space Center in Florida. The brilliant jet from the two solid-fuel rocket boosters (one of which is in the foreground) provides five times more thrust than the shuttle's three main engines (on the right).

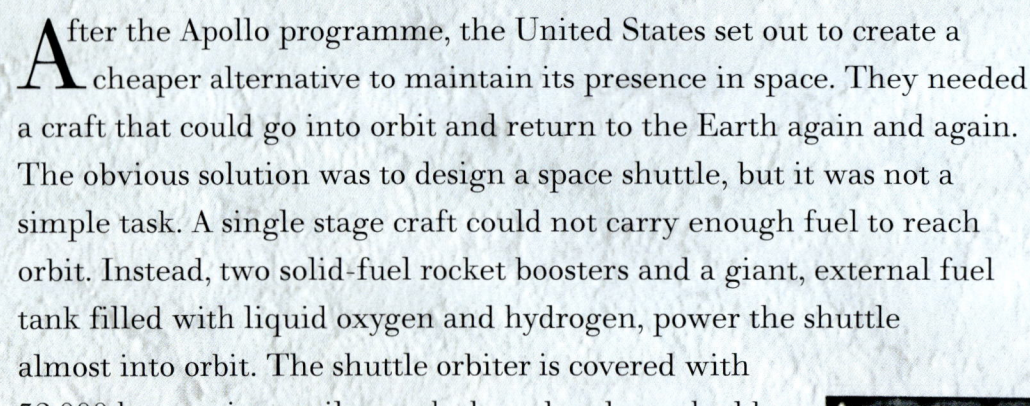

Life in orbit

Life aboard a shuttle is more comfortable than that inside the cramped quarters of the Apollo modules. There is a wash room and bunk beds. The food is much better and there is plenty to do, with fantastic views of the Earth just outside the windows. After take-off, the crew (of up to eight people) can wear comfortable clothes. There are racks of experiments in the living quarters. In the cargo bay, satellites can be carried for launch, or retrieved for repair. Astronauts put on space suits and go out through an air lock to work outside the orbiter.

△ Once in space, the shuttle orbiter can open its 18-metre-long cargo bay doors to deploy satellites, perform experiments, or point instruments at the Earth or space.

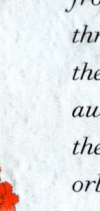

△ At blast-off, the shuttle's main engines (using fuel from the external tank) and rocket boosters provide thrust equivalent to 140 jumbo jets. Two minutes later the boosters break away. Then the external tank falls away and it is MECO (Main Engine Cut-Off). After the mission is complete, the main engines slow the orbiter and it begins to fall, glowing red from friction on re-entry. It lands like a glider on a runway.

136

EXPLORING SPACE

◁ *Attempts to design a fully reusable spaceplane are now underway. Unlike the shuttle, spaceplanes will be able to take off as well as land on runways like conventional aeroplanes.*

Challenger *disaster*

No one wants a space mission to fail, but when there are people on board, safety is the most important issue. Launches are often delayed or called off at the last moment because of a slight change in the weather, a minor computer glitch or a faulty sensor. On January 28, 1986, however, one fault proved fatal. A frosty night before the launch of shuttle *Challenger* caused the rubber 'O' rings sealing the sections of its rocket boosters to become brittle. After take-off, a flame from the rockets broke through a seal sending a jet of fire onto the huge external fuel tank. Little more than a minute into the flight, the tank exploded and the seven astronauts were killed.

Satellite triumphs

After the *Challenger* disaster, shuttle missions were suspended for two and a half years. Since then, among the shuttle's biggest triumphs have been the refurbishment and repair of satellites. For example, after its launch in 1990, the *Hubble Space Telescope* was found to be faulty. In 1993, shuttle astronauts retrieved the telescope and repaired it in space.

▽ *One of the two solid-fuel rocket boosters veers away from the exploding wreckage of the* Challenger *shuttle just 73 seconds after lift-off.*

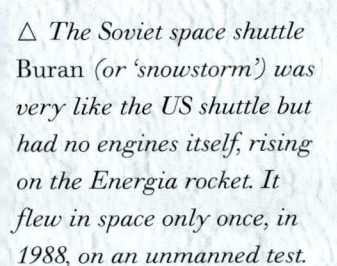

Unmanned competition

Although the shuttle is the most versatile manned spacecraft the unmanned satellite launch market is very competitive. The US's leading competitor is the European Ariane rocket, with over 100 successful launches. Russia, China, Japan and India also have rocket programmes.

△ *The Soviet space shuttle* Buran *(or 'snowstorm') was very like the US shuttle but had no engines itself, rising on the Energia rocket. It flew in space only once, in 1988, on an unmanned test.*

△ *The* Ariane 5 *rocket sits on its launch pad in French Guiana in June 1996. The first flight was a disaster (a computer fault caused it to veer off course), but the second succeeded. Unlike its rivals,* Ariane 5 *can launch up to four satellites at once.*

137

▷ The International Space Station *as it may look by 2003. Largely US-built and serviced by the space shuttle, it also carries modules from Russia, Europe and Japan.*

△ *Spacelab is a pressurized module that flies in the cargo bay of the space shuttle. On this mission, in 1993, there were around 90 experiments, including ones on the effects of weightlessness on astronauts.*

▽ *Astronauts train underwater* (inset) *to simulate the effects of weightlessness in space and to practise repairing satellites. In space itself, an astronaut uses the shuttle's robot arm like a cherrypicker to control his or her movements above the open cargo bay.*

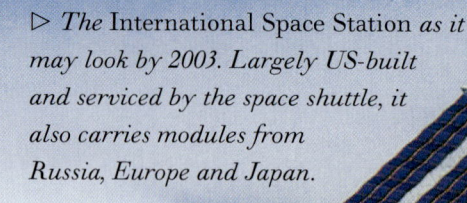

Living in Space

On May 27, 1973, the space station *Skylab* was launched. Made of modified *Saturn V* and *Apollo* units, it offered the first long-stay, orbiting laboratory for microgravity research and for studying the Sun and the Earth. It also provided an opportunity to practise space repairs when the crew had to replace damaged shielding. Its last crew set a space endurance record when they spent 84 days living in *Skylab*. In 1977 the Russians launched *Salyut 6*, the first space station to have two airlocks, allowing one crew to arrive before the other departed. This was replaced in 1982 by *Salyut 7* and then, in 1986, by *Mir* in which the endurance record has been broken over and over again.

Working in space

In space some of the most difficult tasks are Extra-Vehicular Activities (EVAs). A space suit must be worn as protection from the vacuum, radiation and temperature extremes. Large objects, though weightless, still have mass and, once in motion, can cause havoc. Even turning a screwdriver can cause problems. Unless an astronaut is well-anchored, the screw stays in place while the astronaut rotates!

△ *In June 1995, the US shuttle* Atlantis *docked with* Mir *and both crews posed for cameras. It was the start of a collaboration that provided much-needed cash for Russia's space programme and hardware for the US.*

EXPLORING SPACE

△ *The meals served on board the space shuttle are a great improvement on the dried and concentrated capsules given to Apollo astronauts.*

◁ *This unisex toilet is designed for the* International Space Station. *It comes with foot and thigh restraints. Air flow removes the waste, which is then dried and compressed.*

Space stations of the future

The *International Space Station* was launched in the late 1990s. It is a laboratory for microgravity research and provides a testing-ground for future plans. Space stations could serve as assembly points for interplanetary craft and missions to Mars. They could be used as astronomical observatories or even as factories for manufacturing new types of material. A rotating space station with artificial gravity might even one day become a hotel for tourists.

◁ *Huge arrays of solar cells, assembled in space, provide the electrical power for the space station.*

Enduring Mir

The core module of the Russian space station *Mir* was launched in 1986 with a planned life of five years. Ten years later, surrounded by add-on modules, it started to show signs of ageing. First, waste water pumps and air conditioning malfunctioned. The oxygen generators failed next, followed by a potentially serious fire which was caused by an oxygen-releasing candle. Then, in June 1997, an unmanned supply craft crashed into one of *Mir*'s modules, cutting forty percent of the power. Only Russian determination and US money kept *Mir* going.

◁ *This close-up of* Mir, *taken from the Progress M35 supply craft in July 1997, shows damage to a solar array* (right) *and a thermal radiator* (left). *The damage was caused by another unmanned Progress supply craft that crashed into Mir's Specktr module six weeks earlier.*

◁ *Since the Russian space station* Mir *was launched in 1986, several new modules have been added to it, increasing its mass from 21 tonnes to over 100 tonnes. Astronauts live and work in the largest module, which is 13 m long. The other modules are used for experiments and storing equipment. Handrails on Mir's exterior aid astronauts as they work outside.*

EXPLORING SPACE

Using Space

Rocket launches are very expensive and not always reliable, yet governments and businesses are queuing up for slots on board launch craft. Space is potentially so useful that it is well worth the risk and expense. Some satellites look at the Earth, following its weather patterns, monitoring the environment, searching for oil and minerals, or even spying on countries. Others are used by astronomers to look out at the stars. The most popular use of space, however, is for communication. In 1945, the writer Arthur C. Clarke predicted that we would communicate via space. This was before the silicon chip was invented, and Clarke imagined vast space stations with teams of engineers to service the unreliable, bulky equipment.

△ *In 1962, Telstar relayed the first live transatlantic TV transmission, which lasted for 20 minutes.*

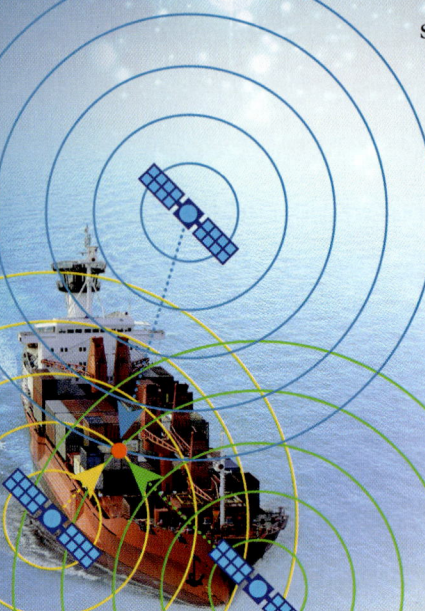

△ *The Global Positioning System (GPS) uses the signals from at least three satellites to calculate any position on land or at sea.*

▽ *The giant radio dish at Goonhilly Downs, Cornwall, was used to pick up the first transatlantic satellite links.*

Staying in touch

One of the most popular satellite orbits is called geostationary orbit, 36,000 kilometres above the equator. Here, satellites orbit at the same speed as the Earth rotates, and so always appear to be overhead. But the distance is so great that either a big dish is needed to receive the signal or the signal must be very powerful, and concentrated in a single beam. Now, networks of satellites are launched into low orbit, so there is always one in range of the hand-held receiver of a mobile phone.

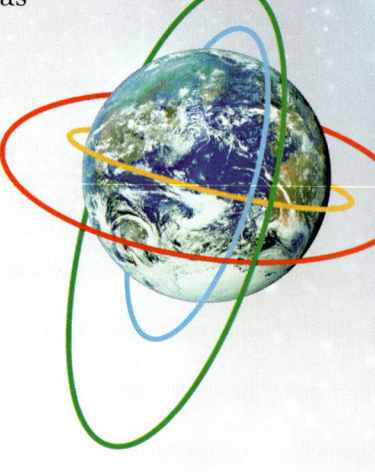

△ *The main satellite orbits around Earth are: low Earth orbit (orange), polar orbit (blue), elliptical or Molniya orbit (green), and geostationary orbit (red).*

△ *In 1997, Tony Bullimore spent five days beneath the hull of his capsized yacht. He was saved when satellites located his distress signal.*

Space junk

As more and more rockets and satellites are launched, unwanted junk accumulates in space. Space junk ranges from dropped spanners and chips of paint to spent rocket motors and defunct satellites. The US Air Force is tracking over 8,500 large objects, but even small pieces can be dangerous – a space shuttle window was once chipped, probably by a flake of paint. Operators are encouraged to put old satellites in unused orbits or force them to burn up in the atmosphere.

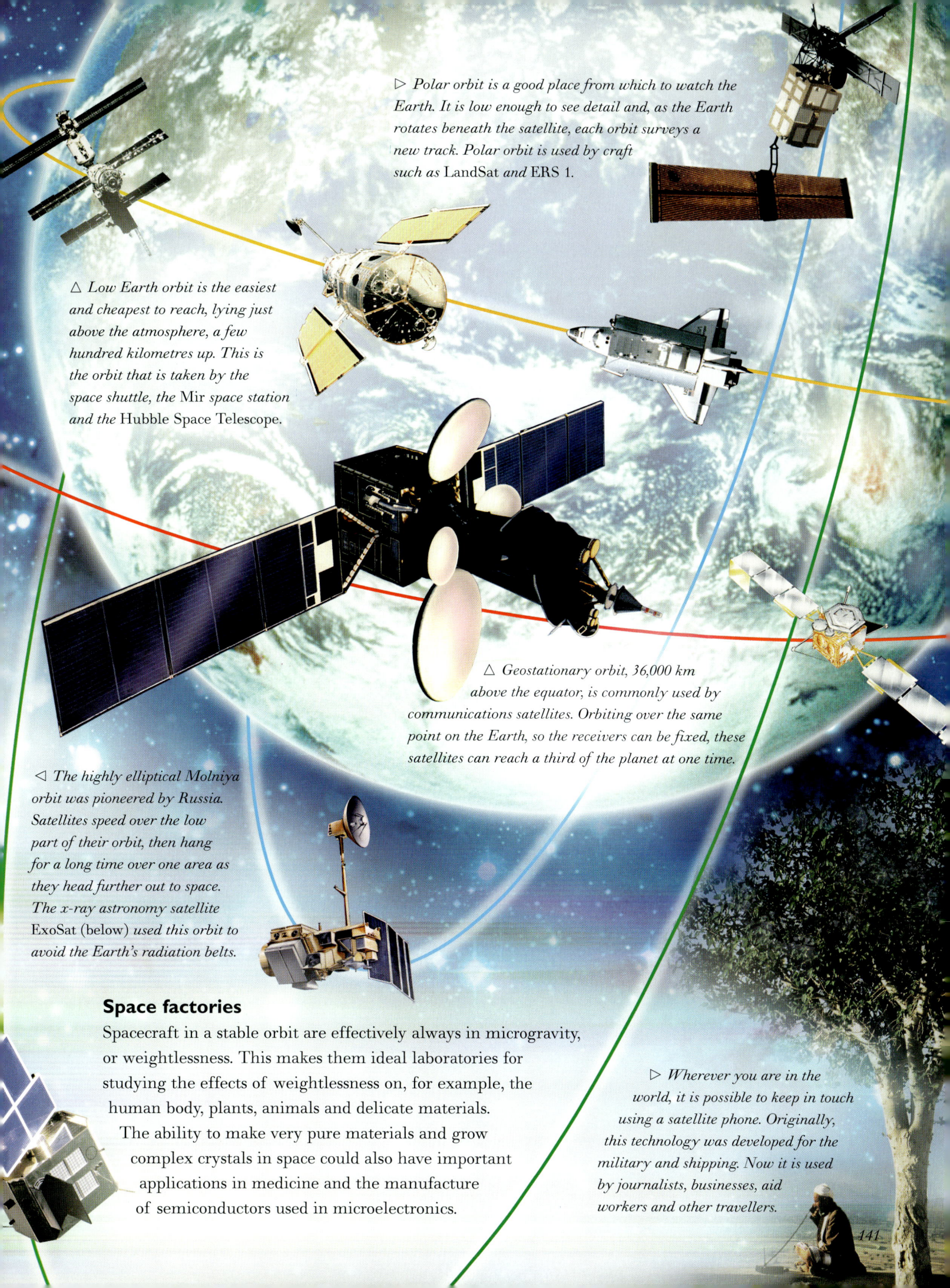

▷ Polar orbit is a good place from which to watch the Earth. It is low enough to see detail and, as the Earth rotates beneath the satellite, each orbit surveys a new track. Polar orbit is used by craft such as LandSat and ERS 1.

△ Low Earth orbit is the easiest and cheapest to reach, lying just above the atmosphere, a few hundred kilometres up. This is the orbit that is taken by the space shuttle, the Mir space station and the Hubble Space Telescope.

△ Geostationary orbit, 36,000 km above the equator, is commonly used by communications satellites. Orbiting over the same point on the Earth, so the receivers can be fixed, these satellites can reach a third of the planet at one time.

◁ The highly elliptical Molniya orbit was pioneered by Russia. Satellites speed over the low part of their orbit, then hang for a long time over one area as they head further out to space. The x-ray astronomy satellite ExoSat (below) used this orbit to avoid the Earth's radiation belts.

Space factories

Spacecraft in a stable orbit are effectively always in microgravity, or weightlessness. This makes them ideal laboratories for studying the effects of weightlessness on, for example, the human body, plants, animals and delicate materials. The ability to make very pure materials and grow complex crystals in space could also have important applications in medicine and the manufacture of semiconductors used in microelectronics.

▷ Wherever you are in the world, it is possible to keep in touch using a satellite phone. Originally, this technology was developed for the military and shipping. Now it is used by journalists, businesses, aid workers and other travellers.

EXPLORING SPACE

▷ *The Earth is ringed by a cosmic necklace of satellites, watching over it from a range of different orbits.*

Earthwatch

Strangely, we sometimes need to go into space to see our own world more clearly. From the perspective of space it is possible to see the overall pattern without being confused by detail. As long ago as 1948, the astronomer Fred Hoyle commented that "when a photograph of Earth, taken from outside, is returned, an idea as powerful as any in history will be let loose". To a great extent, he was right. Astronauts comment on how fragile the Earth appears from space. Scientists use observations to build up a picture of the complex systems on the Earth and how our environment is changing. Satellite pictures can inspire a sense of wonder, which may generate a new ecological awareness. Space also provides a window for monitoring military activities, along with disaster relief, peace-keeping and humanitarian operations.

△ *From low polar orbit,* Landsat 4 *passes over all points on the Earth. This false-colour image, taken over Brazil, shows an area of cleared rainforest*

△ *Weather satellites hang in geostationary orbit watching weather systems such as this hurricane forming over the Atlantic Ocean. This* Meteosat Second Generation Craft *is designed to help forecasters predict weather in the new millennium.*

△ *The* ERS-2 *satellite measures ozone in the upper atmosphere. Here, an ozone hole (in blue) is clearly seen above the Antarctic.*

And now for the weather...

Satellite images are used in weather forecasts to show us what weather to expect. Weather satellites monitor wind speed, cloud temperature and height, sea temperature, and many other factors. Computers then produce detailed forecasts up to a week ahead. These are vital to farmers, sailors and even ice-cream makers. This data can also help predict climate changes, such as global warming, decades into the future

EXPLORING SPACE

△ *The space shuttle sometimes carries remote sensing instruments for monitoring the Earth. These two images were taken by cloud-penetrating radar. They reveal new flows of ash and lava on Mount Pinatubo, an active volcano in the Philippines.*

△ *ERS satellites use radar, ultraviolet and infrared to monitor the Earth. Here, two combined images show ground movements after an earthquake.*

△ *Spy satellites often use powerful telescopes to watch for potential threats. Here, a train carrying Iraqi tanks can be seen heading towards Kuwait in 1994.*

Mapping the Earth

In a few 90-minute-long orbits, a satellite can produce a geological survey of an area of remote and mountainous country that would take years to map on the ground. By looking at the ground, not in just the few colours our eyes can see but using hundreds of different bands of the spectrum, it is possible to reveal mineral deposits, polluted areas, and analyze rocks and soil. Satellites can reveal deforestation or the health of crops. They even detect rocks deep inside the Earth in the search for new oil fields.

Spy in the sky

One of the first uses of space was for military purposes. Many rockets were developed to deliver long-range missiles and more spy satellites may have been launched than any other type. Many take photographs, while others monitor secret radio messages or look for signs of missile launches or bomb tests. In the 1980s, the United States planned a space-based defence system, called 'Star Wars'. Before the technology and finance could be resolved, the Cold War ended and the project was cancelled.

△ *The Solar System was born from a cloud of gas and dust. A knot of gas begins to pull other gas around it (1). The cloud heats up and, as it rotates, it contracts and forms into a disc. Energy is lost in jets of matter from the poles (2).*

△ *A protostar gradually forms at the centre (3) and secondary knots of gas appear in the disc. These will later become the gas giant planets Jupiter, Saturn, Uranus and Neptune.*

△ *Nuclear processes start up in the star (4) and radiation begins to drive gas and ice out of the inner regions of the disc.*

THE SOLAR SYSTEM

The Solar System

The Solar System is dominated by the Sun, our local star. It is circled by nine planets and their moons, together with countless asteroids and comets. The four planets closest to the Sun – Mercury, Venus, the Earth and Mars – are small, rocky worlds. The next four planets – Jupiter, Saturn, Uranus and Neptune – are gas giants. Finally, there is little Pluto, more like a moon than a major planet. Pluto is the smallest of the planets with a diameter of 2,200 kilometres. Jupiter is the largest, with a diameter of almost 143,000 kilometres. But it is the Sun which dwarfs everything else in the Solar System. If the Sun were the size of a football, then the Earth would be smaller than a pea in comparison. Even if all the matter in all the planets was gathered together into a single ball, you could fit seven hundred of these balls inside the Sun and still have room to spare.

△ *The Solar System is nearly formed. The Sun is beginning to shine strongly through its still dusty shroud (5). Planets have formed but the building rubble is still flying around and bombarding the planets.*

Dusty birthplace

About five billion years ago, the material that now makes up the Sun and planets was a great cloud of gas and dust called the solar nebula. This material was composed of a mixture of light elements, mostly hydrogen and helium that had been left over from the formation of our Milky Way galaxy, and heavier elements spewed out by an earlier generation of short-lived stars. A shock wave may have passed through the nebula as it crossed a spiral arm of the Galaxy or as a nearby star exploded. As a result, the nebula began to condense into a nursery of stars.

◁ *The inclined orbit of Pluto together with those of Neptune, Uranus, Saturn and Jupiter are clearly visible. Much further in are the inner planets – Mars, the Earth, Venus and Mercury.*

THE SOLAR SYSTEM

From grains to planets

In one of the protostars, material concentrated to form the proto-Sun. Gas and dust around it collected into a flat, rotating disc. Over the next thousand years, the disc cooled, and grains of solid matter began to freeze. In the hot inner region, they were silicate rock; further out, water ice and further still, frozen methane. The grains collected together into lumps a few kilometres across. These bumped into one another, sometimes breaking up, but sometimes merging to form the planets.

Leftovers

The newly formed planets mopped up most of the remaining lumps and grains. The rest of the gas was blown clear as nuclear processes began in the Sun, sending a wind of atoms out into space. In the outermost reaches of the solar nebula, the icy proto-planetary material was spread so thinly that it did not form planets but remains to this day as a vast cloud of potential comets.

△ *For the past four billion years, little has changed* (6). *The Sun has brightened slightly, a few comets and asteroids have crashed, but the nine planets have remained in stable orbits. Only the Earth has changed significantly as life developed on its surface.*

▷ *The Sun and planets are shown here to scale. The Sun dwarfs everything else in the Solar System, including the gas giants Jupiter and Saturn.*

145

THE SOLAR SYSTEM

Mercury

Mercury, named after the Roman winged messenger of the gods, is an elusive planet. Small, fast-moving and lying closer to the Sun than any other planet, it is only visible from the Earth just after sunset or just before dawn. Mercury is the second smallest planet and only slightly larger than our Moon. It takes just 88 Earth days to orbit the Sun. Its distance from the Sun varies from 46 million kilometres at its closest to 70 million kilometres at its most distant. The Sun's strong gravitational tug on Mercury has dramatically slowed the planet's rotation on its axis. As a result, a day on Mercury lasts the equivalent of 176 Earth days – twice as long as its quicksilver 88-day year.

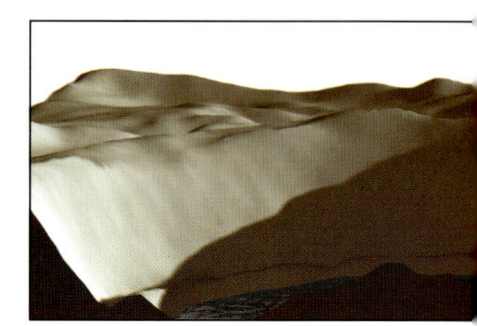

△ *Almost everything we know about Mercury comes from one space probe,* Mariner 10, *which flew past the planet in 1973, 1974 and again in 1975. Here,* Mariner 10 *is shown above a false-colour image of Mercury's cratered surface.*

▽ *Mercury's dry and airless surface creates a very bleak landscape. Pockmarked with impact craters, during the day it is baked by radiation and heat from the nearby Sun.*

Unchanged features

The surface of Mercury is very similar to the Moon's. It is heavily cratered, with evidence of ancient lava flows. With no atmosphere or water to erode them, the craters look almost as fresh as the day they were formed. Yet that must have been more than 4 billion years ago, when debris left over from the formation of the planets was still flying about in the Solar System. This rubble crashed into the surface, throwing up circular craters with characteristic central peaks.

△ *There is evidence from radar images that there may be ice in the craters near Mercury's poles. In deep craters, icy deposits – possibly left-over material from comet impacts – would remain hidden from the Sun's intense heat.*

THE SOLAR SYSTEM

World of extremes

Mercury has no atmosphere (except for a trace of helium given off by the rocks), so there is no wind or rain. There is also no protection against the Sun's searing heat by day, and no blanket to keep the surface warm at night. With days and nights each lasting about three of the Earth's months, and with the planet swinging closer and farther from the Sun, temperatures can range from 420°C to −180°C. These extremes are hot enough to melt some metals or cold enough to freeze air.

△ *Although only about a third the size of the Earth, Mercury is almost as dense. This suggests that a core of iron-nickel takes up about 70 percent of the interior, with a mantle of silicate rock surrounding it. The outer part of the metal core may still be molten.*

◁ △ *More than 4 billion years ago, a huge object must have struck Mercury (above), melting part of the surface and causing ridges and hills to form on the opposite side of the planet. The ridges around the impact crater, called the Caloris Basin (left), were photographed by Mariner 10.*

Wizened world

A surprise discovery by *Mariner 10* was a magnetic field on Mercury. The planet had been thought to rotate too slowly for it to generate a magnetic field. The answer may lie in the planet's large core. If the outer part of the core is still molten, currents in it could produce a weak magnetic effect. A big iron core could also explain Mercury's wrinkles. As it cooled and solidified, the iron shrank, making the planet contract and producing a wrinkled appearance on the surface.

THE SOLAR SYSTEM

Venus

Venus, the brightest planet visible from the Earth, is named after the goddess of beauty. The planet has also been called the Earth's twin. It is almost exactly the same size, is only slightly less dense and is made up of volcanic rocks, but there the similarity ends. The thick atmosphere on Venus means that it is always cloudy, and the pressure on the surface is ninety times greater than on the Earth. The dense atmosphere consists mostly of carbon dioxide – this traps the planet's heat causing a runaway greenhouse effect that makes the worst predictions of global warming on the Earth seem chilly by comparison. The surface temperature is 480°C and if oceans ever existed on Venus they have long since boiled away. If you could withstand the searing heat and bone-crushing pressure on this hostile planet, you would see an orange sky. If it ever rained, you would be drenched in a lethal downpour of sulphuric acid.

△ *Bands of thick, swirling clouds circle Venus at speeds of up to 360 km/h. This ultraviolet picture was taken by* Mariner 10 *in 1974.*

△ *Four Russian Venera probes have landed on Venus and sent back images. In 1982, close-ups taken by* Venera 13 *revealed flat, eroded terrain southeast of a volcanic region called Phoebe Regio. The edge of the Venus lander and its lens cap can also be seen in the picture.*

Global warming

The dramatic contrast with the Earth could simply be because Venus is closer to the Sun. As the young Sun warmed, more carbon dioxide was released from Venus' volcanoes and the surface temperature climbed. The seas began to evaporate, the water vapour adding to the greenhouse effect. Without oceans and plants, carbon dioxide could not be removed as the heat output of the Sun continued to grow. On the Earth, billions of tonnes of carbon are locked up in limestone and chalk. On Venus it is all still in the atmosphere.

△ *The* Magellan *radar mapper revealed that the surface of Venus has rough, mountainous terrain* (bright areas) *and smoother plains* (darker areas).

Revealing geology

The radar mapper on the *Magellan* space probe indicated clear evidence of volcanic activity, including domes of thick or viscous lava and vast floods of liquid basalt. However, it did not detect any drifting plates, which on the Earth create great chains of volcanoes. There must be other forces at work on Venus, still to be identified.

THE SOLAR SYSTEM

▽ *The landscape is a computer-generated view of Maat Mons, one of the largest volcanoes on Venus. This image was created by radar data sent back by the Magellan probe. The fresh lava flows surrounding this 8-km-high volcano suggest relatively recent activity.*

▷ *The* Magellan *probe, seen here as it was released from the space shuttle in 1989, was made up of spare parts from other missions.*

△ *The existence of uneroded craters on Venus indicate that some parts of the surface are much older than areas covered by volcanic lava. The largest of these craters (top left) has a diameter of 50 km.*

△ *This corona, or circular feature, is about 200 km in diameter. It was probably caused by a rising dome of lava from deep below the surface.*

△ *Like the Earth, Venus has a rocky mantle and a crust. Inside is an iron core that may be partly molten. Because the planet rotates very slowly (unlike the Earth), there is no noticeable magnetic field.*

◁ *The atmosphere of Venus is 96% carbon dioxide. Nitrogen, water vapour and traces of other gases such as sulphur dioxide are also present.*

Lengthy days

Venus is best seen from the Earth with the naked eye just after sunset or before dawn. Like the Moon, Venus has phases as the Sun illuminates a crescent, half or full disc. Venus has a slow rotation from east to west. In fact, its rotation rate of 243 Earth days makes a day on Venus longer than the planet's year – the time it takes to revolve once around the Sun.

THE SOLAR SYSTEM

The Moon

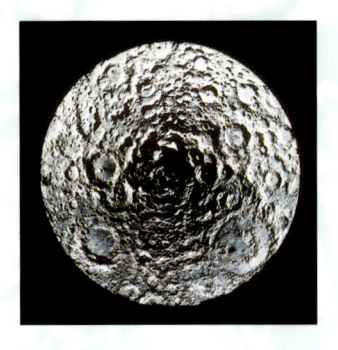

The Moon is the most spectacular object in the night sky and the only world beyond the Earth so far on which people have walked. It is our closest neighbour, orbiting our planet with the same face always pointing towards us. The far side is often called the dark side because it cannot be seen from the Earth. In its monthly orbit, the Moon seems to change shape as different areas of its surface are lit by the Sun. There are five distinct phases called new, crescent, quarter, gibbous and full. When the side we see is dark (a new Moon) the far side is in full sunshine. The Moon is close enough to the Earth for its gravity to pull the water in the oceans towards it, causing the tides.

△ *This mosaic of 1,500 images shows the south pole of the Moon. The dark crater in the centre is permanently in shade and contains an icy layer.*

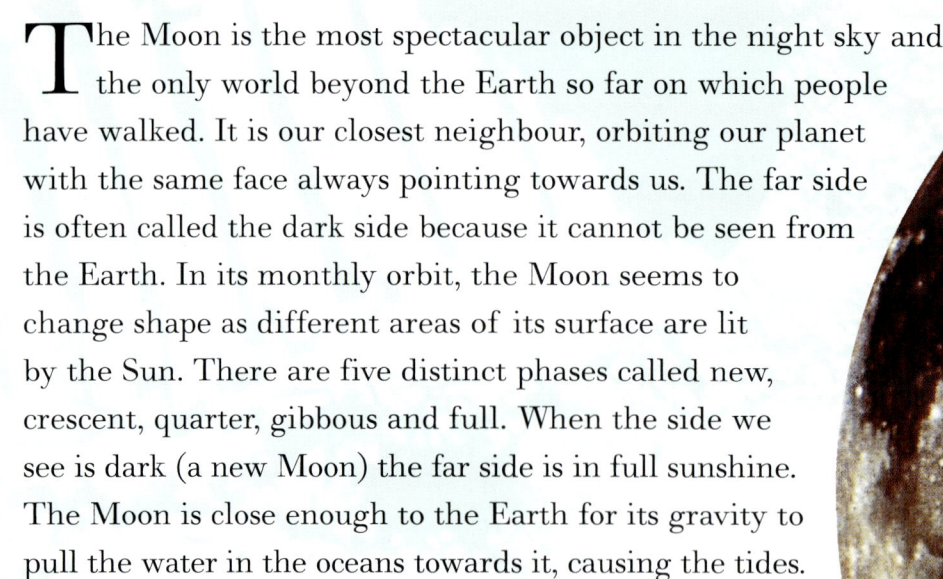

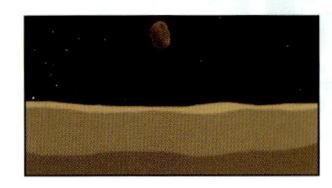

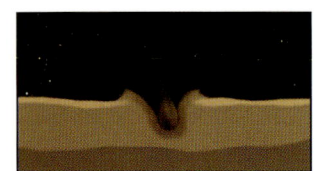

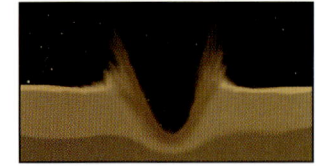

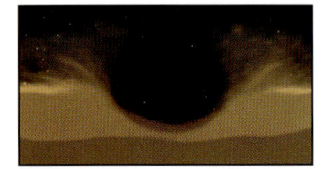

How the Moon formed

There are several theories to explain how the Moon formed. It may have formed together with the Earth from the solar nebula, or perhaps it spun off from a bulge at the Earth's equator. The most popular theory, derived from analysis of Moon rock and computer simulations, is that the early Earth was hit by a protoplanet the size of Mars. Some of the resulting debris merged to form the Moon.

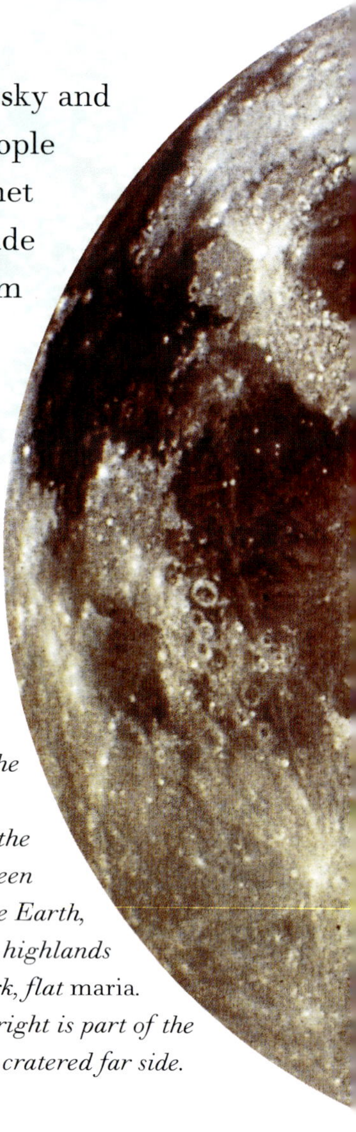

▷ *On the left is a part of the Moon seen from the Earth, with its highlands and dark, flat* maria. *On the right is part of the heavily cratered far side.*

The Moon's surface

The lunar highlands are more than 4.2 billion years old and heavily cratered. Collisions with asteroids were violent enough to melt parts of the Moon's surface, flooding the impact basins with lava and creating great dark regions called *maria*, or seas. Curiously, there are virtually no such features on the far side of the Moon. About 3.8 billion years ago, the asteroid bombardment virtually ceased, apart from the creation of a few craters such as Copernicus. Without wind and water to erode the surface, the Moon has remained the same ever since.

△ *This view of the Moon's craters, lit by sunlight at a low angle, was taken from* Apollo 13 *in 1970.*

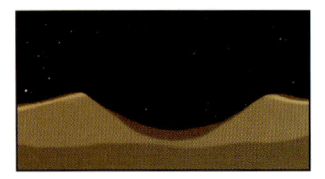

△ *Craters were formed when asteroids plunged into the lunar surface. They can be anything from metres to hundreds of kilometres across.*

▷ *The five different phases of the Moon depend on the direction from which it is illuminated by the Sun. During each monthly cycle it goes through nine different stages.*

| NEW MOON | WAXING CRESCENT | FIRST QUARTER | WAXING GIBBOUS |

150

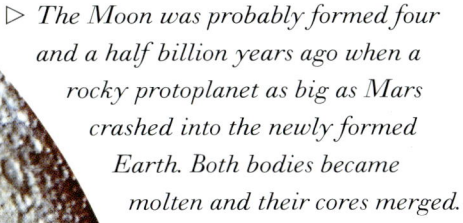

▷ The Moon was probably formed four and a half billion years ago when a rocky protoplanet as big as Mars crashed into the newly formed Earth. Both bodies became molten and their cores merged.

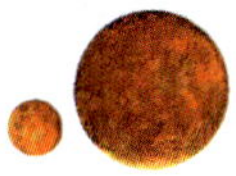

▷ The vaporized rock and fragments from the collision formed a ring around the Earth. Some of the material combined to make an object massive enough to sweep up the debris with its gravity. Finally, only two bodies remained in this area of the Solar System – the Earth and its new Moon.

Tomorrow's Moon

Twelve men have walked on the Moon, leaving landers, rovers, flags and footprints behind. And it is still the goal of many scientists and commercial enterprises. With only one-sixth of the Earth's gravity, the Moon would be a very good place to mine bulk materials for launch into space. With permanently dark skies, no atmosphere and no radio noise, it would also be an excellent site for setting up telescopes. Water, discovered frozen in the rocks of the poles, could be used to supply moonbases. The main obstacle, at present, is the cost.

◁ In the future, the low gravity would make moonbases good staging-posts for interplanetary journeys. And the Moon's airless surface and dark skies would make an excellent laboratory for astronomers and scientists.

| FULL MOON | WANING GIBBOUS | LAST QUARTER | WANING CRESCENT | OLD MOON |

△ There is a thin crust of lighter-coloured granite-like rock on the highlands of the Moon, above a thick, dark, denser rocky mantle.

THE SOLAR SYSTEM

Mars

Mars is smaller, darker and slightly more distant than Venus. It is also the most Earth-like of the planets and has always attracted humans. Mars' reddish colour (with its associations of blood) led to it being named after the Roman god of war and Martians have featured in countless science fiction stories. Speculation about life on Mars was reinforced by changing hues on the surface and reported sightings of canals. When the first Mariner probes flew past in the 1960s, however, all they saw was a barren, cratered surface, rather like the Moon, beneath an atmosphere one hundredth the density of the Earth's. In 1971, *Mariner 9* (the first craft to orbit a planet other than the Earth) explored Mars' fascinating geology. As the dust from a violent storm settled, a giant volcano was revealed, followed by valleys and canyons.

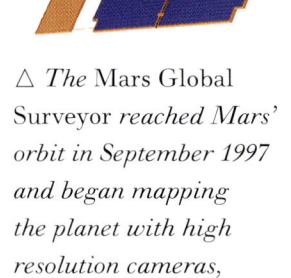

△ *This picture of Mars was taken by the* Hubble Space Telescope *in 1990. It reveals wispy storm clouds around the north pole and thin dust clouds in the south.*

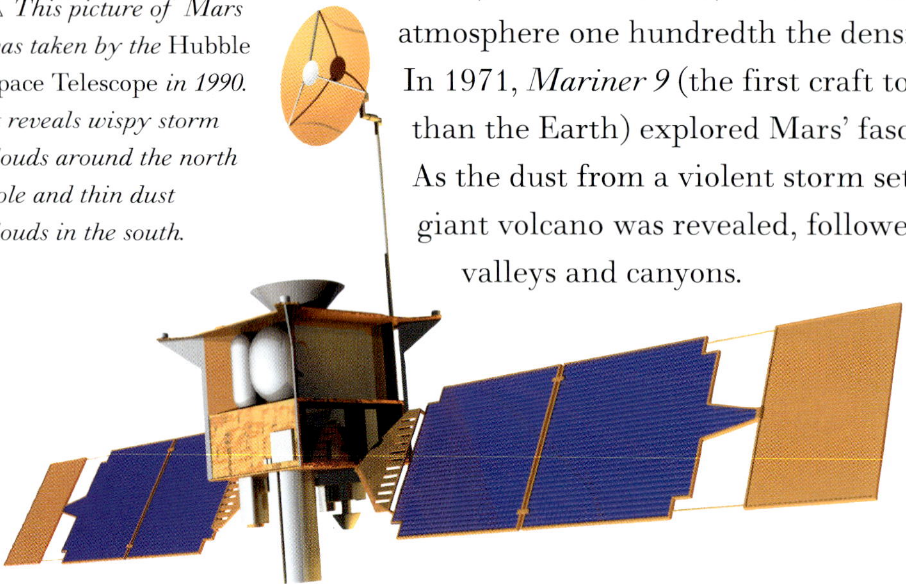

△ *The* Mars Global Surveyor *reached Mars' orbit in September 1997 and began mapping the planet with high resolution cameras, lasers and radar.*

Heat and dust

Like Earth, Mars has a 24-hour day, although its year is nearly twice as long. The thin atmosphere is made almost entirely of carbon dioxide. Swirls of cloud are often visible and, in winter, polar caps of water ice and frozen carbon dioxide form. Temperatures range from a comfortable 25°C in summer to a bitter −120°C on winter nights. Although it no longer rains, there is clear evidence that water once flowed on Mars, scouring out deep channels. Today, strong winds whip up dust storms, which sometimes envelop the whole planet.

◁ *Mars has two tiny moons, Phobos* (top) *and Deimos* (bottom). *Both are probably captured asteroids. Phobos is heavily cratered. Deimos is smoother and darker.*

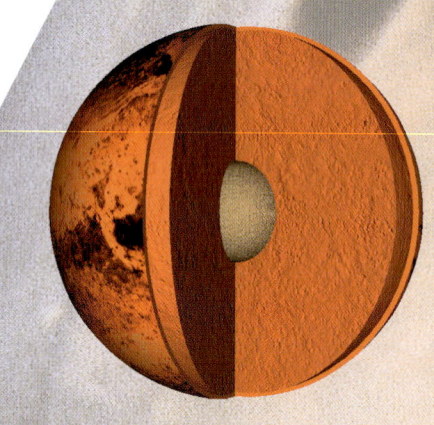

△ *Mars has a weak magnetic field, suggesting that its core must be solid. The thick rocky mantle may circulate slowly beneath a thin, hard crust.*

◁ *The Martian atmosphere is only one hundredth the density of the Earth's. Although it is 95% carbon dioxide, it is too thin to insulate the planet.*

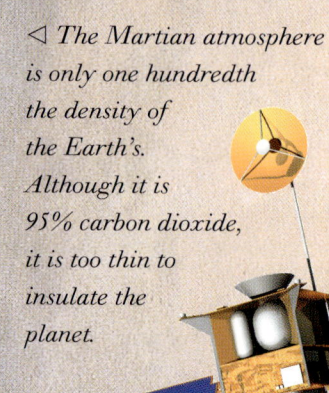

152

THE SOLAR SYSTEM

▷ Unlike Mars' south pole, which is mostly frozen carbon dioxide, its north pole is mostly water ice. Every summer it shrinks leaving a spiral pattern, probably due to wind erosion.

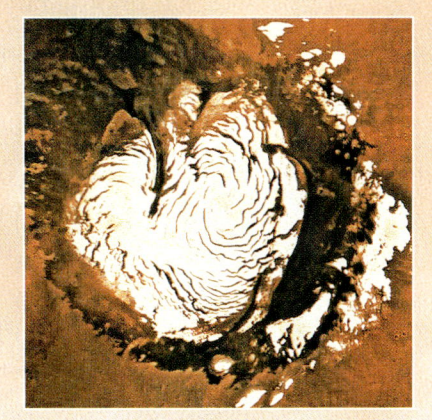

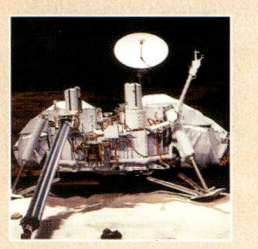

◁ Two Viking Landers touched down on Mars in 1976. The sampling arm (front left) scooped up soil for analysis. The two cylinders with vertical slits are stereo cameras.

▷ Evidence shows that water once flowed down this valley in the Valles Marineris.

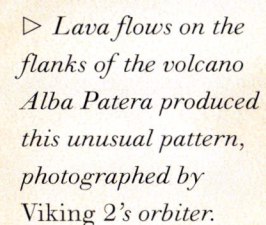

▷ Lava flows on the flanks of the volcano Alba Patera produced this unusual pattern, photographed by Viking 2's orbiter.

△ The Ophir Chasm, in the Valles Marineris, was formed by geological faulting. It has cliffs which are over 4,000 m high. These have seen major landslides, including an avalanche that travelled 65 km.

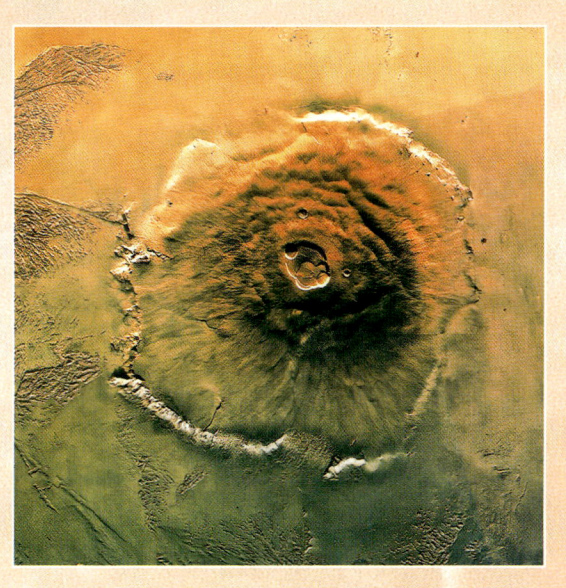

△ The biggest volcano on Mars, and in the Solar System, is Olympus Mons. Like the Earth's biggest volcanoes, it is shield-shaped, and once erupted runny, black, basalt lava. It towers 26,400 m high.

Vikings invade Mars

By the 1970s it was clear that Mars was neither covered in lush vegetation nor populated by Martians. But there might be microscopic life (bacteria or algae) in the soil. In 1976, two Viking space probes set out to investigate. Each comprised an orbiter and a lander. Both landers contained miniature laboratories to test Martian soil samples for signs of life. They fed nutrients into the soil and, when a gas was given off, it suggested that living organisms were using up the nutrients. But the process slowed and stopped. Scientists concluded that all they had detected were lifeless chemical reactions.

The Martian landscape

Some parts of Mars are heavily cratered and very old. Other parts have been smoothed over by newer lava flows from volcanoes. Cracks and canyons indicate past earthquakes. The Valles Marineris canyon (*below*) is four times deeper and six times wider than the Grand Canyon in the US. There are large areas of wind-blown sand dunes. Dust storms change the surface dramatically, covering or exposing rock underneath. Signs of water erosion suggest past flooding along channels and plains. This water may have escaped to space or lie frozen underground.

△ A panorama taken by Viking 2 in the Utopia Planitia region. The sloping ground is strewn with angular lumps of dark, volcanic rock and frosted with a thin layer of water ice.

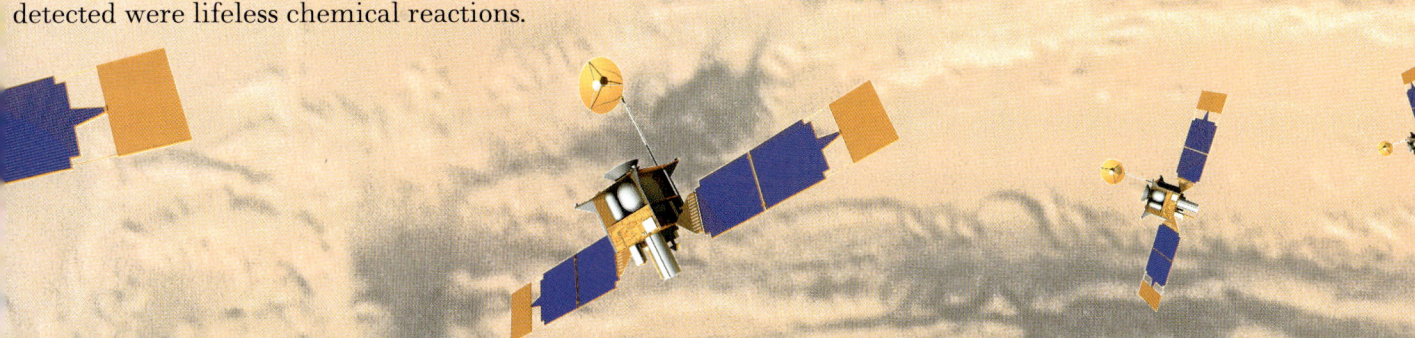

THE SOLAR SYSTEM

Mission to Mars

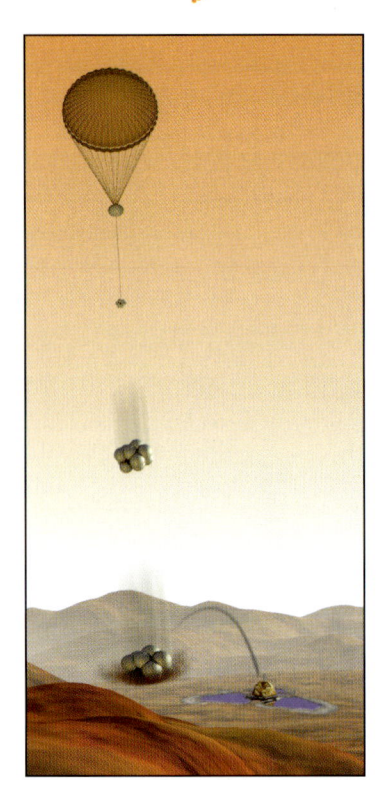

The year 1997 marked the return to the red planet. For almost twenty years, every Mars mission had ended in failure. The two Russian *Phobos* craft failed, the US *Mars Observer* exploded as it prepared to enter the planet's orbit and the mighty Russian *Mars '96* craft did not escape from the Earth. But finally, on American Independence Day 1997, *Mars Pathfinder* parachuted down to Mars, its novel landing technology proving a success. Its little six-wheeled rover, *Sojourner*, spent nearly three months analyzing Martian rocks before the battery went flat. More missions have been planned, including a mission to return rock samples to the Earth and ultimately one to land the first humans on Mars.

Where did all the water go?

Great floods of water once washed down in channels from the Martian highlands and fanned out on the plains below. Now it has all escaped to space, or lies frozen underground or in the icecaps. For water to flow, Mars must once have been warmer and have had a denser atmosphere. About three billion years ago all that changed. The once-molten iron core may have solidified, or the planet been struck by an asteroid. Whatever the cause, it resulted in the cold, barren world we see today.

Meteorite from Mars

In 1984, a grapefruit-sized lump of rock was found in Antarctica. After years of careful research, scientists were able to tell its story. It had formed on Mars 4.5 billion years ago, when the planet was still young. Then, 16 million years ago, an impact threw it out into space, and 13,000 years ago it landed on the Earth. The meteorite contains chemicals and microscopic structures that some NASA scientists suggest are evidence of life — fossils from another world.

△ *As* Mars Pathfinder *neared the surface, the tether to its parachute was cut and balloons inflated. The craft bounced to a standstill and opened up to reveal instruments, solar cells and a little rover* (inset below).

▽ Mars Pathfinder *landed in a wide flood plain. The camera revealed a panorama of low hills, and a surface littered with rocks of all sizes and textures for the rover* Sojourner *to analyze.*

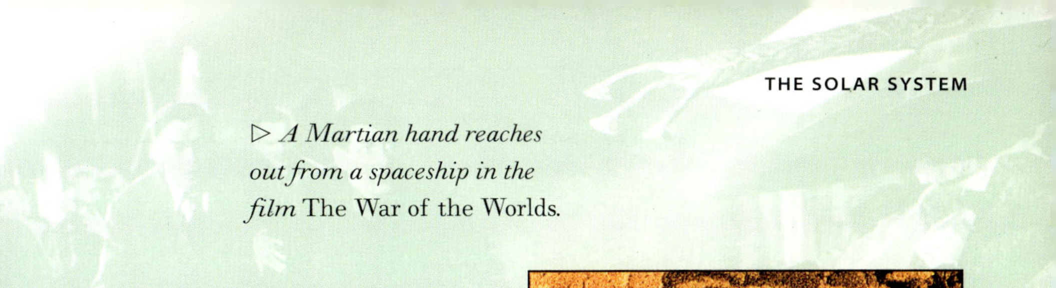

THE SOLAR SYSTEM

▷ *A Martian hand reaches out from a spaceship in the film* The War of the Worlds.

◁ *Sojourner used an x-ray spectrometer to measure the composition of rocks. Here, it is examining the rock given the name 'Barnacle Bill'.*

◁ *The six-wheeled* Sojourner, *the size of a microwave oven, moved from rock to rock, navigating with its own camera and laser, as well as instructions from the Earth.*

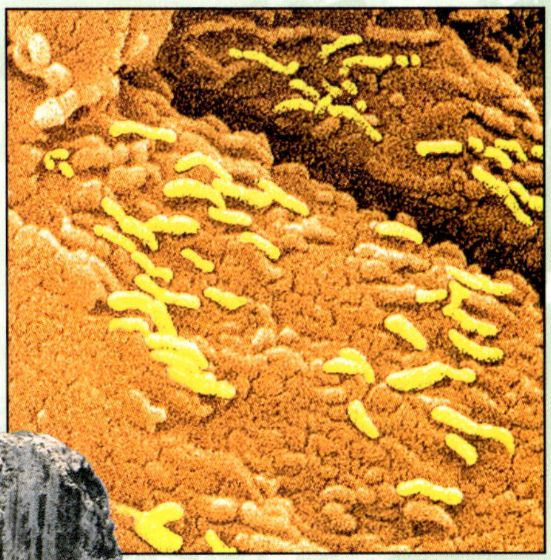

△ *AH84001* (left) *is a Martian meteorite that was found in Antarctica. It contains possible fossil evidence of life. Under a powerful electron microscope, a segment of rock reveals structures that could be tiny fossil bacteria* (above).

Alien invaders

Evidence on the Earth suggests that life can endure extremes of temperature and even survive in cracks within rocks. Although Mars appears to be a barren planet, life may once have thrived there in similarly hostile conditions. Fossil hunters of the future will want to explore any ancient hydrothermal springs they may find on Mars. Returned samples are likely to be put into quarantine – just in case microbes are still alive and choose to invade the Earth!

Home from home

Sending people to Mars – and returning them to the Earth – might be more feasible if the fuel for the return journey were to be made on Mars. A robot craft could make propellant from the Martian atmosphere before astronauts arrived. More fanciful is the idea of using orbiting mirrors to warm the South Pole of Mars. This would release more carbon dioxide to warm the planet. Bacteria might release oxygen and ultimately make the atmosphere breathable by human colonists.

▽ *In the distant future, Mars may be made more Earth-like. A thicker atmosphere and warmer climate would allow liquid water to remain on the surface – just as it did some four billion years ago.*

▽ *The asteroid belt, between Mars and Jupiter, contains rocks of all sizes. Although they frequently collide and break up, the belt is made up mostly of empty space. All together the asteroids would form an object smaller than the Moon.*

THE SOLAR SYSTEM

Asteroids & Meteorites

Between the orbits of Mars and Jupiter is a gigantic belt made up of more than 4,000 lumps of rock. They range in size from a few metres across to the biggest, called Ceres, which is about 1,000 km across. These chunks of rock are called asteroids. Scientists believe they were formed from material similar to that of the rocky planets, such as the Earth and Mars. Stirred up by the immense gravitational influence of Jupiter, this material was unable to stick together to form a single planet. However, mini-planets with iron cores may have formed, only to be smashed up by impacts with smaller debris. Collisions between asteroids are thought to be quite frequent. Some of the asteroids are composed mostly of iron, like the core of the Earth.

△ *On June 30, 1908, a huge fireball exploded near Tunguska, Siberia flattening more than 3,000 km² of forest. It was probably caused by an asteroid exploding in the atmosphere.*

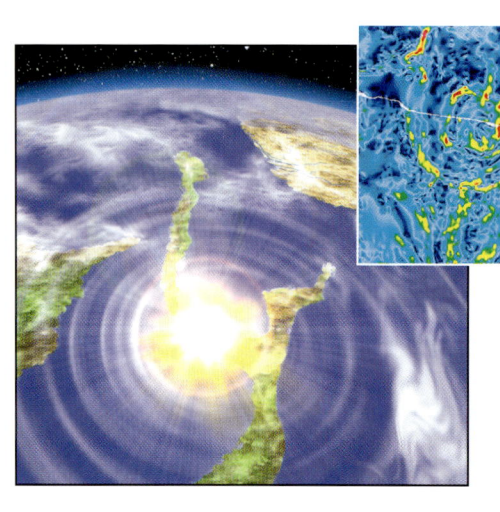

◁ *When a large asteroid hit Central America 65 million years ago, it caused a great fireball and climate change that may have ended the age of the dinosaurs. A satellite map (inset) of the Yucatan peninsular, Mexico, shows the rim of the 180-km-wide crater.*

A big impact

Not all asteroids remain in orbit between Jupiter and Mars. Some have elliptical orbits that bring them close to the Earth. Craters on the Moon were caused by asteroid impacts. Asteroids must have bombarded the Earth too, but most of that evidence has eroded. Geologists have identified the traces of enormous ancient craters. One in the Gulf of Mexico was caused by an asteroid 30 km across that fell 65 million years ago. It threw up thousands of tonnes of water and rock, shutting out the Sun and contributing to the extinction of the dinosaurs.

156

Could it happen again?

Occasionally, asteroid-sized rocks still hit the Earth. Small asteroid strikes may occur once every 100 years, probably over uninhabited land or sea. A two-km-sized object may hit only once in a million years, but it could change the climate and, indirectly, kill millions of people. Telescopes now look out for rocks that pose a threat, in the hope that missiles or lasers can be used to deflect them.

▷ *Wolf Creek crater* (above) *in Western Australia was formed about 10,000 years ago and still looks fresh. Deep Bay* (below) *in Reindeer Lake, Canada, is 150 million years old. It is so eroded that it was not thought to be an impact crater until 1957.*

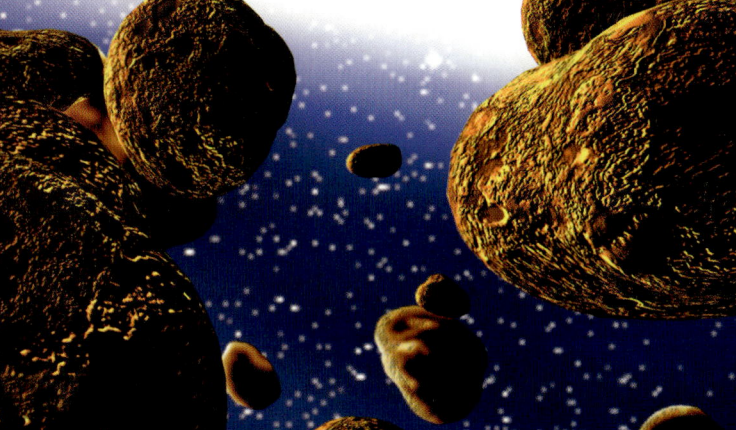

Meteorites

Hundreds of tonnes of rock hurtle towards the Earth each year, but most burn up in the atmosphere to form shooting stars. Lumps that reach the surface are called meteorites. A few are chips off comets, the Moon or even Mars, but most are asteroid debris. Collectors scour Australia and Antarctica to recover them. Even the bigger ones, which vaporize on impact, leave traces. Meteorites can enrich sediments many kilometres away.

△ *The commonest meteorites are stony ones made of silicate rocks* (1). *Glassy tektites* (2) *form on impact from vaporized rock. Meteorites made of iron* (3 and 4) *are rarer.*

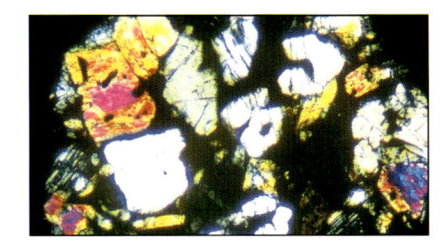

△ *Metallic asteroids may be very valuable due to the iron, copper, cobalt and nickel they contain. This imaginary scene shows one captured for mining in orbit around the Earth.*

◁ *Under the microscope, a thin slice of meteorite reveals crystals formed at high temperatures, surrounded by dark, carbon-rich material created at lower temperatures.*

Jupiter

Jupiter is the giant among the planets. If all the others were combined, they would still not add up to half of Jupiter's mass. It is a great gas bag made up of 90 percent hydrogen, with a lower density than the Earth. Down in its thick atmosphere, the pressure rises to a point where hydrogen behaves as a liquid rather than a gas. Deeper still, it is like a liquid metal, with huge circulating electrical currents. Here, a powerful magnetic field is generated, strong enough to emit radio waves that can be received on the Earth. Jupiter is still contracting from its formation, a process that generates heat and makes it glow in the infrared. If Jupiter were much bigger, the heating would start nuclear fusion in its core and the planet would become a star.

△ This ultraviolet image shows the glow at Jupiter's poles, as charged particles from the Sun stream along its magnetic field lines.

Turbulent planet

Jupiter's incredibly fast 9 hour 55 minute rotation (or day) makes it bulge 9,000 kilometres wider at its equator than its poles. It whips up violent winds and stretches the clouds out into bands parallel to the equator. Essentially, there are about 14 alternating bands of dark, low pressure regions that circulate with the planet's rotation, and light, high-pressure regions blowing the other way. Swirling storm systems form where they meet, especially in the turbulent polar regions. High white clouds of ammonia ice are tinted yellow and orange lower down by sulphur compounds.

△ Two bright lines at the top of this picture reveal Jupiter's thin rings, as seen by Voyager 2 from a distance of 1,450,000 km.

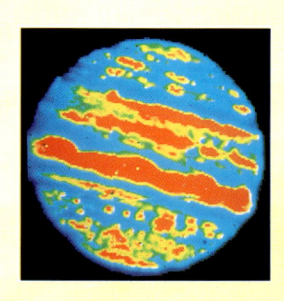

△ The red bands in this infrared image are gases from the deeper atmosphere, heated by the planet's continued contraction.

THE SOLAR SYSTEM

◁ *Voyager 2 went on a grand tour of the giant planets, passing Jupiter in 1979, Saturn in 1981, Uranus in 1986 and Neptune in 1989.*

Cosmic fireworks

In 1993, comet hunters David Levy and Gene and Carolyn Shoemaker spotted a strange comet. It had come so close to Jupiter that gravitational forces had torn it apart into what looked like a string of pearls. Calculations showed that the fragments would crash into the planet (*left*) in July 1994. No one knew what to expect. The impacts would be just out of sight over Jupiter's horizon, so perhaps nothing would be seen. In fact, the fireballs were clearly visible and, as the impact sites rotated into view, they were revealed as great brown marks larger than the Earth.

Visitors to Jupiter

Five spacecraft have visited Jupiter. *Pioneer 10* and *11* and *Voyager 1* and *2* sped past, giving valuable but tantalizingly brief glimpses (they discovered a thin ring of particles as fine as smoke.) But, in December 1995, *Galileo* went into orbit around the giant planet. Although the spacecraft's main antenna failed to open properly, *Galileo* has still returned spectacular pictures and data. On arrival, it released a probe that descended into Jupiter's atmosphere before being destroyed by the heat. The probe found less water than was expected, but it may just have missed the moist clouds.

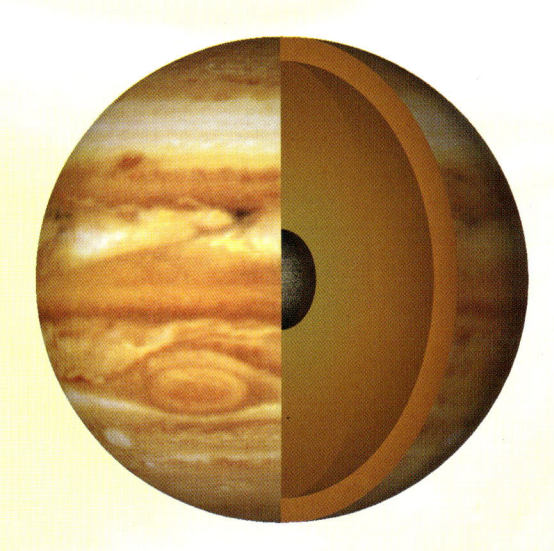

△ *The Red Spot, a 40,000 km storm system, has been raging for over 300 years. It has a dramatic effect on surrounding weather systems* (inset). *Nearby white ovals are huge temporary storms.*

△ *Jupiter's clouds lie in a thin layer on the surface. Below this, the atmosphere of hydrogen and helium becomes more and more compressed until it behaves as a liquid metal. Inside is a compressed rocky core, slightly bigger than the Earth.*

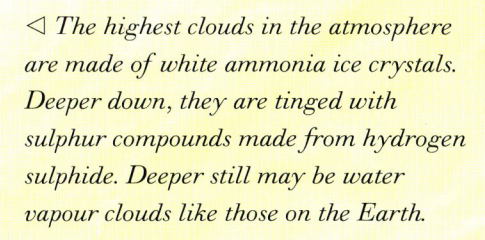

△ *The southern part of Jupiter, photographed in July 1994 by the Hubble Space Telescope. Dark chemicals welling up from deep in the atmosphere mark the impact sites of fragments of comet Shoemaker Levy 9. Each mark lasted for several months.*

◁ *The highest clouds in the atmosphere are made of white ammonia ice crystals. Deeper down, they are tinged with sulphur compounds made from hydrogen sulphide. Deeper still may be water vapour clouds like those on the Earth.*

159

Jupiter's Moons

△ *In the shadow of Jupiter lies the frozen world of Europa. A faint greenish light penetrates cracks in the ice. Some scientists think that under the ice there could even be liquid water.*

When Galileo first looked at Jupiter through his telescope in January 1610, he saw three, then four, tiny star-like objects moving close to the planet. He quickly realized that these were moons orbiting Jupiter. Each of these moons – Callisto, Ganymede, Europa and Io – is a world in its own right. We now know of 12 other moons. These include four that orbit inside Galileo's moons. Outside them lie four more, 11 million kilometres from Jupiter. Finally, at twice that distance, are another four. These may have been passing asteroids, captured by Jupiter's gravity.

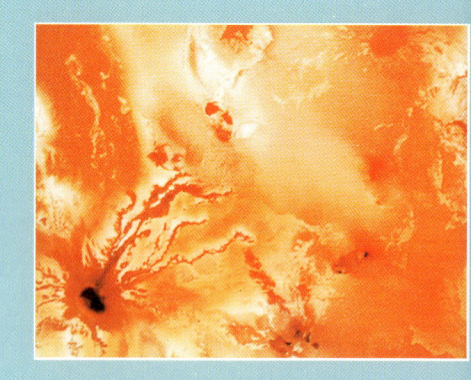

△ *The orange, sulphurous surface of Io is churned up by Jupiter's gravity, resulting in these fresh lava flows from a volcanic crater. The volcanic gases escape into space to form a ring around Jupiter.*

Callisto and Ganymede

Callisto is the same size as Mercury and is covered almost entirely with craters. Its crust is a mixture of ice and rock. One huge impact structure, called Valhalla, consists of rings up to 3,000 km across. Under the dark, dirty surface, the crust may be 300 km deep, with water or slush lying underneath. Ganymede is the largest moon in the Solar System at 5,276 km across. Its icy surface has large, dark patches that are heavily cratered. Ganymede's magnetic field raises the possibility that it still has an active interior.

◁ *The grooved surface of Ganymede appears to be made up of separate slabs of icy material.*

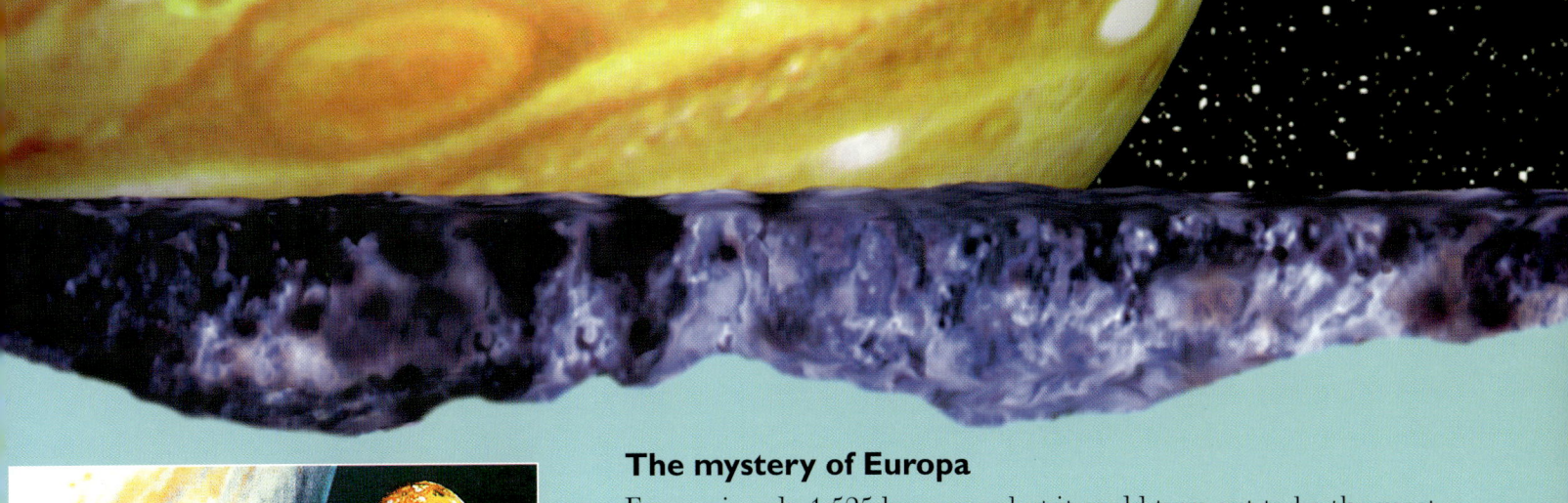

The mystery of Europa

Europa is only 1,525 km across but it could turn out to be the most exciting of all Jupiter's moons. The smooth, white surface has very few craters, but is crazed by numerous cracks. The cracks look very similar to those in pack-ice on the Earth. This suggests that the ice is floating on an ocean of liquid water. Hydrothermal vents in the ocean floor might provide energy as they do on the Earth, and it is just possible that life could have developed in the cold, dark water.

Io, world of fire

Io is the most volcanically active world in the Solar System. It is tugged so hard by Jupiter's gravity that tidal forces churn up the interior, keeping it partly molten. The Voyager craft saw eruptions taking place, with sulphur dioxide spewing 300 km up into space. *Galileo* saw several new volcanoes. Some have left dark lava flows and red and yellow patches of sulphur, making this moon look like a mouldy orange.

△ This composite picture shows Jupiter dwarfing its four main moons. Closest to the great planet is Io (top), followed by Europa, Ganymede – the largest moon – and Callisto.

◁ If oceans do exist beneath Europa's icy surface, there is also the possibility of life flourishing in the cold water. Volcanic vents on the ocean floor could provide the energy to support life, whatever form it might take.

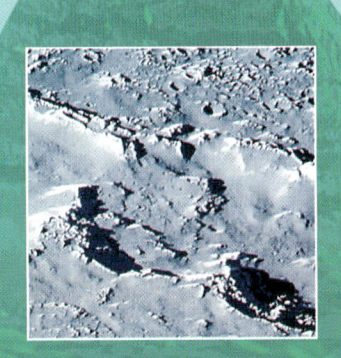

▷ Callisto's ancient surface is pockmarked by billions of years of impacts.

△ *Voyager 2* revealed the cracked, icy surface of Europa. In close-up the structures resemble those found in pack-ice around the Earth's poles, with tilted slabs, cracks and icebergs.

THE SOLAR SYSTEM

Saturn

After Galileo discovered Jupiter's moons he turned his attention to what appeared to be a triple planet – Saturn. Then the objects to the sides seemed to disappear, making him suspect they were gas clouds. It was the Dutch astronomer Christiaan Huygens who finally realized, in 1675, that Saturn was a ringed planet. Just under two hundred years later it was shown that the rings could not possibly be solid discs, but must be made up of millions of smaller particles of rock or ice, each acting like a tiny moon. When space probes *Pioneer 11* (1979), *Voyager 1* (1980) and *Voyager 2* (1981) flew past Saturn, it quickly became clear that there are thousands of separate bands of different density within the main rings (which are named A, B, C, D and E). There is also a very thin F ring outside these, its particles kept in line by two tiny moons. The rings are less than 30 metres thick and may have formed from the break-up of a giant comet that strayed too close to Saturn.

△ *Voyager 1* found dark lines running across Saturn's rings, like spokes on a wheel. Since the rings orbit at different speeds, the spokes were difficult to explain. They are now thought to be caused by ice crystals charged with static electricity.

△ An image, taken by the *Hubble Space Telescope* in 1990, enhanced to show the clouds. An elongated Great White Spot of ammonia ice crystals has formed high up in the atmosphere. The false colours pick out the top of the spot in red.

Stormy weather

A constant dull yellow haze of high ammonia clouds masks most of the deeper structure of Saturn's atmosphere. Occasionally, telescopes can make out a huge, swirling, white storm system. Computer enhancement of the Voyager images revealed circulating bands of cloud similar to Jupiter's. The fastest winds race around Saturn's equator, reaching up to 1,800 kilometres per hour. To the north and south of the equator are alternating bands of slow and fast winds.

△ As *Voyager 2* drew away from Saturn, it photographed the rings illuminated from behind. By tracking a star passing behind the rings, thousands of individual ringlets were recorded.

▷ Two pictures of Saturn taken by the *Hubble Space Telescope*. In the top picture, the shadow of the rings and Titan, Saturn's largest moon, are visible. In the bottom picture, Saturn appears with its rings tilted.

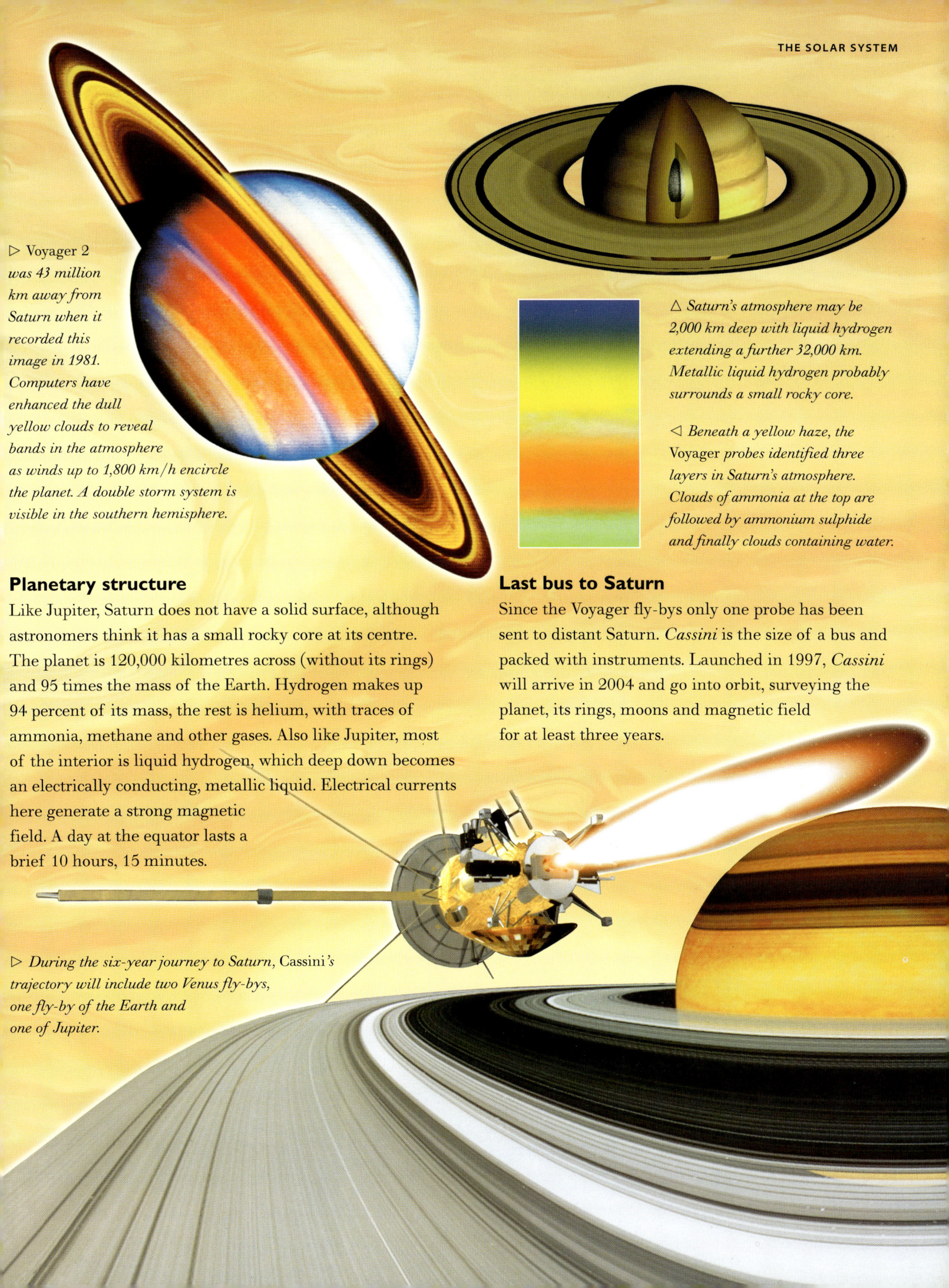

THE SOLAR SYSTEM

▷ Voyager 2 was 43 million km away from Saturn when it recorded this image in 1981. Computers have enhanced the dull yellow clouds to reveal bands in the atmosphere as winds up to 1,800 km/h encircle the planet. A double storm system is visible in the southern hemisphere.

△ Saturn's atmosphere may be 2,000 km deep with liquid hydrogen extending a further 32,000 km. Metallic liquid hydrogen probably surrounds a small rocky core.

◁ Beneath a yellow haze, the Voyager probes identified three layers in Saturn's atmosphere. Clouds of ammonia at the top are followed by ammonium sulphide and finally clouds containing water.

Planetary structure

Like Jupiter, Saturn does not have a solid surface, although astronomers think it has a small rocky core at its centre. The planet is 120,000 kilometres across (without its rings) and 95 times the mass of the Earth. Hydrogen makes up 94 percent of its mass, the rest is helium, with traces of ammonia, methane and other gases. Also like Jupiter, most of the interior is liquid hydrogen, which deep down becomes an electrically conducting, metallic liquid. Electrical currents here generate a strong magnetic field. A day at the equator lasts a brief 10 hours, 15 minutes.

Last bus to Saturn

Since the Voyager fly-bys only one probe has been sent to distant Saturn. *Cassini* is the size of a bus and packed with instruments. Launched in 1997, *Cassini* will arrive in 2004 and go into orbit, surveying the planet, its rings, moons and magnetic field for at least three years.

▷ During the six-year journey to Saturn, Cassini's trajectory will include two Venus fly-bys, one fly-by of the Earth and one of Jupiter.

THE SOLAR SYSTEM

Saturn's Moons

Saturn is at the centre of a solar system in miniature. Apart from the billions of particles making up its rings, 23 different moons have been identified. Some are lumps of rock only a few kilometres across that lie close to the planet and shepherd the rings into place. Saturn's most distant moon, Phoebe, is nearly 13 million kilometres from the planet. The biggest of all the moons is Titan. At 5,150 kilometres across, it is bigger than Mercury and has a thick atmosphere. It is the only atmosphere astronomers know of, apart from the Earth's, that is made up mostly of nitrogen. The surface of Titan is very cold (about −180°C) and the atmospheric pressure is double that of our own planet. Titan's atmosphere resembles the early Earth's, but kept in frozen lifelessness.

△ *Discovered by Christiaan Huygens in 1655, Titan is the second largest moon in the Solar System. Voyager 2 was only able to see this orange ball of smog, made by the action of sunlight on Titan's atmosphere.*

▽ *High in Titan's nitrogen atmosphere is a layer that absorbs ultraviolet rays. A thin blue haze of carbon chemicals sits above an unbroken layer of orange smog. Below this, the sky may have clouds of methane.*

△ *In November 2004, after a seven year journey, the* Huygens *probe will be released above the clouds of Titan from the* Cassini *Saturn orbiter. After an initial fiery entry, the heat shield will fall away and the probe will parachute down to the surface of the moon.*

A giant among moons

The interior of Titan is probably a mixture of rock and ice, with a rocky core that has an ice mantle. The ice could never melt, but there may be lakes or oceans on Titan, not of water but of liquid natural gas or methane. Methane rain or snow may fall from the clouds. The Voyager probes were unable to see any features on Titan because it is wrapped in a thick, butterscotch yellow, chemical smog.

Mysterious worlds

Saturn's other large moons are equally strange. Enceladus has an ancient, cratered landscape with signs of newer activity in the form of smooth plains and series of ridges. Iapetus, the outermost of Saturn's big moons, is little denser than water, suggesting it is mostly ice. One side is bright and cratered but the opposite side is as black as anything in the Solar System. Dione has light, wispy markings that may be trails of frost sprayed out from ice volcanoes. Mimas, just outside the rings, has an enormous crater, like a great black eye. Tethys is made up mostly of pure ice and has a huge crack, 100 kilometres across and five kilometres deep, running almost pole to pole.

Landing on Titan

On November 27, 2004 the *Cassini* Saturn orbiter will release the *Huygens* probe above the clouds of Titan. No one knows what the probe will find. It may land on rock or ice, or even in a sea of liquid methane. If waves do not sink it, the probe will use sonar to measure depths, as well as recording temperatures and composition. It may even find the basic chemicals needed for life, suspended in a deep freeze.

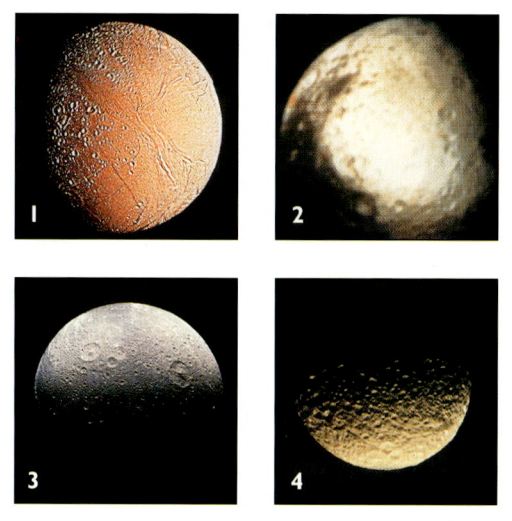

△ These *Voyager* images show five of Saturn's large moons: Enceladus (1), Iapetus (2), Dione (3), Mimas (4), and Tethys (5).

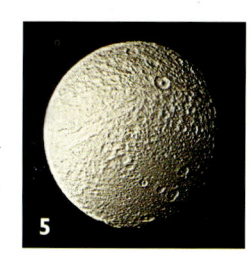

▽ The *Huygens* probe will have 2.5 hours to make its readings as it descends through the smog of Titan. It is designed to survive landings on both solid and liquid surfaces.

THE SOLAR SYSTEM

Uranus

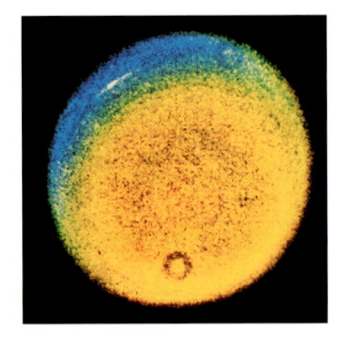

Mercury, Venus, Mars, Jupiter and Saturn are all visible to the naked eye and have been known since ancient times. Uranus was the first planet to be discovered through a telescope. One March night in 1781, the astronomer William Herschel noticed what he described as "either a nebulous star or perhaps a comet". He had actually become the first person to discover Uranus. Although it is four times the size of the Earth, Uranus is twice as far away as Saturn and, even through a telescope, only appears as a tiny greenish disc. Herschel wanted to name the new planet after the English king, George III, but in the end it was named after Uranus, the Greek god of the sky.

△ *By using computers to stretch blues and greens into a wider spectrum, scientists were able to see white clouds of methane near Uranus' equator (top left).*

▽ *Combining images taken by Voyager 2 through orange, blue and green filters revealed Uranus as a featureless blue ball.*

Cloudy world

Only one probe, *Voyager 2*, has visited Uranus, on January 24, 1986. No one knew what it would find as the planet appears totally featureless through telescopes on the Earth. When the probe's pictures were enhanced they revealed clouds on the surface. These show that the planet rotates once every 17 hours, 14 minutes, with winds blowing at up to 300 kilometres per hour.

Surprise discovery

In March 1977, astronomers noticed a star passing behind Uranus. Hoping to record how it dimmed as it disappeared behind the atmosphere, they tracked it with an infrared telescope. To their amazement, the star flickered on and off. The only explanation was that Uranus is encircled by rings.

△ *Voyager 2 confirmed that Uranus has rings, 11 in all, of very dark, boulder-sized fragments. Here, fine dust is revealed between the main rings as they are backlit by the Sun.*

◁ *This colour-enhanced picture, taken as Voyager 2 approached Uranus' south pole, indicated that a high altitude haze had formed during the southern hemisphere's 42-year-long summer.*

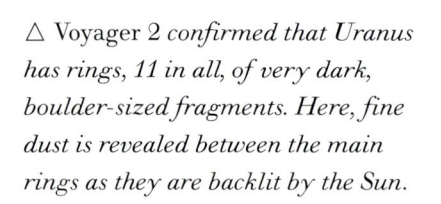

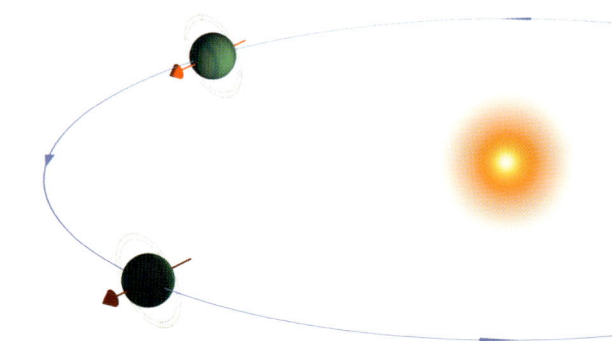

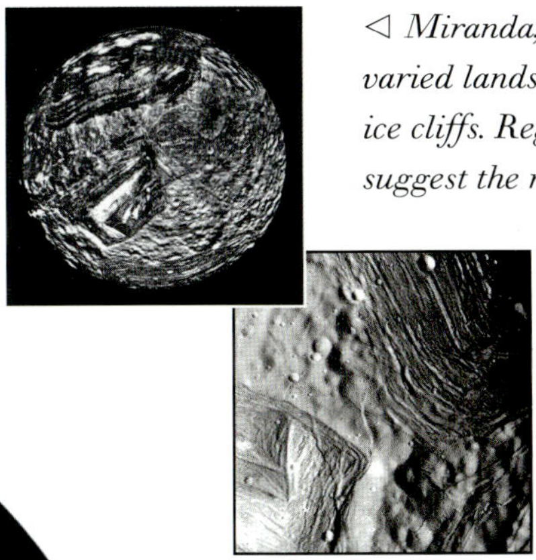

THE SOLAR SYSTEM

◁ *Miranda, only 480 km across, has a very varied landscape with old, cratered plains and ice cliffs. Regions like the Chevron (below) suggest the moon was once almost completely shattered by a major impact.*

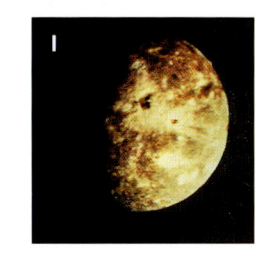

Multiple moons

Until the *Voyager 2* mission, Uranus was known to have five moons – Oberon, Titania, Umbriel, Ariel and Miranda (all named after characters from English literature). As *Voyager 2* approached, another moon was spotted and named Puck. A further nine small, dark moons were also found. The two innermost moons, Cordelia and Ophelia, on opposite sides of the outer ring, help shepherd the ring particles into line. One astronomer commented that God must have taken a shaker and scattered moons in all directions.

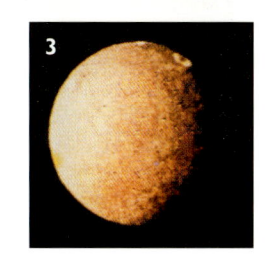

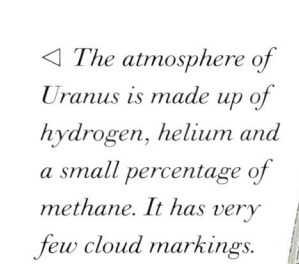

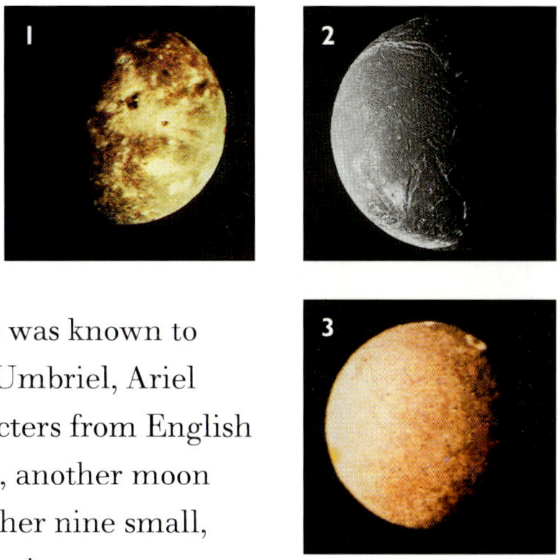

△ *Three of Uranus' main moons are shown here. Oberon (1) has big impact craters, containing dark, carbon-rich material. Ariel (2) is covered in places by small craters and resurfaced in others by eruptions of lava or water. Umbriel (3) has a dark, cratered surface, but no signs of geological activity.*

◁ *The atmosphere of Uranus is made up of hydrogen, helium and a small percentage of methane. It has very few cloud markings.*

△ *The blue-green gas giant Uranus is four times the size of the Earth. It has a strange magnetic field aligned at 60° to the rotation axis and off-centred 10,000 km from the heart of the planet. It may be generated by electrical currents in the watery mantle.*

◁ *Uranus probably has a rocky core with a mantle of ammonia, methane and water ice that may be partially liquid.*

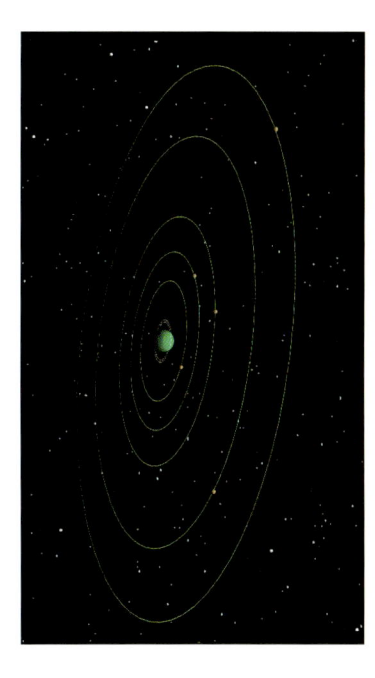

Strange rotation

Unlike the other planets, Uranus' axis of rotation is at right angles to its orbit around the Sun. So, as *Voyager 2* approached Uranus' south pole, the rings and moons seemed to circle the planet like a target. This also gives Uranus very strange seasons. The poles are the warmest places on the planet. The south pole has a summer lasting 42 years, when the Sun never sets, while the opposite pole is plunged into total darkness for 42 years.

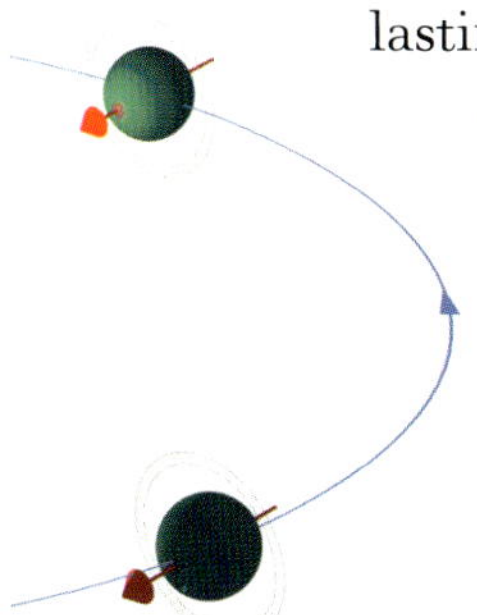

▷ *The orbits of Uranus' five main moons are shown here. From the outside in they are: Oberon, Titania, Umbriel, Ariel and Miranda. They orbit in circular paths in the same direction as the planet's rotation.*

◁ *Uranus rotates at an angle of 97° to the Sun during its 84-year orbit.*

167

THE SOLAR SYSTEM

Neptune

After the discovery of Uranus, astronomers were unable to make sense of its orbit around the Sun – it seemed as if something was pulling it off course. In 1845, Cambridge graduate John Couch Adams proposed that this movement was caused by an eighth planet, and a year later his professor, James Challis, began a search. In France, Urbain Leverrier had made similar predictions and, although Challis had seen the new planet without recognizing it, Berlin astronomers using the French predictions actually made the discovery of Neptune in 1846. They named the blue-green planet after the Roman god of the sea. It is 4.5 billion kilometres from the Sun and takes 165 years to orbit it (a Neptunian year).

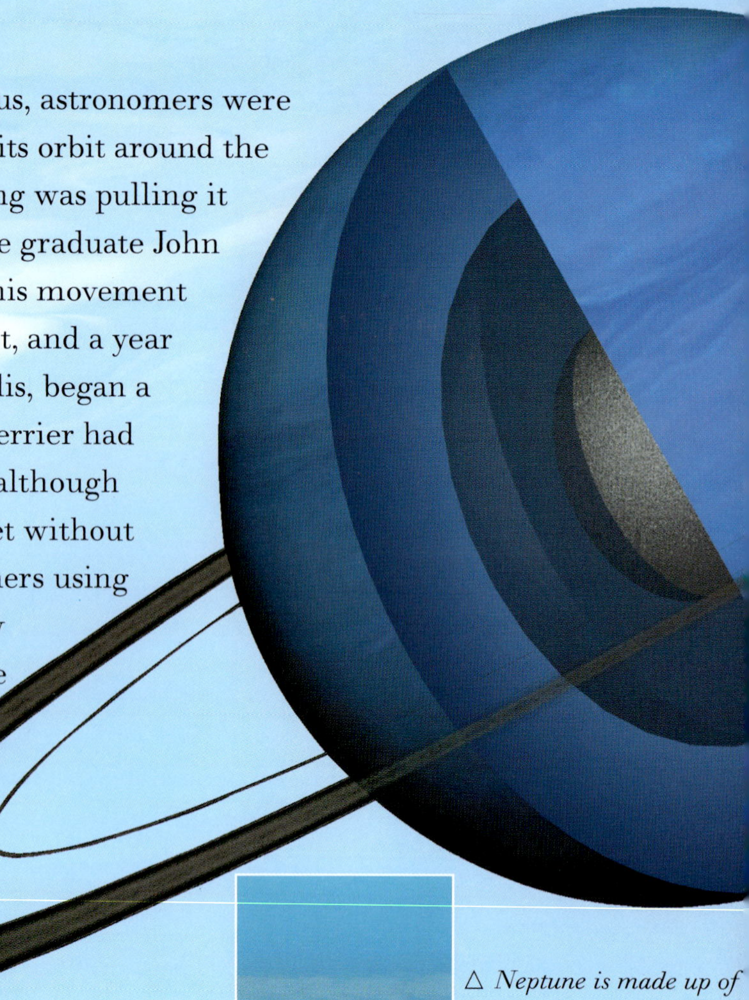

△ *This image, made by* Voyager 2 *in 1989, has been enhanced to reveal a haze high in the atmosphere and white clouds of methane ice.*

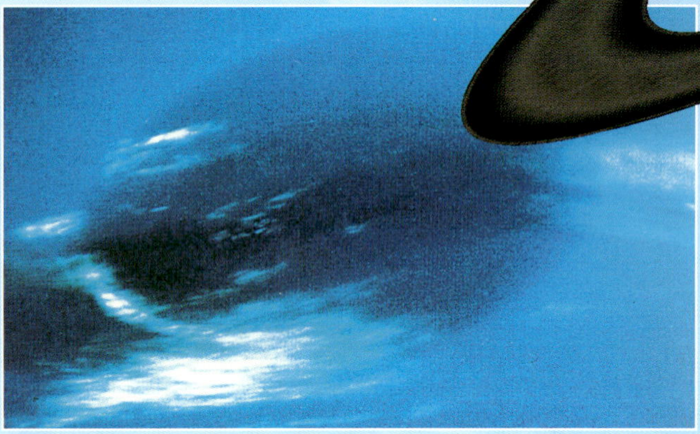

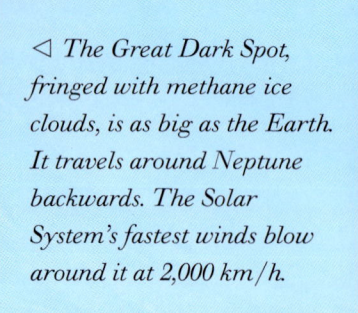

◁ *The Great Dark Spot, fringed with methane ice clouds, is as big as the Earth. It travels around Neptune backwards. The Solar System's fastest winds blow around it at 2,000 km/h.*

△ *Neptune is made up of a thick mantle of liquid water and gases around a rocky core. It has a magnetic field inclined at 50° to its axis and 10,000 km off-centre. It has rings made up of large particles and broad bands of finer dust.*

Weather forecast

Neptune's atmosphere consists of 85 percent hydrogen, thirteen percent helium and two percent methane. It is bitterly cold (the cloud tops are −210°C) but heat is produced in the interior. Neptune is a very active planet. Clouds of methane rise through the atmosphere and violent winds blow at over 1,000 kilometres per hour. One cloud pattern, the Scooter, speeds around the planet passing another feature, the Great Dark Spot, every few days.

△ *The atmosphere is topped by a thin haze with cirrus clouds of methane ice. Sunlight causes reactions in the methane, producing hydrocarbon snow. As this falls it reverts to methane gas and rises again.*

◁ *High-speed winds have stretched out these high cirrus clouds of methane into streamers. They cast shadows onto the blue main cloud deck, 50 km below.*

THE SOLAR SYSTEM

◁ *Neptune's two main moons, Triton and Nereid, have very different orbits. Nereid's long elliptical orbit lasts 360 days. Triton's 5.9-day orbit circles the planet backwards. Both may have been caught by Neptune's gravity as they passed.*

Rings and moons

Before *Voyager 2*'s fly-past of Neptune in 1989, only two moons and partial rings were known to astronomers. The craft's cameras confirmed complete rings, bands of dust and six new moons. The largest of these is Proteus. It is 436 kilometres across and has a giant 150-kilometre crater. Next in size is Larissa at 208 kilometres. The other four moons lie between the rings. The outermost moon, Nereid, may be a captured comet. Neptune's largest moon, Triton, is 2,706 kilometres across. With no high mountains and few craters, its surface may have been flooded by eruptions of liquid water and ammonia. Most of its surface is ice, but the poles are capped with a pink snow of frozen nitrogen.

▽ *Triton's south pole is capped by a light, pinkish substance that is probably frozen nitrogen accumulated during its long winter in shadow. The grooved and wrinkled surface to the north has a red tint, possibly due to hydrocarbons produced by the action of sunlight.*

△ *This imagined view from the surface of Triton shows Neptune on the horizon and an active nitrogen geyser erupting from the surface. Pressure keeps nitrogen liquid deep below the ground. As it rises it explodes as a mixture of ice crystals and vapour. The eruption carries the plume 30 km high, before it blows away in the thin wind, raining a dark streak of dust down onto the surface.*

169

THE SOLAR SYSTEM

Pluto

In order to explain the orbit of Uranus, astronomers realized they had to discover something else. An American astronomer, Percival Lowell, predicted a planet larger than the Earth and searched for it in vain (Pluto appeared on his photographs, but he failed to recognize it). However, Clyde Tombaugh, a successor at the observatory Lowell founded in Arizona, USA, painstakingly compared star after star and, finally found an object that moved. Named Pluto (after the Greek god of the underworld) at the suggestion of an eleven-year-old girl, it is six billion kilometres from the Sun and one four-hundredth the mass of the Earth.

△ *This image of Pluto is made up from measurements taken by the* Hubble Space Telescope. *The lightest patches may be nitrogen ice.*

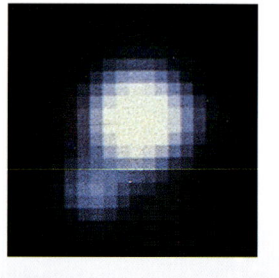

△ *Even the most powerful Earth-based telescopes can only just make out the faint disc of Pluto and its moon, Charon. No probe has visited Pluto and there is still much to learn about it.*

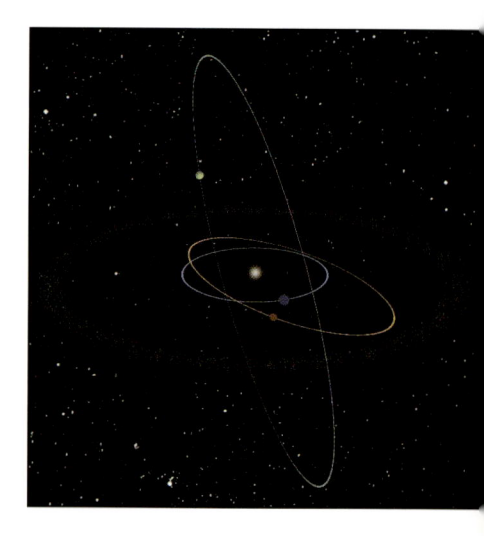

△ *Pluto is usually the furthest planet from the Sun, but its elliptical orbit* (orange) *briefly brings it closer than Neptune* (blue). *Some astronomers suggest that a Planet X* (green) *follows a steeply inclined orbit far outside Pluto. The Kuiper Belt – a ring of small, icy objects lies beyond the planets.*

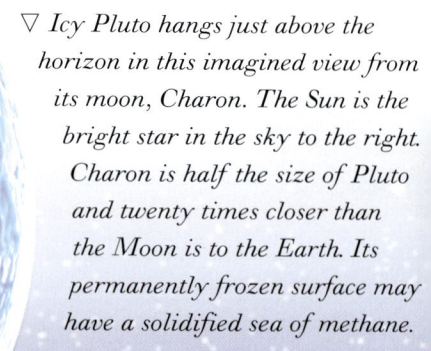

▽ *Icy Pluto hangs just above the horizon in this imagined view from its moon, Charon. The Sun is the bright star in the sky to the right. Charon is half the size of Pluto and twenty times closer than the Moon is to the Earth. Its permanently frozen surface may have a solidified sea of methane.*

Seeing double

When it was first discovered, Pluto's mass and density were unknown, so no one knew if it was the final explanation for the outer planets' orbits. If Pluto had a moon, however, the masses could be calculated from that moon's orbit. There the matter rested until 1978, when Jim Christy was trying to make precise measurements of Pluto at the US Naval Observatory. At first, his picture seemed pear-shaped. Suddenly, he realized he was seeing not one object but two. He named the moon Charon after his wife, and also after the mythological ferryman of the ancient Greek underworld.

▷ *Both Pluto and Charon are denser than the other outer planets and their moons. They must have big, rocky cores covered by a thick layer of water ice, frozen methane and nitrogen.*

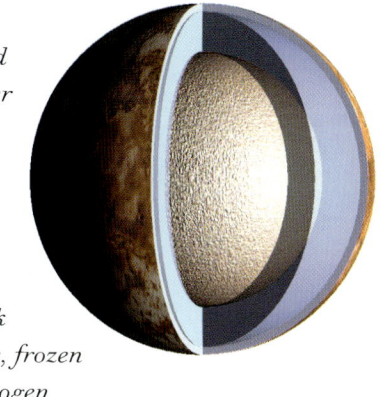

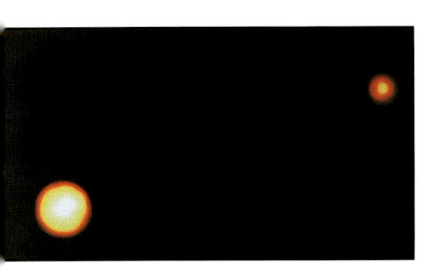

△ *This picture taken by the* Hubble Space Telescope *shows Pluto and Charon. Pluto at 2,300 km across is far smaller than our Moon, while Charon is less than 1,200 km across.*

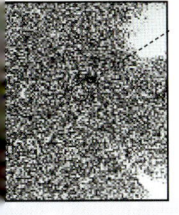

◁ *A faint line among the points of stars reveals an object in the Kuiper Belt. Only a few kilometres across, a few hundred of these objects have been observed with powerful infrared telescopes.*

Planet X and beyond

Pluto, however, did not account for all the discrepancies in Uranus' orbit and astronomers started searching for a tenth planet, Planet X. Clyde Tombaugh searched for 13 years, plotting the positions of 45 million stars and identifying 775 asteroids in the process. Some people predicted that a planet would be found in an orbit angled to the other planets, while others thought that the Sun has a distant, dark companion. There may also be billions of comets beyond the planets, all adding their own gravitational effect. A belt of icy objects has been discovered far beyond Pluto, known as the Kuiper Belt. Each object is only a few kilometres across and may be the frozen left-overs from planetary formation.

△ *Pluto has a thin atmosphere of nitrogen and methane. This thickens as the planet's elliptical orbit brings it nearer the Sun and warms it up. Polar caps of methane ice may be deposited as Pluto cools again.*

THE SOLAR SYSTEM

Comets

Comets are among the most beautiful and exciting sights in the sky. They are made all the more mysterious by their unpredictability, leading people in the past to think that they were omens of either good or evil. Five hundred years ago, they were thought to be within our atmosphere. Then, in 1577, Danish astronomer Tycho Brahe worked out the distance to a comet and showed that they came from beyond the planets, and rounded the Sun before returning to deep space. We now know that there must be a vast number of comets in the outer regions of the Solar System, far beyond the planets. In fact, there could be billions waiting in the deep-freeze of space.

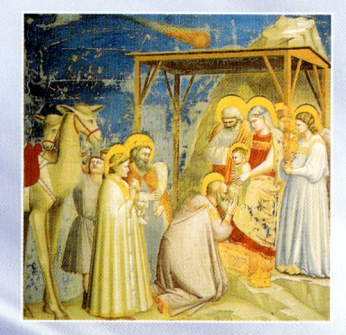

△ *This engraving from the* Nuremberg Chronicle *(published in 1493) depicts the sighting of Halley's Comet in AD684.*

△ *In the* Adoration of the Magi *by Giotto, Halley's Comet is shown as the Star of Bethlehem, above the stable.*

Halley's Comet

Edmond Halley (1656–1742) studied the records of comets and realized that the comets of 1531, 1607 and 1682 were actually the same object. He predicted correctly the comet's return in 1759, although he never lived to see it. In fact, Halley's Comet has been seen 30 times since 240BC. It is depicted in the Bayeux Tapestry, which shows the Norman Conquest of England in 1066, and in a painting of the Nativity by the Italian artist Giotto, based on his sighting of the comet in 1301. In 1986, a probe named *Giotto* visited Halley's Comet.

△ *This computer simulation shows how the front dust shield of* Giotto *looked after speeding past the nucleus of Halley's Comet. Dust particles punched holes in the metal.* Giotto *took a close-up picture of the comet's dark nucleus (right) silhouetted against brighter jets of gas.*

▽ *In 1997, Comet Hale-Bopp gave a great display. Its nucleus was unusually large and it started to brighten beyond Jupiter's orbit.*

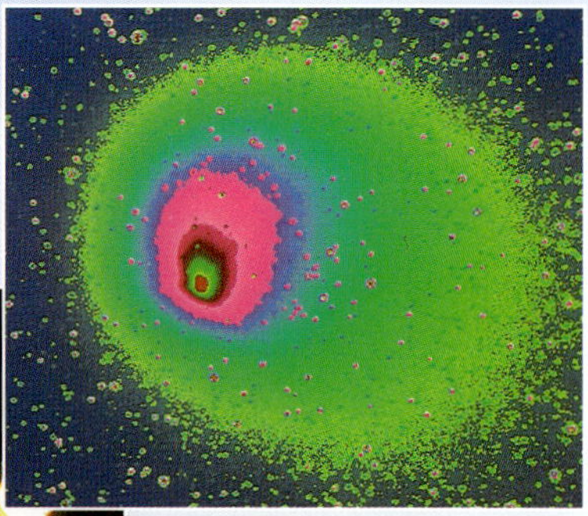

△ *This image of Comet Hale-Bopp, taken in 1996, is coloured to show the bright coma as well as the dark nucleus embedded deep within it.*

The core of a comet

Comets are all show and very little substance. The head of a comet is made up of a small nucleus only a few kilometres across. It may contain lumps of rock, but they are loosely bound by ice and comets often break up. As the nucleus approaches the inner Solar System, ice begins to vaporize, creating the bright coma (a sphere of gas and dust around the nucleus), and tail, which can be millions of kilometres long. A crust of black, carbon-rich material covers the surface with jets of gas breaking out through cracks. Each time a comet passes the Sun it loses millions of tonnes of ice, eventually leaving a dead, dark nucleus or just a trail of dust.

THE SOLAR SYSTEM

▽ *The nucleus of a comet is like a huge, dirty snowball. Jets of gas and dust escape through fissures in its black, asphalt-like surface, blown by the solar wind to form a tail. Here, the surface has been cut away to reveal the icy interior, surrounding a loosely-bound, rocky core.*

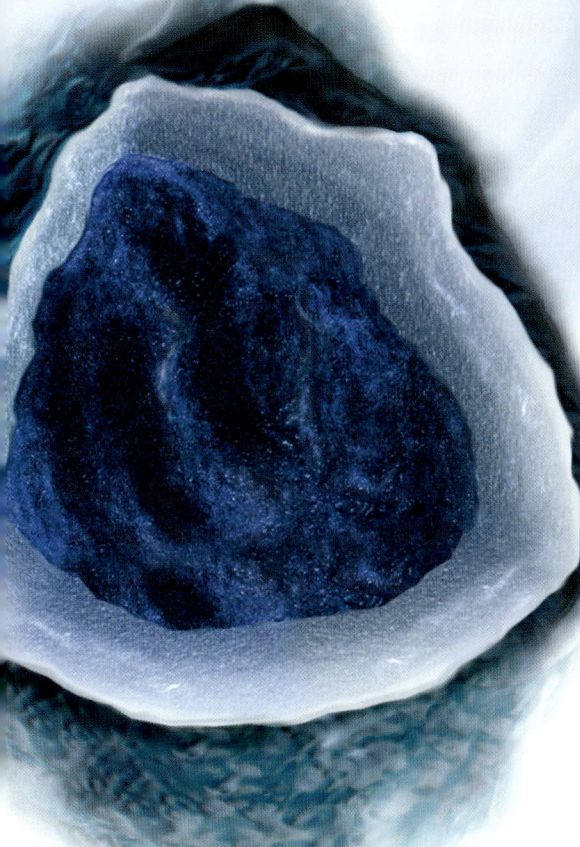

△ *Comets have two tails. Electrically charged ions of gas always point directly away from the Sun. The yellower dust tail lags slightly and curves with the comet's motion.*

Dead comets and shooting stars

Long after a comet has run out of bright gas and faded for good, anything that is left of the nucleus, along with a stream of dusty particles, continues in the same orbit. When the Earth passes through this orbit, thousands of the particles burn up as shooting stars in the atmosphere. These are the meteor showers that seem to radiate out from the same place in the sky at the same time each year. Spectacular storms look as if they emerge from particular constellations. For example, the Perseid shower, which follows Comet Swift-Tuttle, appears from the constellation Perseus, while the Orionids, which follow Halley's Comet, seem to come from Orion.

△ *Blown back by the solar wind (a constant stream of electrically charged particles emitted by the Sun), a comet's tails always point away from the Sun. The tails are longest closest to the Sun, when gas production is at its highest.*

The Oort Cloud

Far out, on the edge of the Solar System, lies a gigantic cloud of billions of frozen comets, called the Oort Cloud. Some comets are concentrated in a disc beyond the orbit of Pluto, while others are randomly distributed up to a light year or more away. The gravity of nearby stars 'knocks' these comets from their orbits so that they fall towards the Sun. About ten comets a year are newcomers to the inner Solar System, where many become trapped. The Oort Cloud may be debris left over from when the Solar System formed. If so, comets may be able to tell us what conditions were like when the Sun was born.

△ *An exposure of only a few seconds captured the bright streaks of the Leonid meteor shower, which seems to radiate from the constellation Leo and follows Comet Tempel-Tuttle.*

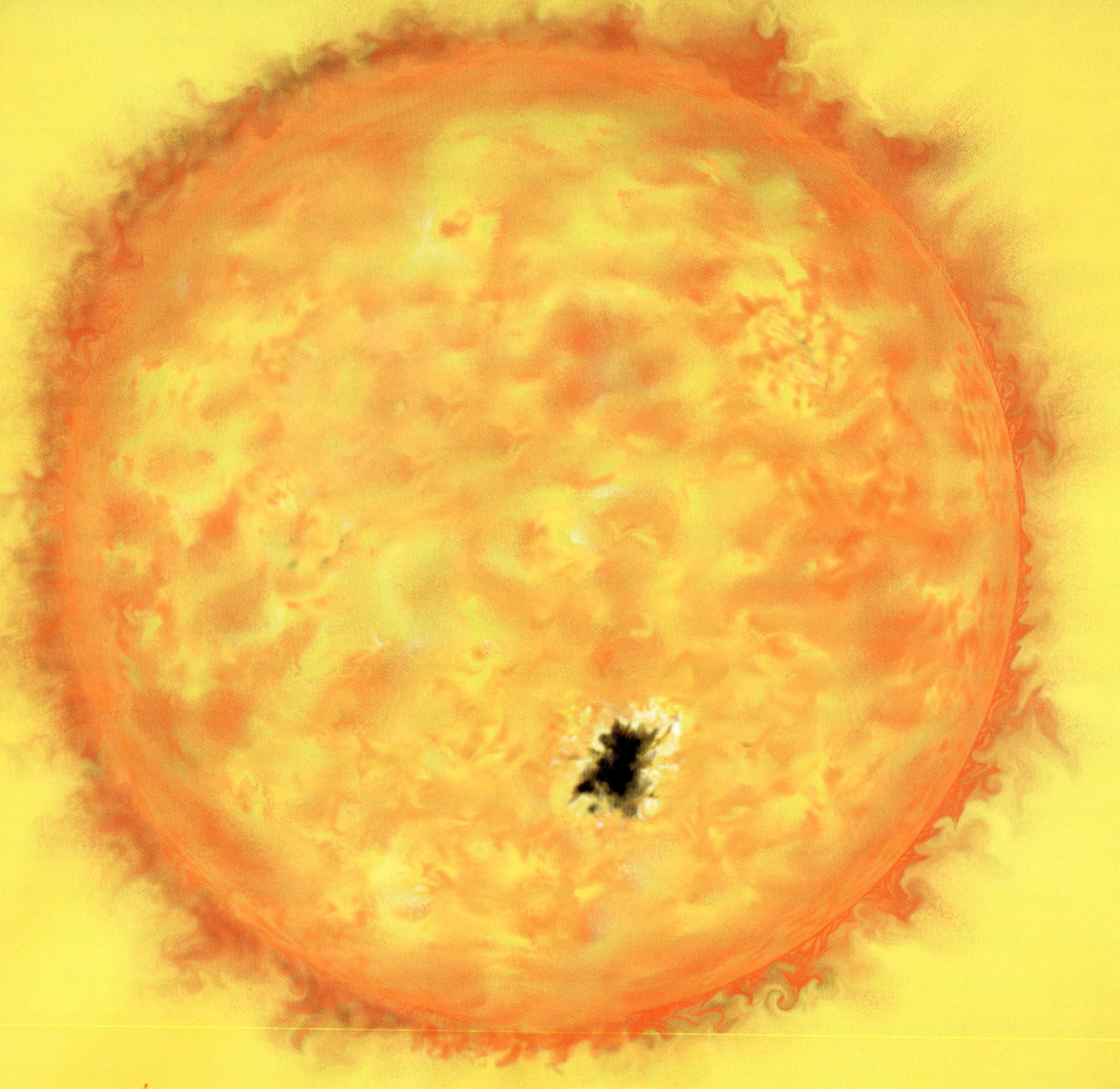

◁ The Sun has been burning for about five billion years. Like all stars, it is a huge ball of very hot gas. Its constant stream of sunshine keeps our planet warm, enables plants to photosynthesize and ultimately sustains all life.

▽ During a total eclipse, the corona – the outer layer of the Sun's atmosphere – becomes visible. It can reach temperatures of up to 2,000,000°C.

The Active Sun

△ Sunlight scatters off dust and clouds in the Earth's atmosphere to produce spectacular sunrises and sunsets.

The Sun is our nearest star, the centre of the Solar System and the source, directly or indirectly, of almost all the energy we use. The Sun is extremely hot – about 6,000°C at the surface, or photosphere, and 15,000,000°C at the core. The core temperature and pressure are high enough for an energy-generating process called nuclear fusion to take place. Protons, the nuclei of hydrogen atoms, fuse together to make deuterium or heavy hydrogen, then helium. At each stage, mass is lost in the form of energy. Altogether the Sun loses four million tonnes of mass every second, which is converted into the four hundred billion billion megawatts of energy it needs to support itself and to shine. Most of the energy radiates as heat, light and gamma rays, taking thousands of years to reach the surface. But some escapes straight through the Sun, carried by ghostly particles called neutrinos, produced in the nuclear reactions.

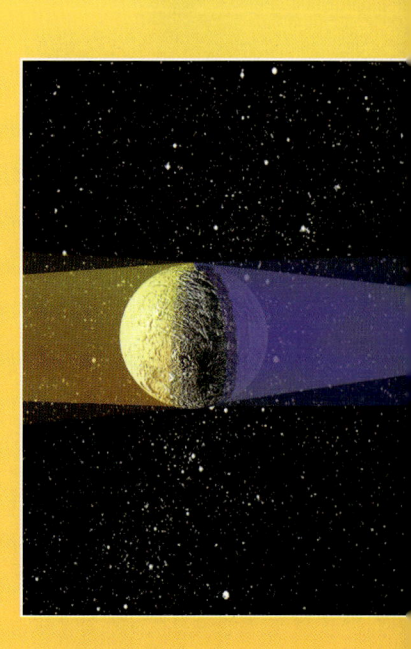

STARS

△ *This x-ray image of the Sun and its corona was recorded by the Japanese satellite* Yohkoh *in 1992. The brightest and hottest areas occur above sunspots, where hot gases flare up.*

▷ *Nuclear reactions take place inside the core of the Sun and the energy slowly radiates out to a distance of about 600,000 kilometres. Huge bubbles of hot gas continue the transfer of energy to the surface.*

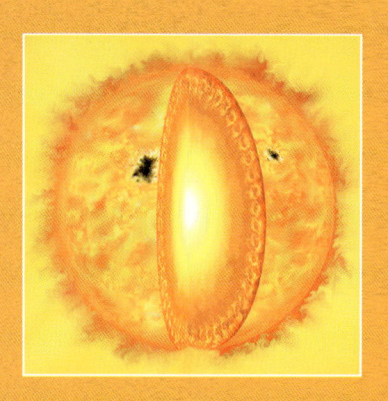

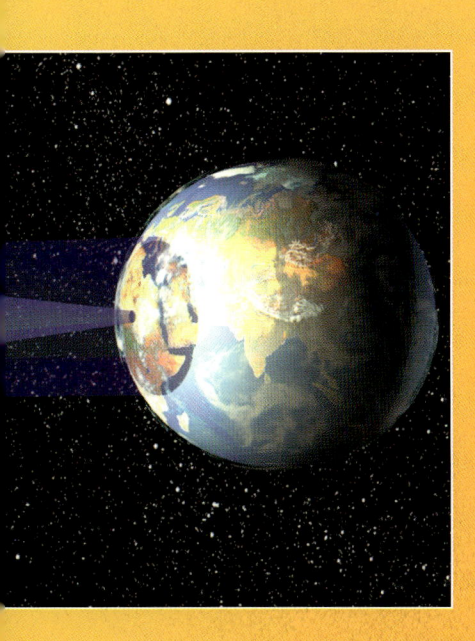

Observing the Sun

You should not look at the Sun directly and certainly never through a telescope or binoculars – you risk being blinded for life. It is possible, however, to project an image onto a sheet of paper using binoculars, a lens or even a pinhole in a sheet of cardboard. This is essentially what solar astronomers do, focusing the light down long tubes, through filters and onto an observation table.

Unobstructed view

The Sun is best viewed from beyond our turbulent atmosphere. From space the Sun can be seen in other wavelengths such as x-rays, revealing the superhot flares that leap from the surface. Several spacecraft have studied the Sun directly, including *Skylab* in the 1970s and *SolarMax* in the 1980s. *Ulysses* has left the plane of the planets to study the magnetic field and solar wind above the poles of the Sun. And Europe's *SOHO* craft hangs between the Earth and the Sun looking at sunquakes and flares, and spotting storms of particles on their way to the Earth.

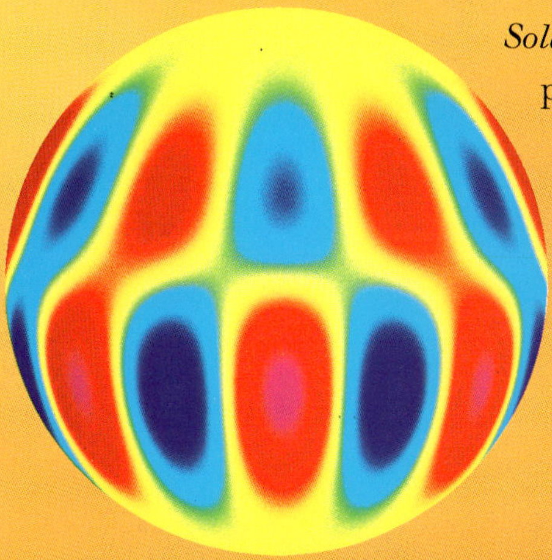

Eclipse!

About once a year, the Moon comes between the Sun and the Earth, casting a shadow. When the Moon is close enough to the Earth in its orbit, it masks the Sun's disc entirely, causing a total eclipse.

▽ *During a total eclipse, part of the world is plunged into darkness. People in the outer shadow see a partial eclipse.*

△ *The Sun is ringing like a bell. Scientists can record the vibrations by seeing how the movement stretches or compresses light from different regions. The sound waves are created in the solar convective zone – the outer layer of the Sun.*

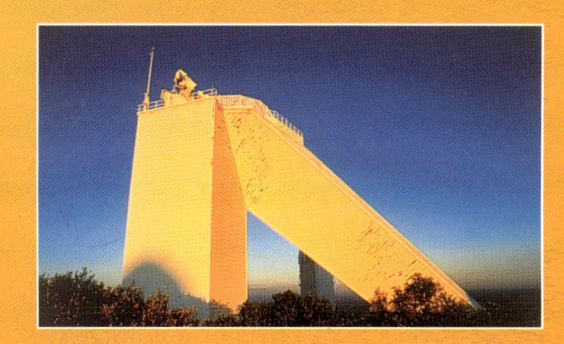

△ *The McMath Solar Telescope on Kitt Peak in Arizona, focuses the Sun's image down a 152 m diagonal tube to instruments below.*

175

STARS

Outside the Sun

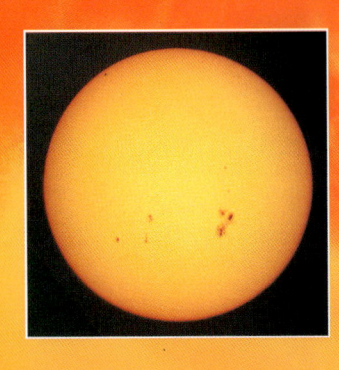

The hot, electrically-charged gas within the Sun generates very powerful magnetic fields. Where these break the surface, great jets or loops of hot gas called prominences lift off into space. Dark, relatively cool patches on the Sun's surface are called sunspots. These form in pairs or groups, and represent points where the magnetic field lines leave and re-join the surface. Rapid eruptions called solar flares also arise along these lines. They usually last no longer than ten minutes and release the energy equivalent of a million hydrogen bombs. Together with the solar wind (a constant stream of charged particles flowing from the Sun), they create a vast envelope, known as the heliosphere, around the Solar System.

△ *A visible light image of the Sun, taken with the McMath Solar Telescope in Arizona. Several sunspots can clearly be seen on the photosphere, or the visible surface of the Sun.*

△ *Prominences of hot gas break free from the Sun's surface and can leap out hundreds of thousands of kilometres into space.*

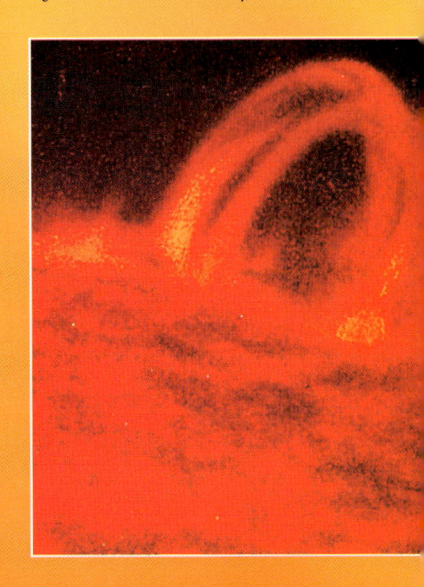

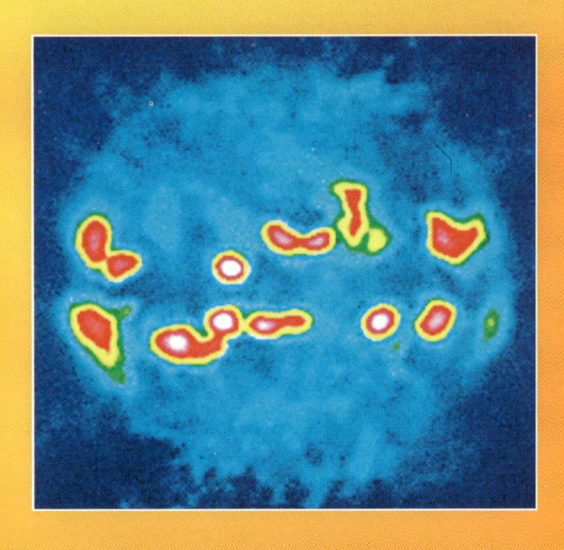

△ *The Sun emits strong radio waves that were first noticed in the 1940s. The brightest areas in this radio image occur where gas flares off into space above pairs of sunspots.*

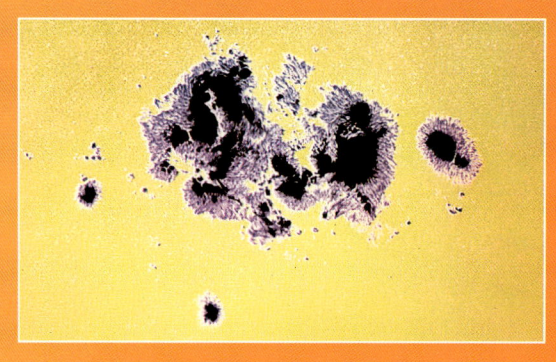

△ *This false-colour photograph shows a group of sunspots. The spots form in pairs with opposite magnetic poles. The dark centres of the spots are the coolest, lowest regions where strong magnetic fields slow the upward flow of heat. Around them, bubbles of gas rise, cool and move away.*

The changing Sun

The Sun is not as constant as it appears. By tracking sunspots, it is clear that it rotates at the equator once every 25 days, and at the poles once every 35 days. This difference results in magnetic field lines getting wrapped around the Sun until they break through the surface at sunspots. The pattern of sunspots changes in a cycle of about 11 years. At the start, spots begin to appear near the poles. As they fade, spots appear nearer and nearer the equator, where they cause a peak of solar activity.

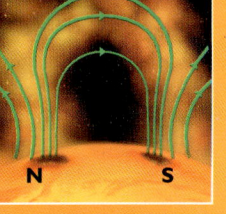

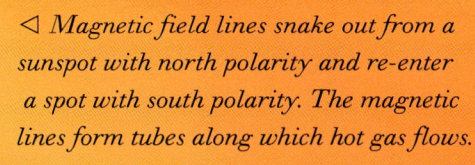

◁ *Magnetic field lines snake out from a sunspot with north polarity and re-enter a spot with south polarity. The magnetic lines form tubes along which hot gas flows.*

Solar weather

There are less dramatic changes, too. Between 1645 and 1715, there were virtually no sunspots. This coincided with extreme winters in Europe, a period sometimes known as the 'Little Ice Age'. Evidence from other Sun-like stars suggests that, for up to 20 percent of their time, they have no sunspots.

◁ *These great loops of hot gas were photographed in ultraviolet by* Skylab *in 1973. They arch up between pairs of sunspots and can remain relatively stable for many hours or even days.*

The end of the Sun

It probably took the Sun 3.5 billion years to reach its present brightness, during which time plants were slowly using up carbon dioxide from the Earth's atmosphere, reducing the greenhouse effect and keeping the climate more or less constant. The Sun will probably continue to shine at its present level for another two billion years. But in about six billion years' time, hydrogen will begin to run out at the core, and the Sun will begin to expand rapidly and cool as it becomes a dying star called a red giant. This will engulf the inner planets, including the Earth.

△ *In about six billion years' time, the Earth's atmosphere and oceans will boil away as the dying Sun becomes a red giant. As the giant star expands, the baked husk of our planet will be swallowed up and become part of a new generation of stars and planets.*

▽ *Swirling nebulae of dust and gas are the nurseries of stars. Often, they are themselves the ashes of earlier generations, cooked and spewed out from short-lived massive stars.*

STARS

Star Birth

△ *Knots form in the gas as gravity pulls it together. As the gas compresses it begins to heat up*

△ *Below the line of three stars that form the belt of Orion is Orion's Sword. At its centre lies the distinctive Orion Nebula, a birthplace of stars.*

The backdrop of stars used to be thought of as constant and unchanging. Over human lifetimes, there is little detectable change, but over the billions of years of galactic life, stars are born, live their lives, grow old and die. Space, by human standards, appears very, very empty. But collect together all the gas and dust of supposedly empty space and there is more matter than all the stars and planets put together. It is out of these clouds, or nebulae, that new stars are born. Over 12 billion years ago, when the Universe itself was young, clouds of hydrogen and helium created the first stars that ever shone. Now, all kinds of other elements are mixed in, the ashes of earlier generations of stars. These combine to make the stars we see forming in dusty nebulae today.

Conception!

Stars tend to be born not singly but in nurseries, where sufficiently dense clouds of gas have accumulated. Star formation can be triggered simply by the gravitational pull of the gas, or when a shock wave passes through it from, for example, a nearby exploding star or intergalactic collision.

▷ *Altogether, 700 young stars have been spotted in the dust and gas clouds of the Orion Nebula, illuminated here by visible and ultraviolet light.*

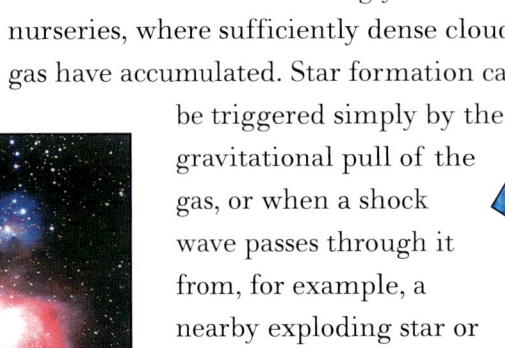

◁ *An infrared image* (left) *of the Orion Nebula taken by the* Hubble Space Telescope *reveals that many young stars lie inside the teeming mass of gas and dust* (above).

△ *The gas begins to spiral around in a disc. The protostar expels jets of gas from its poles.*

△ *Nuclear fusion begins in the hot core. Gas is expelled in a wind that blows the dust away.*

△ *Finally, the star begins to shine steadily.*

Getting warm

As knots of gas inside the cloud become compressed, they begin to warm up. This contraction causes the cloud to rotate faster, making the gas form into a disc. Matter falling inwards from the disc is ejected in jets from the poles. Eventually the central protostar becomes so hot and compressed that the process of nuclear fusion begins at its core. This in turn causes more material to be blown off and, finally, the remains of the disc blow away – apart from any lumps that are forming into planets – and the new star shines into clear space.

Seeing cool, seeing deep

At the different stages of a star's birth and life-cycle, matter glows with different wavelengths. When stars begin to form, warm gas radiates in infrared wavelengths, while cooler dust and molecules glow at sub-millimetre radio wavelengths. Infrared and radio waves can also penetrate the thick clouds, so it is at these wavelengths that astronomers peer into the nebulae and watch stars being born.

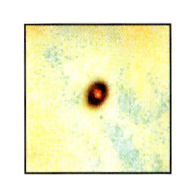

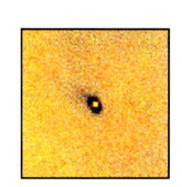

△ *Baby stars hatch from EGGs (Evaporating Gaseous Globules), the finger-like tips emerging from this pillar of gas in the Eagle Nebula. This picture was taken by the* Hubble Space Telescope.

▷ *The* Hubble Space Telescope *has revealed more than 150 of these disc-like knots in the Orion Nebula. They provide the best evidence so far that planetary systems can form at the same time as stars.*

STARS

Star Life

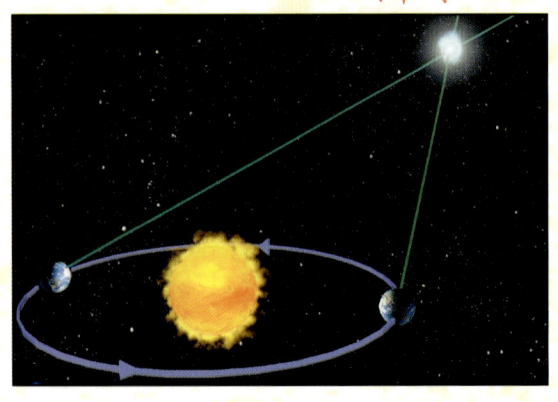

Stars come in all sizes and colours. Look up on a clear, dark, night and you will see hundreds, perhaps thousands of stars. Look with a powerful telescope and you will see millions, perhaps even billions. Some are bright, others faint. Some look blue, others white, yellow or red. There are stars that are bright simply because they are nearby. Certain stars are, in absolute terms, hundreds of times brighter than the Sun, others thousands of times dimmer. A star's colour reflects its surface temperature. Blue stars are very hot, while red ones are cooler. Their ages vary as well. Some are almost as old as the Universe, others are babies in comparison. It is the smaller stars that live longest. Big stars burn up their nuclear fuel much faster and only last a few million years.

△ *As the Earth moves in its orbit around the Sun, nearby stars appear to move against the distant background. This displacement is called parallax, and it is used to measure the distances to stars.*

The main sequence

Most stars follow a fixed relationship between their temperature and brightness. They begin as red dwarfs and become hotter and brighter. This period of a star's life – when it is shining almost constantly – is known as the 'main sequence'. How long it lasts depends on the star's mass. When the hydrogen burning in its core runs out, the star expands and cools into a red giant, leaving the main sequence. Eventually the star sheds its outer layers, leaving a slowly cooling white dwarf.

▷ Hipparcos, *the European satellite, has measured the precise position of more than 120,000 stars. It found that some are closer than we previously thought.*

△ *The Pleiades open cluster of stars is sometimes known as the Seven Sisters, after the seven bright stars clearly visible to the naked eye. This cluster contains, in fact, nearly 500 young, blue stars.*

How far to the stars

To find out how bright a star really is, you need to know how far away it is. The brightest star in the sky, Sirius, is quite close (8.6 light years) and, although it is in reality 26 times brighter than the Sun, it is not nearly as bright as some more distant stars. A nearby star's distance can be calculated by measuring its position twice, six months apart, when the Earth is on opposite sides of the Sun. You can see how this works by moving your head from side to side. Objects close to you seem to move against the background. This shift – known as parallax – can be used to calculate the object's distance. Similarly, the apparent motion of stars (caused by the Earth's orbit against the distant background) gives a measure of distance.

A sense of scale

The distances to the stars is vast. Proxima Centuri, the nearest, is 40,000 billion kilometres away, while others are hundreds of times further. Clearly, kilometres are not very convenient units at such scales. Instead, astronomers use light years – a measurement of distance not of time. One light year is the distance light travels in one year. Proxima Centuri is 4.2 light years away, distant indeed.

△ *One of the best-known constellations is Orion the hunter. It contains stars at all stages of life, including new-born stars in the Orion Nebula (lower centre), bright blue-white Rigel (lower right) and red giant Betelgeuse, near the end of its life (top left).*

Pairs and clusters

Our Sun shines alone in space, but most stars are members of groups. Frequently, they are in pairs known as binaries. Some are in less stable groups of three, or in double binaries of four. Stars turn up in larger groups too, such as the Pleiades. Some of the closest-packed groups of stars, called globular clusters, may contain millions of stars, light months rather than light years apart.

△ *The life story of a star like the Sun begins in a cloud of gas from which a bright, young protostar condenses. For eight billion years it shines as a yellow star, then expands into a red giant before becoming a white dwarf.*

Variable stars

Some stars appear to vary in their brightness, either erratically or in a regular cycle. Sometimes it is because they are in binary pairs and one eclipses the other. Young and unstable stars flare out great masses of hot gas into space, while old, red, supergiants send out black sooty clouds of carbon. Others pulsate regularly. One type, the Cepheid variables, alternately inflates and contracts, brightening and fading at a rate directly related to its overall brightness. This makes these stars useful for measuring distances in the Universe.

▷ *This globular cluster in our neighbouring galaxy, Andromeda, has at least 300,000 stars. From the amount of helium that has built up, astronomers have estimated that the stars are almost as old as the Universe itself.*

STARS

Star Death

Stars the size of our Sun swell up as hydrogen runs low in their core and they shed layers of gas to form what are known as planetary nebulae. Left behind at the centre is a white dwarf star, which slowly cools to a cinder over billions of years. Bigger stars live briefer, more violent lives. Within them, a constant battle rages between the crushing force of gravity and the outward pressure of heat. If a star's mass is more than 40 percent greater than that of the Sun, not even electrons can hold it up when its nuclear fuel runs out. Electrons in the core become squashed so hard that they fuse with protons to make neutrons. The resulting matter has a density of 300 million tonnes per cubic centimetre and forms a star no bigger than a city, but weighing more than the Sun. The energy released as the core collapses tears through the outer layers of the dying star in a huge supernova explosion.

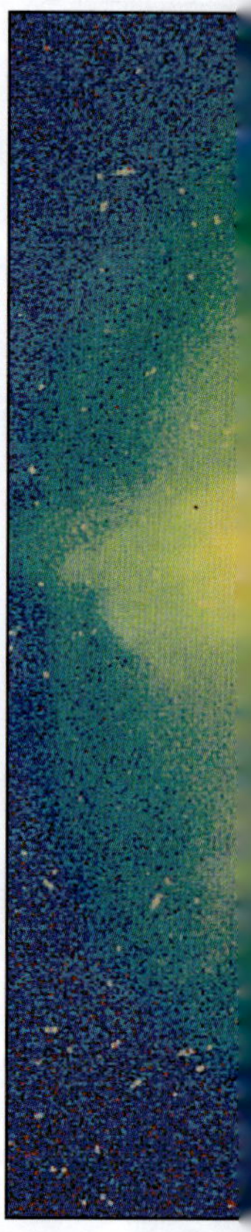

△ *The Egg Nebula consists of concentric shells of gas ejected by a red giant star near the end of its life. The 'searchlights' are areas where light and jets of particles penetrate gaps in the swirling clouds of dust.*

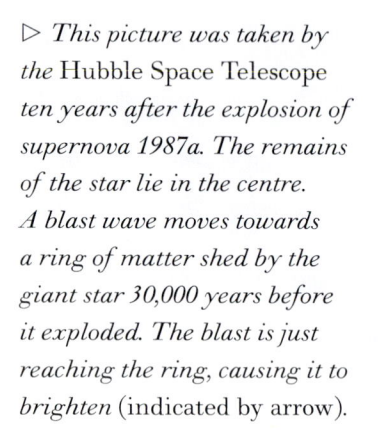

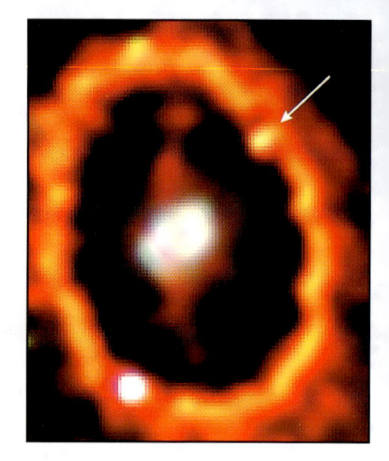

▷ *This picture was taken by the Hubble Space Telescope ten years after the explosion of supernova 1987a. The remains of the star lie in the centre. A blast wave moves towards a ring of matter shed by the giant star 30,000 years before it exploded. The blast is just reaching the ring, causing it to brighten* (indicated by arrow).

Going supernova

On February 23, 1987, Canadian astronomer Ian Shelton was making routine observations using a telescope in Chile when he noticed a very bright star which he did not remember seeing before. He soon realized that he had spotted an exploding star, a supernova lying 170,000 light years away. A few hours earlier, special underground detectors in the United States and Japan had picked up a pulse of ghostly neutrinos, particles created when the iron core of a giant star collapses and a neutron star forms. The process had caused a tremendous explosion that tore the star apart in a blaze of hot new radioactive elements.

△ *Tadpole-like knots of material in the Helix Planetary Nebula plough into gases ejected earlier from a dying star. Each knot is larger than our own Solar System.*

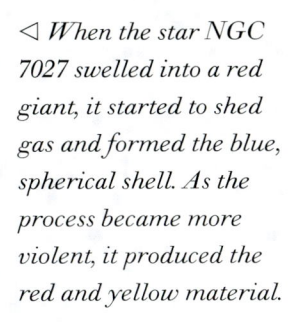

◁ *When the star NGC 7027 swelled into a red giant, it started to shed gas and formed the blue, spherical shell. As the process became more violent, it produced the red and yellow material.*

▷ *The Hourglass Nebula has formed around a star reaching the end of its life. A stellar wind has blown out from the poles creating the double ring.*

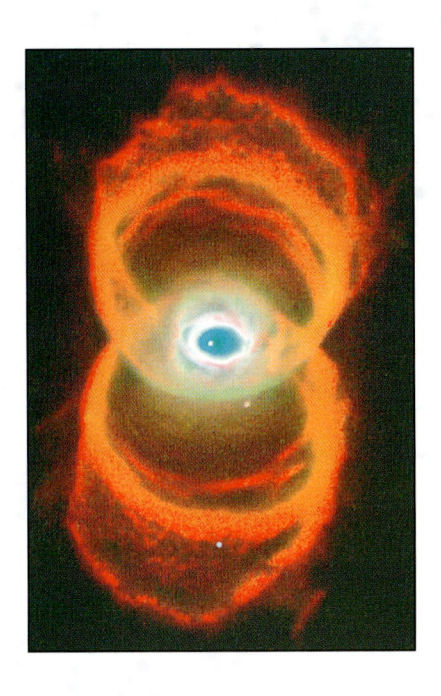

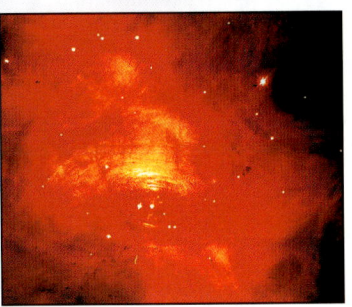

◁ *The Crab Nebula is the remnant of a star that exploded in AD1054. At its centre is a tiny, superdense neutron star, pulsing as it spins thirty times a second and ejecting particles that interact with the gas.*

The stars, our ancestors

The first matter in the Universe was almost all helium and hydrogen. All the other elements around us today, including carbon, silicon, oxygen, and nitrogen were cooked up in the nuclear furnaces of stars, scattered into space and reformed into solar systems such as ours. All elements that are heavier than iron were created and spewed out in supernova explosions. Our world and even our bodies are made, quite literally, of stardust.

Pulsars

Every year, several supernova explosions are spotted in distant galaxies and there is plenty of evidence for past explosions nearer home. In AD1054, Chinese astronomers recorded a bright new star, or nova, in the direction of the constellation of Taurus. Today, it is still visible as the Crab Nebula, a bright, expanding shell of radioactive gas and debris. At its centre is a small white star sending out radio pulses thirty times a second. When it was discovered in 1965, it was given the name LGM1 (L for little, G for green and M for man). But this is no alien distress beacon. It is a pulsar, an ultra-dense neutron star, flashing a beam of light and radio waves as it spins. Hundreds have been found since, some spinning up to a thousand times a second.

△ *The bright ray of a pulsar sweeps across space as a neutron star spins on its axis. Escaping electrons are funnelled by the intense magnetic field, sending out a radio beam and light.*

◁ *"Oh my ears and whiskers, how late it's getting!"* At least both Alice and the White Rabbit agree what time it is as Alice sets out on a journey into a black hole.

Black Hole!

While some dying stars turn into superdense neutron stars, others collapse even further. In a star that is more than three times the Sun's mass, gravity violently crushes matter inwards. It continues to collapse before disappearing into an incredibly dense but dimensionless point called a singularity. A black hole is the space around a singularity, and nothing that falls in can ever go fast enough to escape – not even light. Black holes vary in size – the more massive the singularity, the wider the black hole.

Time for a change

A black hole plays strange tricks on the fabric of space and time, curving it in on itself. If you were able to watch someone falling towards a black hole's outer edge, or event horizon, you would see their clock running slower and slower. At the same time, they would become redder and redder until they faded from view.

The long stretch

If you were the unfortunate person falling in to a black hole, your clock would seem to tick normally and you would remain your usual colour. But you would have other things to worry about. The gravity would pull so hard that it would stretch you out like spaghetti. Your remains would rapidly spiral in, like water down a cosmic plug-hole, and friction would heat them up until they gave off x-rays.

△ *Gas is dragged off a massive star* (above right) *and spirals violently into a black hole. The spinning disc of gas heats up until it emits x-rays and a jet of matter shoots from the poles.*

STARS

▷ *The gravitational well of a black hole or even a massive star distorts the fabric of space-time. A ray of light travelling from a star to the Earth is bent as it shines past, changing the apparent position of the star.*

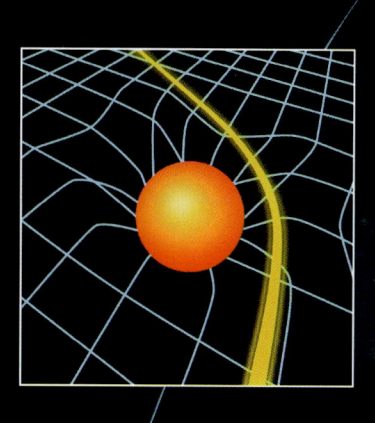

▽ *As Alice gets close to the black hole, its gravity begins to act more on her feet than her head and she starts to stretch. It also stretches the light, and her feet grow redder. Alice notices no change in the rate her watch ticks, but already the Rabbit sees her watch running slow.*

Hunting the invisible

Although astronomers cannot see black holes directly they can detect them through their effects. Stars often come in pairs and if one of the pair has collapsed into a black hole it may also pull in gas from the companion star. As the gas spirals in, it emits x-rays. By looking at these x-ray sources, astronomers can study the invisible black hole.

▽ *In what to Alice are the next few seconds, she will be beyond the point of no return – the event horizon. Meanwhile, the Rabbit is getting later and later.*

▷ *Now Alice has really got problems. She becomes 'spaghettified' as the gravitational forces begin to pull her apart. Compared to the Rabbit's watch, her time is running slower and slower.*

The great escape

Although you could never escape from a black hole, something does emerge from them. Pairs of particles, created on the event horizon itself, end up with one falling in, one coming out. The loss of energy is known as 'Hawking radiation'. It is so faint, however, that it would take a hundred billion billion billion billion billion billion years for a black hole with the mass of our Sun to evaporate.

OUT IN SPACE, BACK IN TIME

The Milky Way

We have seen how ideas have changed from the ancient notion of our Earth at the centre of the Universe to one where the Sun rules the planets. Today, we know that the Sun is just one among about 200 billion stars in the great star city of our galaxy, the Milky Way. This spiral galaxy is like a vast disc with a bulge in the middle (a bit like two fried eggs, put back to back), with great arms of stars. About three-quarters of the way out along the Orion Arm is our local star, the Sun. The Milky Way is about 100,000 light years across and rotates in space, spinning fastest at its centre (the Solar System is only about 12 light hours across).

△ *This fish-eye view of the entire night sky above Australia is dominated by the billions of stars that make up the Milky Way.*

Highway of stars

Look up at the sky on a clear, dark night, away from city lights and you can see the great highway of stars that is the Milky Way. It is densest towards its centre, in the constellation of Sagittarius. You will see nearby bright stars, clusters of stars and a faint haze of millions of distant stars. The darker patches that look like holes are really great clouds of dust. The faint remains of ancient supernova explosions show up as a wispy structure of gas all around.

Among the crowd

We cannot see the centre of the Galaxy (it is shrouded in gas and dust), but infrared and radio waves can penetrate the clouds, giving hints of violent processes at work. It is a very crowded place, with millions of stars and immense quantities of gas. There is a bar-like structure and clouds of molecules. Strong magnetic fields have drawn out gas into thin filaments and a fountain of antimatter rises thousands of light years from the galactic plane.

△ *This near-infrared view of the Milky Way clearly shows the central bulge of the Galaxy from our edge-on position within it.*

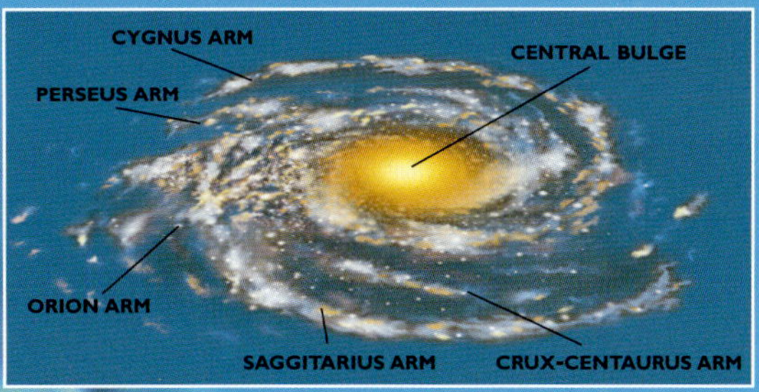

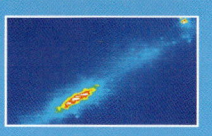

OUT IN SPACE, BACK IN TIME

◁ The Milky Way has a complex structure of spiral arms and a densely-packed central bulge of older stars. Some of the main features can be seen above. The Sun is in the Orion arm.

△ Infrared telescopes can see through the clouds of dust and give a tantalizing glimpse of the Milky Way's centre, where a black hole may lurk.

Shifting heart

Three hundred light years from the Galaxy's core lies a gamma ray source called the Great Annihilator. Once thought to be the centre of the Milky Way, it produces jets of antimatter and emits gamma rays. It is probably a black hole. The true centre is now known to be Sagittarius A*. This may be a monster black hole more than a million times the mass of the Sun. But if it is, the beast at the centre of the Galaxy appears to be sleeping right now.

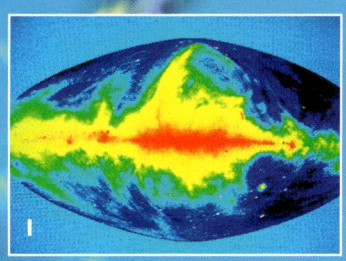

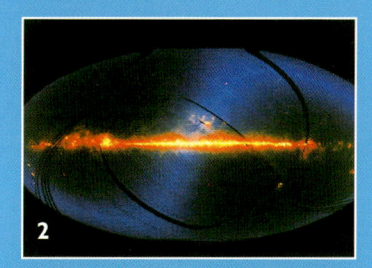

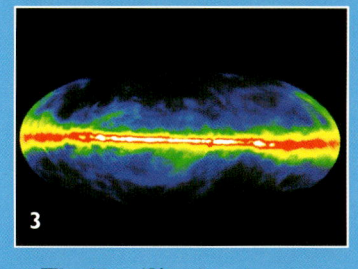

△ The 73 cm wavelength radio map (1) reveals high-velocity electrons moving in a magnetic field. It helps astronomers to plot the magnetic field of the Galaxy. The infrared map (2) is especially bright where there are dust clouds warmed by hot, new stars. The blue 'S' is dust in our Solar System. The 21 cm radio map (3) shows up atomic hydrogen in gas clouds between stars. The gas emits a very precise frequency, helping scientists trace its motion in the rotating galaxy.

OUT IN SPACE, BACK IN TIME

Our Local Group

The Milky Way and the Andromeda galaxy are immense spirals of stars, island universes in their own right. They are the two largest and most important members of the Local Group, a cluster of galaxies stretching five million light years across space. The Local Group contains some thirty galaxies, loosely bound together in each other's gravitational pull. Andromeda, which has twice as many stars as our own galaxy, is situated near another small spiral. The other members of the group are smaller still and are either irregular blobs of stars, like the Magellanic clouds near our own spiral galaxy, or are dwarf galaxies.

Cannibal galaxies

It appears that over billions of years, the big spirals, including our own Milky Way, have grown by eating up their neighbours. Some of the nearby dwarf galaxies will be gobbled up by our galaxy in a few million years time. And even the great spiral Andromeda galaxy itself is coming towards our own galaxy at about 300 kilometres every second. It still has a long way to go, but eventually the two galaxies may pass through one another or even merge. The distances between stars are so immense that few will collide, but great clouds of gas and dust might be stirred up into star formation.

▽ In 1912, Henrietta Leavitt discovered that stars called Cepheid variables change their brightness in a predictable way.

▽ The Virgo cluster contains more than 1,000 galaxies. Virgo is over 50 million light years away and is the centre of our supercluster.

△ Henrietta Leavitt

△ Virgo cluster

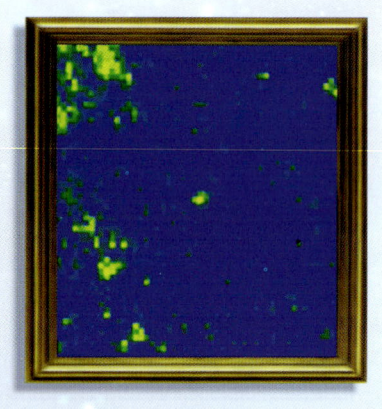

△ Cepheid star (dim)

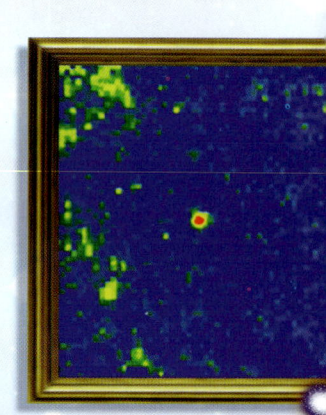

△ Cepheid star (bright)

△ The changing brightness of a Cepheid variable star, seen here on the left at its dimmest and on the right at its brightest, allows astronomers to measure the distance to the galaxies. After the discovery of this type of star, the painstaking mapping of the Universe, galaxy by galaxy, could begin.

△ The Local Group consists of about thirty galaxies. Our own spiral galaxy, the Milky Way, is surrounded by dwarf galaxies and a few irregular galaxies. To the right is the great Andromeda galaxy and its smaller companions, including the spiral M33. The other irregular galaxies are more isolated.

TYPE OF GALAXY

| Dwarf galaxy
| Irregular galaxy
| Spiral galaxy

▽ **Fritz Zwicky** discovered that galaxies are grouped in clusters, some of them thousands strong and millions of light years across.

▽ **The Hubble Space Telescope** revealed that the core of the Andromeda galaxy has a double nucleus. This may have resulted from a merger with another galaxy.

◁ **The Andromeda galaxy** has a spiral form similar to the Milky Way. Andromeda is 2.2 million light years away, and 150,000 light years across.

Rotating galaxies

The spiral shape of many galaxies gives the impression that they are rotating. However, it is not the stars that are going round and round, but the arms, with the stars passing through them. The arms rotate over hundreds of millions of years, their outside ends trailing behind the faster inner regions. In our own galaxy it takes the Sun over two hundred million years to complete an orbit and come back to the same position. This period is sometimes called the cosmic year.

△ *Andromeda galaxy*

ANDROMEDA

M33

△ *Andromeda's core*

MILKY WAY

△ *Fritz Zwicky*

Superclusters

Even the vast Local Group is a small backyard on the intergalactic scale. We are part of a much larger grouping of other clusters which together form the Local Supercluster. Our Local Group is being pulled by gravity towards the Virgo cluster, the centre of the Local Supercluster (sometimes also known as the Virgo Supercluster), at a speed of 270 kilometres per second. Superclusters are among the largest structures seen in the Universe, but even the Local Supercluster is just one of many others stretching billions of light years across the Universe.

OUT IN SPACE, BACK IN TIME

Expanding Universe

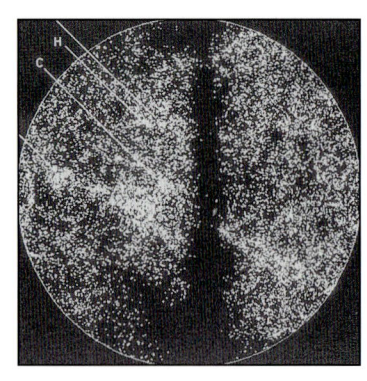

The speed of galaxies is one of the easier things to calculate in the Universe. The light from stars and galaxies comes with a very convenient measure. If a galaxy is moving away from us, the wavelength of its light is redshifted, or stretched. If it is coming towards us, the wavelength gets squashed and shifted towards the blue end of the spectrum. In 1929, Edwin Hubble discovered that the more distant a galaxy is, the more its light is redshifted. And it soon became clear that the further a galaxy is from our own, the faster it is speeding away. Hubble concluded that the reason for this is not that our galaxy is at the centre of the Universe, but rather that the entire Universe is expanding. If this is so, then there must have been a time when all the galaxies were much closer together.

△ *The dark, vertical band in this map of galaxies is where our own galaxy, the Milky Way, blocks the view. We are moving at 600 km/sec towards the Great Attractor, the dense, bright cluster near the centre.*

Mapping the Universe

By using redshift to measure the distances to galaxies, astronomers have begun to map the Universe in three dimensions. It is an enormous task but already some very large structures have been revealed. Some areas are like voids or bubbles with very few galaxies in them. Around them are slabs and filaments rich in galaxies. One particular structure forms what has been called the Great Wall, and is at least a billion light years across. There might be a repeating structure of such walls, a bit like a picket fence, with walls about 400 million light years apart.

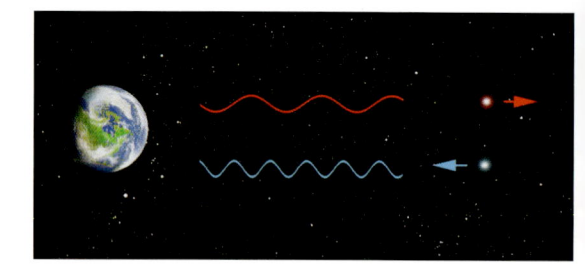

▽ *On the largest scale, the Universe is like a vast foam, with superclusters and walls of galaxies situated along the boundaries of giant bubbles or voids in space.*

△ *If a galaxy or star is moving towards us, the waves in its light become squashed together, or blueshifted, and so it looks bluer. If, on the other hand, the object is receding from us, the light becomes stretched or redshifted.*

190

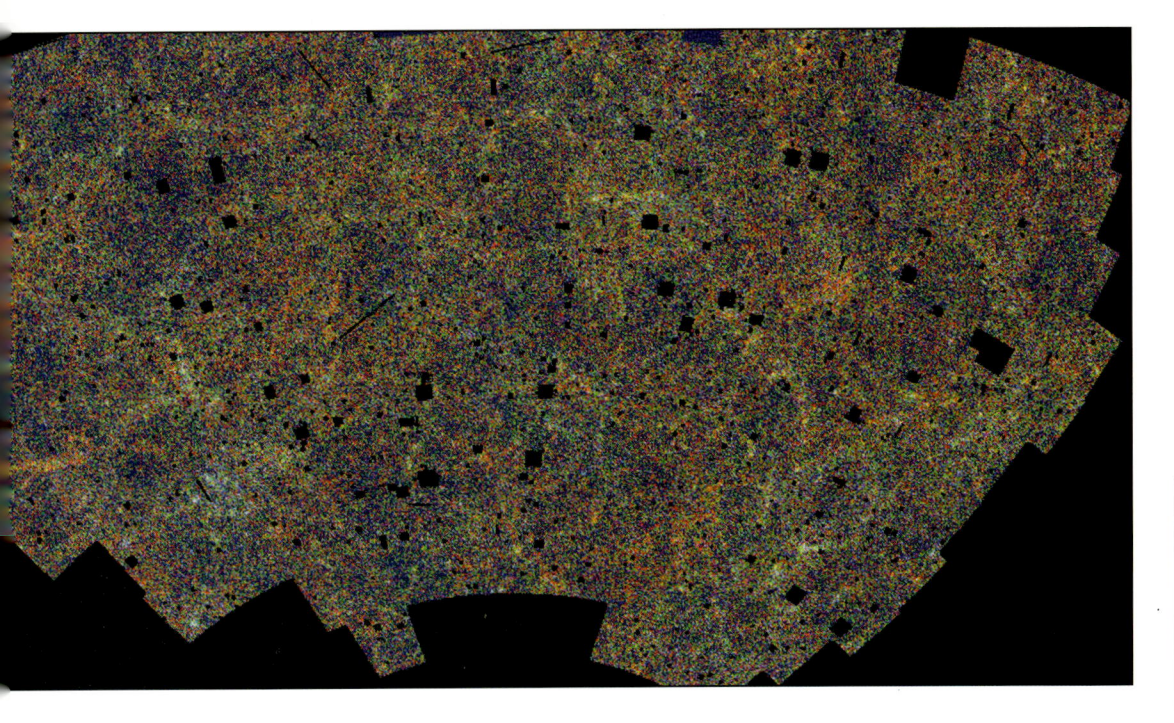

◁ *This slice through the Universe shows all the galaxies that have had their redshifts measured. Faint structures are visible. Black areas have not yet been fully surveyed.*

▽ *The 2DF instrument on the Anglo-Australian Telescope can measure the redshifts of up to 400 galaxies at once.*

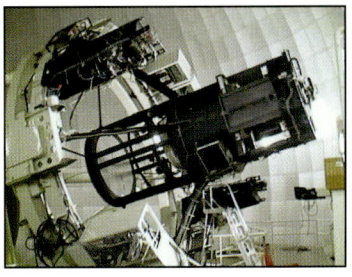

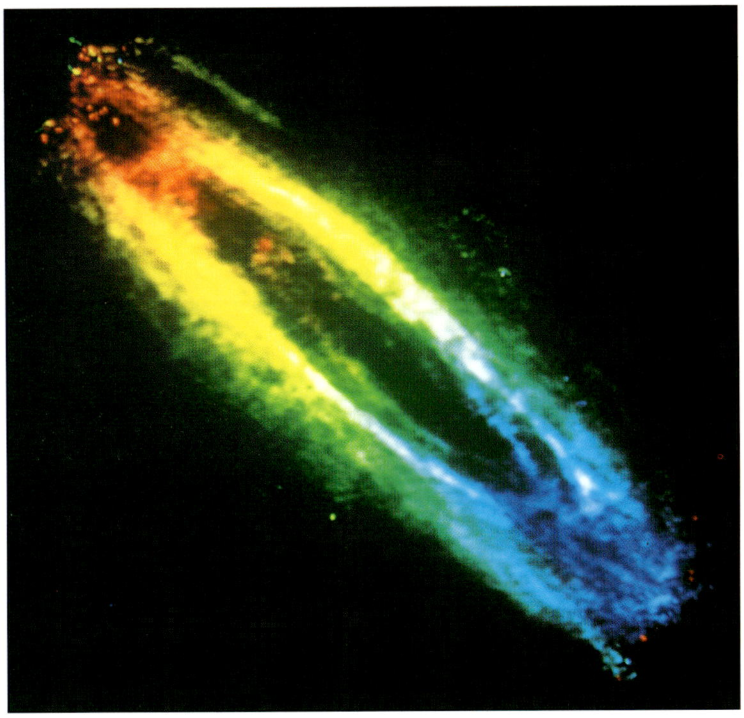

The Great Attractor

The Universe does not expand evenly in every direction. Huge concentrations of galaxies put a gravitational brake on the process. Whole streams of galaxies end up resisting the expansion – we are part of such a stream. Beyond the great Virgo Supercluster there appears to be something pulling us and thousands of other galaxies towards it. It has been called the Great Attractor, and it lies in the approximate direction of the constellation Perseus. It acts as if it has a mass of fifty million billion suns, equivalent to hundreds of thousands of galaxies. At one time it was thought that the Great Attractor might be some monster black hole or other strange object. Now it is generally believed to be an irregularity, or a knot, in the clouds of galaxies. Even so, it has enough gravity to pull our whole local group of galaxies towards it at a velocity of about 600 kilometres per second.

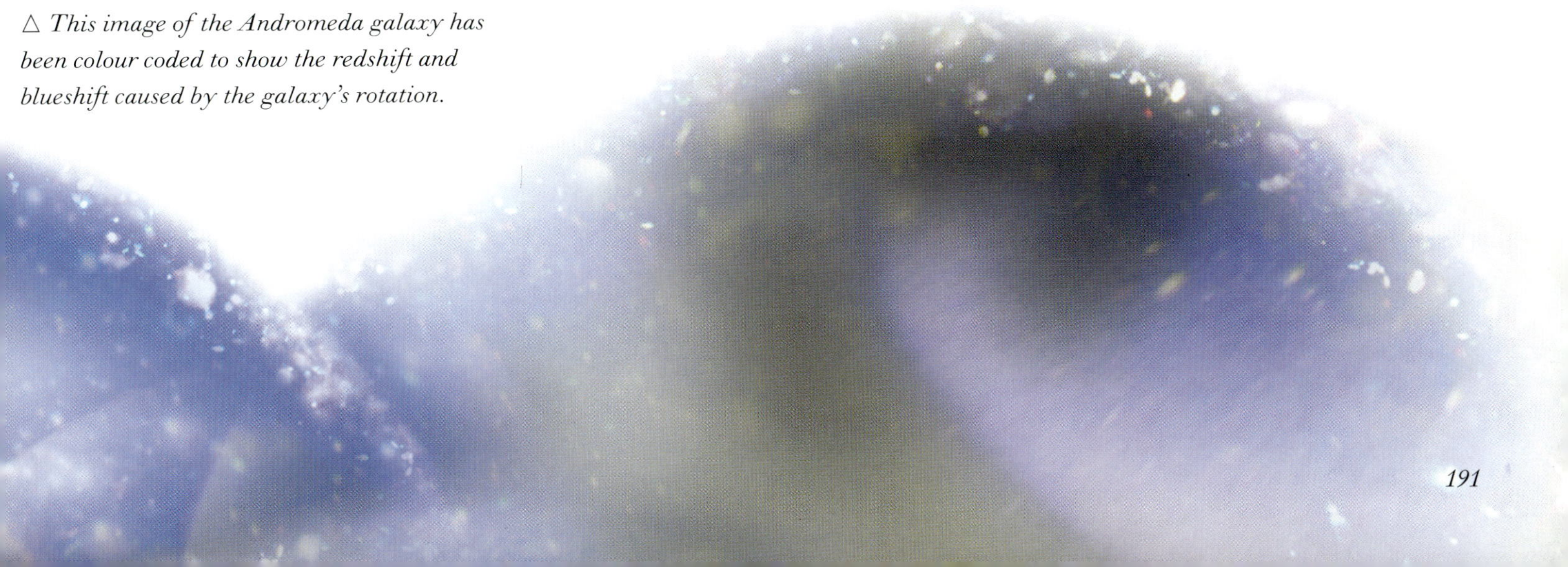

△ *This image of the Andromeda galaxy has been colour coded to show the redshift and blueshift caused by the galaxy's rotation.*

OUT IN SPACE, BACK IN TIME

The Galactic Zoo

The Universe contains around one hundred billion galaxies and each galaxy, on average, is made up of about one hundred billion stars. Galaxies come in many different shapes and sizes. Spiral galaxies can be tightly wound or loose, while others have a broad bar across their centre. Some galaxies have no obvious shape and are classed as irregular.

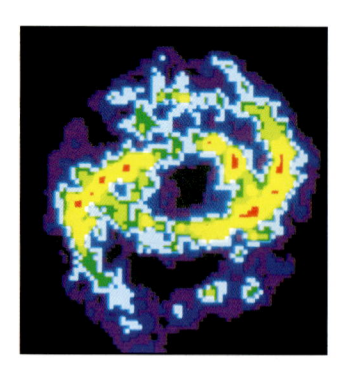

The largest of all galaxies are elliptical. Starbirth does not take place in elliptical galaxies. It could be that most galaxies begin as spirals but, as they interact with one another, all their gas is pulled into the stars. The spiral structure disappears and becomes an elliptical galaxy.

△ Some galaxies, such as NGC 1300, appear to lose their tightly wound spiral structure as they evolve and develop a broad bar.

Looking back in time

The most distant galaxies ever seen are probably more than ten billion light years away. This means that light has taken ten billion years to reach us so what we are seeing is the light that left them when the Universe was ten billion years younger. By peering back across such distances, it is possible to see galaxies as they form. In one particular study by the *Hubble Space Telescope*, no less than 18 dwarf galaxies were spotted moving together under the influence of each other's gravity. This suggests that galaxies are formed when much smaller galaxies merge together. The final stages of this process can be seen today in our own galaxy as it swallows up a few remaining dwarf galaxies.

◁ Giant elliptical galaxies such as M49 are the final stage in galactic evolution. They contain almost no young stars.

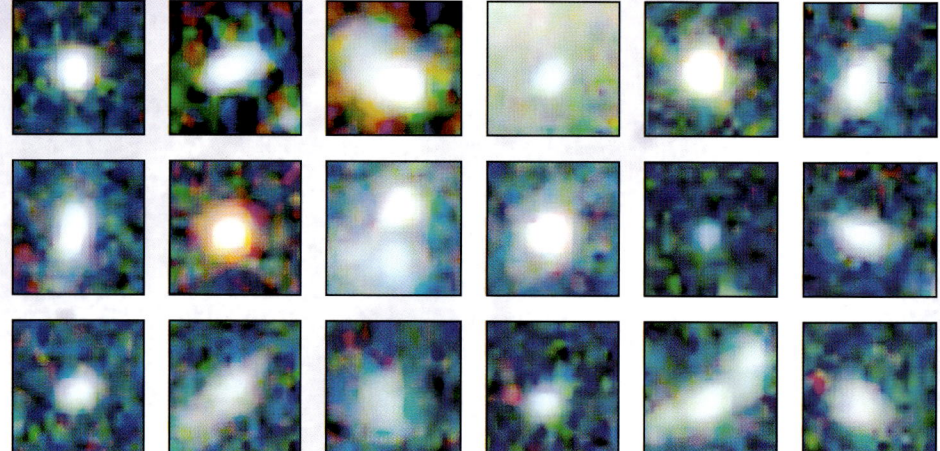

△ The central hub of the whirlpool galaxy, M51, is made up mostly of old, yellow stars. The spiral arms contain young, blue stars while a bridge of gas and dust connects it to a second galaxy.

▷ Astronomers believe that these faint smudges of starcluster, eleven billion light years away, are the building blocks that will merge to form the core of a new galaxy.

192

OUT IN SPACE, BACK IN TIME

▽ *M82 is a spiral galaxy, seen here almost edge-on. The disturbance at the centre is probably caused by the galaxy ploughing into a gas cloud.*

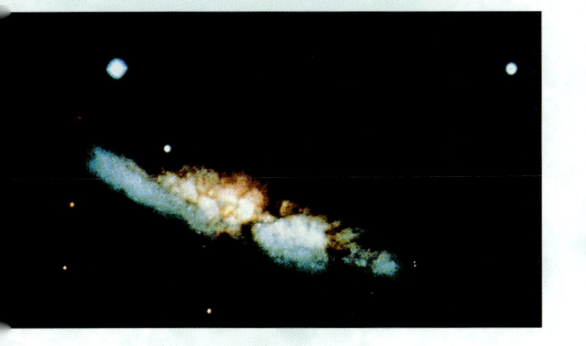

Starburst

There must have been a time when the first stars started to shine, a spectacular period in the history of the Universe which had been dark since the Big Bang of creation. When astronomers peer through the great clouds of dust in which stars are made, they can see whole galaxies shining brightly with the sudden birth of millions of big, hot stars. More recent starburst galaxies are also seen where galaxies have smashed into one another, stirring up the dust lanes and triggering a new burst of star formation. In one of these, called Arp 220, the rate of star formation is probably a hundred times that of our entire Milky Way galaxy, but concentrated into a nucleus a hundred times smaller.

△ *Arp 220 is a starburst galaxy, packed with very new, hot young stars. It probably formed when two spiral galaxies merged.*

The Hubble Deep Field

In December 1995, the *Hubble Space Telescope* was pointed at a single stretch of sky for ten consecutive days. It revealed no less than 1,500 galaxies at various stages of evolution. Some are four billion times fainter than can be seen by the naked eye and date back to near the beginning of the Universe. This so-called Hubble Deep Field is beginning to give astronomers clues about how many galaxies there are in the Universe and how they formed.

△ *This is what the* Hubble Space Telescope *saw when it took a ten day exposure of a patch of sky close to the constellation of the Plough. The Hubble Deep Field is made up of 342 exposures and contains 1,500 galaxies, some of them among the faintest and most distant ever seen.*

193

OUT IN SPACE, BACK IN TIME

Violent Galaxies

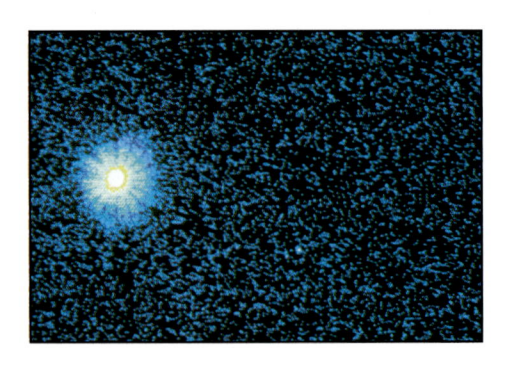

In 1963, Maartin Schmidt, an astronomer in California, was examining the spectrum of light from a faint, blue star-like object known as 3C 273. To his astonishment, he realized that, although it was small, it was more than three billion light years away, moving away from us at 50,000 kilometres per second and giving out intense radiation. These distant objects became known as quasi-stellar radio sources or quasars for short. The *Hubble Space Telescope* has revealed that quasars are, in fact, blindingly bright objects embedded in the centres of distant galaxies. They appear star-like because they emit a hundred times more energy than our entire galaxy, but from an area not much bigger than our Solar System.

△ *The first quasar to be identified was 3C 273, viewed here in x-rays. Although star-like in appearance, quasars are very distant and intensely active galaxies.*

Monster black holes

There is only one power source that could generate the immense energy of quasars — black holes. Most quasars are found in colliding galaxies. As the galaxies merge, gas and stars are stirred up and begin to spiral around a black hole that lies at the centre of one or even both galaxies. As matter is sucked in, an accretion disc is created, similar to those around black holes formed from dying stars in our own galaxy. But in the case of quasars, the black holes must be incredibly massive, each perhaps a billion times the mass of the Sun.

▽ *The galaxy M87, in the Virgo cluster, sends out a narrow jet of matter from its core. The activity in this galaxy is probably caused by a giant black hole.*

△ *A great cloud of swirling gas and star debris spirals down towards a black hole millions of times the mass of the Sun. At the same time it gives out x-rays and powerful jets of radio-emitting gas. Many of the violent processes taking place in the cores of galaxies are probably similar events seen from different angles.*

OUT IN SPACE, BACK IN TIME

△ *In this computer simulation, two spiral galaxies have collided and passed one another. Spiral arms have been dragged out into a bridge of matter between them.*

Galactic activity

Not all galaxies fit into the neat classification of spiral, elliptical, irregular or even quasar. Many are being torn apart by immense explosions. Others, like M87 in the Virgo cluster, have a single great jet of matter spiralling out from the core. It seems likely that all these different galaxies have a massive black hole at their centre. In some cases the black hole becomes active each time it is fed with gas and stars. In other galaxies the black hole remains dormant. There is good reason to believe that every galaxy, including our own, has a black hole at its centre.

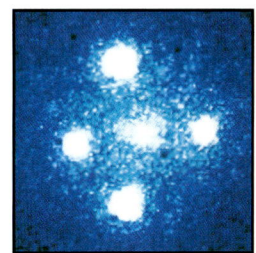

△ *The Cartwheel galaxy is the result of a collision in which one galaxy passed straight through the middle of another spiral galaxy.*

◁ *Light bent by gravity creates the illusion of a cluster of five different quasars when, in fact, there is only one. It is called Einstein's cross.*

Gravitational lens

When astronomers identified two identical quasars lying next to each other they were puzzled. The explanation quickly dawned – it was something first predicted by Einstein, who realized that light is bent by a strong gravitational field. If there is a massive object such as a cluster of galaxies between us and the quasar, the light from the quasar becomes bent, as if through a lens. If the alignment is right, light will be bent through several routes and create a multiple image. This can take the form, for example, of a cross or even a clover leaf.

195

OUT IN SPACE, BACK IN TIME

Echoes of Creation

The Universe is flying apart. Trace all the lines of the expanding galaxies back in time and it appears they all originated from the same place. If so, they must have been blown apart by an incredible explosion. In the 1950s, the English astronomer Fred Hoyle and others suggested a different explanation. They argued that the Universe, though expanding, remains essentially the same, with new matter created to fill the expanding gaps. This is known as the 'Steady State' Universe and Fred Hoyle called the alternative the 'Big Bang' Universe. Other scientists remained unconvinced by Hoyle's theory and predicted that there should be a way of proving that the Big Bang had really happened. If the Universe did begin in an explosion, it would have left an echo. The incredible heat of the explosion would now have cooled to just a few degrees above absolute zero (−273°C), but even so it should be detectable.

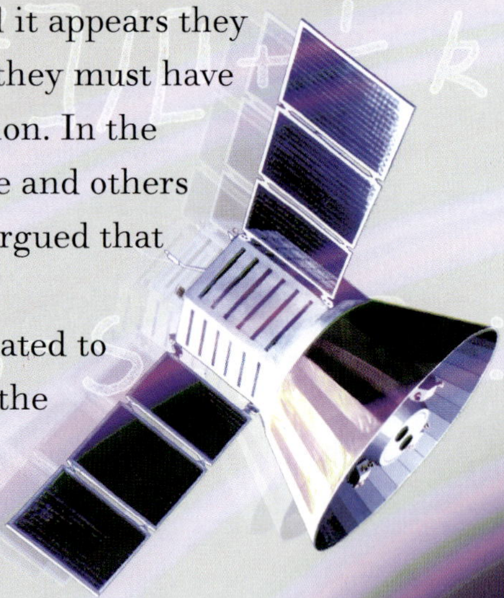

◁ *The Cosmic Background Explorer satellite, COBE, was launched in 1990 to study the microwave background radiation left over from the Big Bang over twelve billion years ago. Scientists are now beginning to build up a quite detailed map of the early Universe.*

▽ *You can listen to the sound of the Big Bang in your own home! If you tune your television between stations, the picture will 'snow', and the sound will hiss. About one percent of this noise is from the microwave background reaching us from the Big Bang itself.*

Whispers from space

When the first transatlantic communications satellite, *Telstar*, was launched in 1962, a big radio antenna was constructed in New Jersey, United States, to receive its signal. But it also received a faint background hiss which would not go away even when two astronomers, Robert Wilson and Arno Penzias, removed pigeon droppings from the receiver! The hiss seemed to come from every direction and radiated energy at a temperature just 2.73 degrees above absolute zero. They realized that this must be the background radiation left from the Big Bang itself. To date, this is the best evidence that the Universe did indeed begin in a fireball.

OUT IN SPACE, BACK IN TIME

▽ *The map of the cosmic background radiation is not a true map as some of the signal was due to warmth in* COBE's *instruments. Even so it confirmed that the present structure of the Universe originated in the Big Bang. When the discovery was made, the leader of the project described it as "like seeing the face of God".*

Cosmic ripples

In 1990, NASA launched *COBE*, the *Cosmic Background Explorer* satellite. Its purpose was to stare at the microwave background. The first result was a spectacular confirmation that the radiation is a perfect example of so-called 'black body' radiation – radiation that is simply due to heat. *COBE* then started to map it and look for features. The radiation turned out to be very, very smooth in every direction. Eventually, patterns began to emerge and, in 1992, scientists announced that they had seen ripples in the background. This caused a sensation. The fluctuations are only thirty millionths of a degree, but they provided the early Universe with enough variation in density for the very first stars and galaxies to be born. Without them, the Universe would still be a diffuse haze of gas.

▽ *Robert Wilson and Arno Penzias stand in front of the radio antenna with which they discovered the microwave background radiation in 1962. The antenna was originally designed to pick up signals from the communications satellite,* Telstar.

First light

The fireball of the Big Bang gave off no light. Light could not travel in straight lines without bumping into things – atoms had not yet formed and the Universe was a seething mass of particles. After about 300,000 years, the Universe had cooled enough for atoms to form. The Universe became transparent and radiation could shine freely. The microwave background radiation is the cooled remnant of that first light.

△ *The discovery of the background radiation sent out ripples through astronomy. The theory of the Steady State Universe (which rejects the Big Bang theory) was finally discredited.*

OUT IN SPACE, BACK IN TIME

The Big Bang

Astronomers can trace the expanding Universe back to a time when all the stars and galaxies they can see must have been squashed together into a tiny space. They can look back directly to the cosmic background radiation emitted when our Universe was about 300,000 years old and only slightly larger than our own galaxy. To journey back further, towards the Big Bang itself, it is necessary to turn to physics. Scientists have studied conditions back to within a hundredth of a billionth of a second of the start of the Universe by recreating them in high energy particle colliders. And their theories take them even further.

A note on scale

The numbers in cosmology are so vast and the numbers in sub-atomic physics are so tiny that scientists use a special shorthand. Ten multiplied by itself (ie a hundred) is written as 10^2. A thousand is 10^3. Similarly, a tenth is 10^{-1}, a thousandth 10^{-3} and so on.

△ Einstein's famous equation $E=mc^2$ shows that it takes a lot of energy to make a little matter. In the first instant of the Big Bang (1) all four fundamental forces of Nature act as one, and even space and time are unified.

△ By 10^{-32} seconds (2), the Universe is a hot, seething mass of particles, expanding at the speed of light. At 10^{-11} seconds (3), the weak nuclear force separates from electromagnetism. Quarks and antiquarks are spontaneously created and annihilate each other.

In the beginning

The entire Universe may have been born from a single sub-atomic particle! Today, every speck of seemingly empty space is a seething well of potential energy. Physicists suspect that a whole range of particles are being born from it every instant. Usually, they die again before they have had time to do anything, go anywhere or be seen by anyone. But, just occasionally, they can get trapped and become 'real'. No one really knows, but this is possibly how the Universe came into being.

Superforce

There are just four fundamental forces at work in the Universe – gravity, the strong and weak nuclear forces, and electromagnetism. But they may all have been united into a single superforce that governed the Universe at the moment of its birth. As the Universe cooled, so each of the forces separated. Gravity was the first to separate, at just 10^{-43} seconds after the start. The strong force followed at 10^{-35} seconds; the weak force and electromagnetism went their separate ways at 10^{-11} seconds.

OUT IN SPACE, BACK IN TIME

▽ *After 300,000 years (6) radiation is no longer strong enough to break up atoms. The Universe becomes transparent and light shines through it. After one billion years (7) clumps of gas are pulling together to form protogalaxies. Inside them the first stars are beginning to shine.*

▽ *Today (8), after 12 billion years, clusters of galaxies have formed superclusters. Matter has been processed through several generations of stars to form the building materials for planets and life.*

△ *At 10^{-4} seconds (4), the Universe is about the size of the Solar System and the temperature has fallen sufficiently for quarks to form protons, neutrons and other so-called baryons. After 100 seconds (5), protons and neutrons link up.*

△ *The background image shows the tracks of subatomic particles. Scientists create these in high-energy collisions to explore conditions similar to those after the Big Bang.*

Inflation

A process called inflation might explain how something smaller than an atom grew to a universe the size of a grapefruit in the first 10^{-32} of a second. If a little bubble of the Universe continued expanding after the strong nuclear force should have separated out, it might have created a false vacuum, a sort of antigravity. This would allow the bubble to expand 100 times faster than the speed of light. When inflation froze, it released so much energy that it produced all the matter in our Universe.

First atom

When the strong force separated, the Universe heated up to 10^{27} degrees. Matter and antimatter were created in equal proportions. An imbalance in the process led to a build-up of matter, which is why there are no anti-galaxies today. The first particles were quarks and electrons. As the Universe cooled, quarks combined to form protons and neutrons. Some of them clustered together to make helium nuclei and, after 300,000 years, the electrons joined them to make the first atoms.

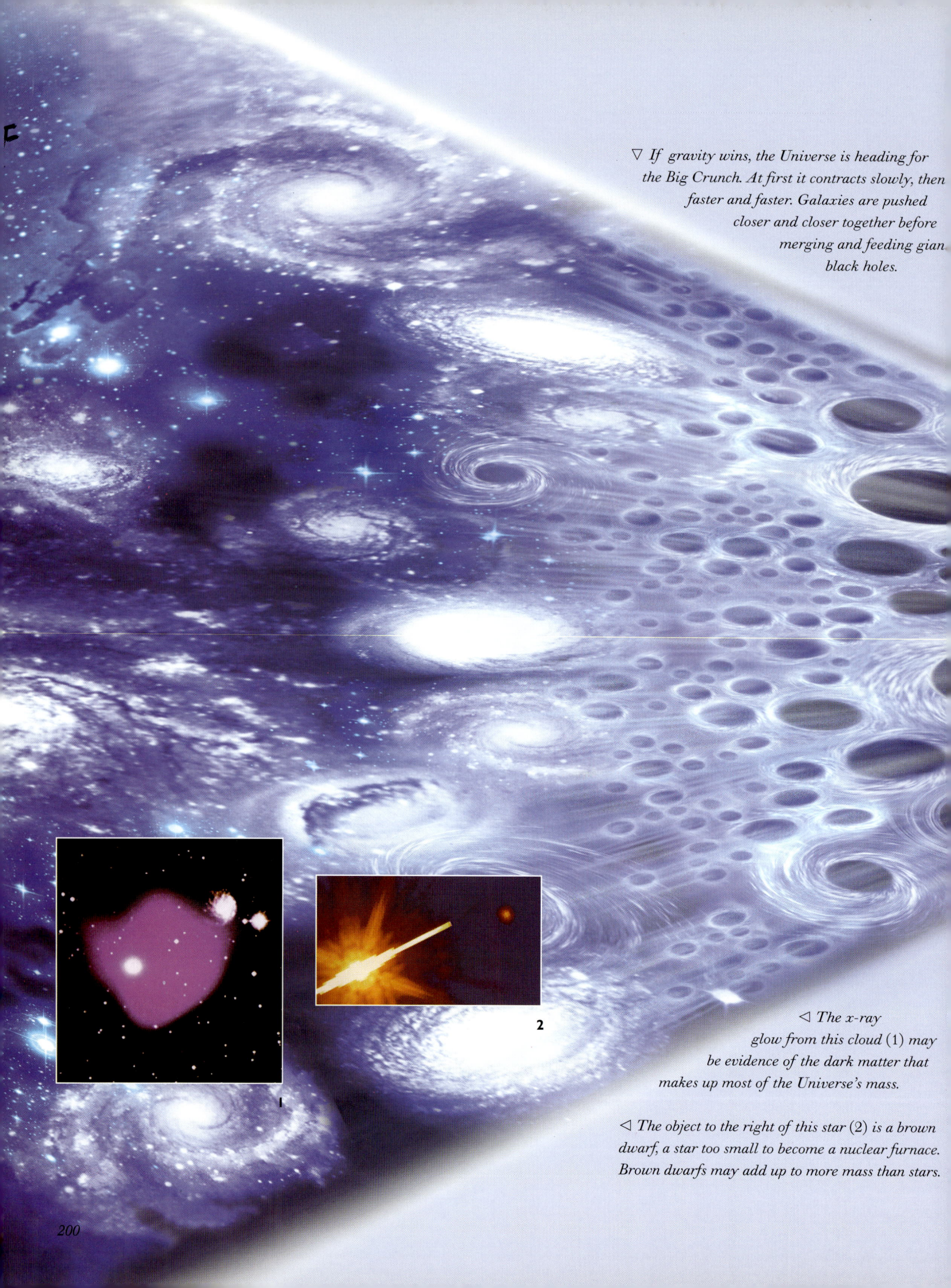

▽ *If gravity wins, the Universe is heading for the Big Crunch. At first it contracts slowly, then faster and faster. Galaxies are pushed closer and closer together before merging and feeding giant black holes.*

◁ *The x-ray glow from this cloud (1) may be evidence of the dark matter that makes up most of the Universe's mass.*

◁ *The object to the right of this star (2) is a brown dwarf, a star too small to become a nuclear furnace. Brown dwarfs may add up to more mass than stars.*

OUT IN SPACE, BACK IN TIME

The Great Unknown

There are some questions about the nature of the Universe that, until recently, seemed to be unanswerable. What makes up the Universe? How heavy is it? How old is it, and how will it all end? Astronomers still do not have all the answers, but at last they feel they might be able to begin to find out. To do so will take some very strange telescopes indeed. As well as using the best measurements possible from optical, infrared and radio telescopes on the ground and in space, there are also instruments deep underground attempting to weigh the Universe and predict its ultimate fate.

△ *The Universe could end in three ways. The closed or Big Crunch Universe (1) is so massive it collapses under its own weight. In the flat Universe (2) expansion slows down, but never quite into collapse. The open Universe (3) expands forever.*

◁ *As the Universe approaches its end, the remaining matter spirals into black holes. Nothing can hold the Universe back from the final inferno. But perhaps it could bounce back in a new Big Bang.*

Dark matter

All that we can see is only a fraction of the Universe. Some matter is detectable only by its gravitational effects on the rotation of galaxies. This is called dark matter and no one knows its composition. Dark matter could be conventional matter, such as small stars called brown dwarfs, or even black holes.

Ghostly particles

Dark matter may also include neutrinos – ghostly particles once thought to have no mass. These are so numerous that any mass at all would make them far heavier than all the stars. Other particles are predicted by physicists, but are yet to be detected. If found they could make up ninety-nine percent of the Universe.

The fate of the Universe

From its birth, now thought to be between twelve and fifteen billion years ago, the Universe has continued to expand. The latest evidence suggests that the expansion may even be accelerating. If the Universe contains a hundred times more matter than we can see, gravity might halt the expansion and make the Universe contract into a Big Crunch. This could be the end of everything or the start of a new Universe.

Heat death

If gravity cannot halt the expansion, stars will slowly age and die. Galaxies will fade away and even black holes will disappear. After billions and billions of years the Universe will become a cold, dull place, containing only a few, widely spaced particles.

△ *Alice enters a wormhole in space-time. It could take her to another time, or even into another universe.*

COSMIC QUESTIONS

△ *Space itself can be curved, so a wormhole might act as a short-cut between two seemingly distant places.*

Beyond Time

Time is relative. The rate your clock ticks relative to someone else's depends on how fast you are moving relative to each other. This was the conclusion Albert Einstein came to in 1905. He established that, as the speed of light must be the same for everyone, no matter how they are moving, then space and time themselves must be intertwined. Einstein developed these ideas in his general theory of relativity, taking gravity into account and showing how gravity bends space-time. Many science-fiction writers and some scientists have seized on Einstein's theories to show that one day time travel may just be possible.

△ *Time appears to run in one direction only. Broken eggs do not reassemble themselves. This tendency to disorder is one of the few natural arrows in time.*

Time's arrow

We all have a strong sense of passing time, and for all of us time seems to run in one direction only. People age, cups of tea cool down, smashed glasses do not spontaneously reassemble. However, according to the laws of physics, there is nothing to prevent most processes from reversing. In fact, in many processes, especially at the level of particles, there is no distinguishable arrow of time.

Warping space and time

The fundamental speed limit of the Universe seems to be the speed of light – 300,000 km per second. Even though a spaceship could never travel faster than light it might, in theory, be possible to warp the space around it, shrinking space ahead and expanding it behind. The snag is that to distort space in this way would require at least a million times the energy locked up in the Sun!

202

▷ *Tweedledum and Tweedledee are identical twins. Tweedledum sets out on a round trip to a nearby star, at almost the speed of light. The journey seems to him to have taken only a few years. When he returns he finds that time has passed more quickly for Tweedledee, who is now twenty years older.*

Wormholes

One possibility for time travel, in theory at least, is a wormhole – a cosmic tunnel built from exotic matter between different regions of space-time. Just as in a black hole, time in a wormhole slows to a standstill and the laws of our Universe break down. But if one could be kept open long enough, it might be possible to emerge from a wormhole unharmed.

Time paradoxes

Time travel raises many paradoxes. For example, if you could travel back in time, you would have the chance to kill your own grandfather before your father was born. That would mean that you also were never born, so how could you begin your journey? Either reverse time travel is forbidden or there are an infinite number of universes, one for every possibility. Perhaps it is simpler to stick to the here and now!

▷ *When Alice steps through the wormhole, she appears instantaneously in another part of the Universe.*

The Search for ET

Are people on the Earth alone in the Universe? As yet, there is no certain evidence of life anywhere else, much less intelligent life. But there are hundreds of millions of stars in our galaxy. If a fraction have habitable planets and a fraction of those developed life, there could be millions of civilizations other than our own. However, the distances between the stars is so great it is unlikely that extra-terrestrials – if they exist – have visited our planet. We do not even know exactly how life began on the Earth. The evidence we do have, however, suggests that it takes several billion years of evolution for intelligent life to arise and to develop the technology capable of sending messages to the stars.

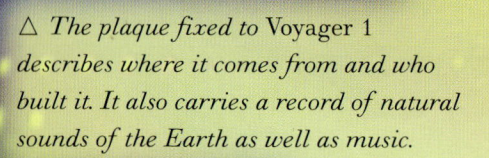

△ *The plaque fixed to* Voyager 1 *describes where it comes from and who built it. It also carries a record of natural sounds of the Earth as well as music.*

The search for distant planets

Our best telescopes could never see a distant planet against the glare of its star. But big planets make stars wobble as they orbit and several wobbling stars have been detected. Most are due to big, Jupiter-like planets, but some may be far enough away from their stars to be hospitable. Far out in space, away from the dust in the inner Solar System, arrays of telescopes may in the future see planets directly as they orbit other stars. They may even be able to detect gases, such as ozone and water vapour, that indicate life.

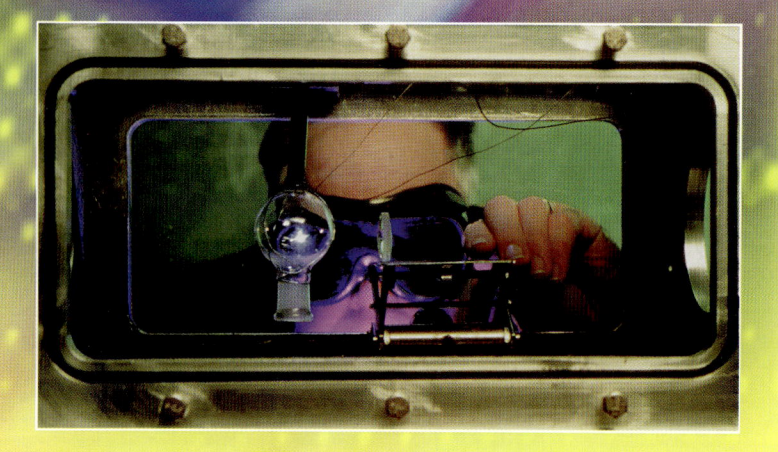

△ *In 1974, the first signal to possible alien life was broadcast from the world's biggest radio dish at Arecibo in Puerto Rico. Arecibo has remained the centre for the search to identify alien signals.*

The search for extra-terrestrial intelligence

Since the first radio broadcast, radio signals have been travelling out beyond our planet at the speed of light. The signals have passed many stars and planets, but unless aliens were listening for them they would not notice. The most powerful radio signal to have left the Earth was sent from a radio telescope at Aricebo, Puerto Rico, in 1974. It was a brief digital signal describing who and where we are, and it was directed at a cluster of stars known as M13. Even at the speed of light, however, it will take 25,000 years to reach its destination. Many teams are taking part in SETI (the Search for Extra-Terrestrial Intelligence). They scan Sun-like star systems with radio telescopes, analyzing millions of radio frequencies by computer in the search for a signal.

△ *A scientist discharges an electric field across a mixture of water, hydrogen, methane and ammonia. In this experiment, amino acids – the basis of life on this planet – accumulate after a time, just as they may once have done on the early Earth.*

△ Will aliens look like these mounds of bacteria? Similar structures may have been among the first inhabitants of the Earth more that 3,500 million years ago.

△ Alien existence is a subject clouded by fiction and fraud. The 'flying saucer' above was proved to be a child's toy photographed at close range. Though many people claim to have been visited or abducted by aliens, there is still no evidence of the presence of other beings in the Universe.

Alien life on other planets

If there are aliens out there, what would they be like? Life on the Earth shows great variety and ingenuity and it is probable that life on another planet would do the same. It might be based on a different chemistry entirely, with boron or silicon taking the place of carbon, or with the role of water being played by liquid ammonia. Physically, life forms will need to do some of the same things as humans. They may need to move about, sense their environment, eat and defend themselves. They would probably have a front and a back, but eyes, hands and so on could all be replaced by other tools, and not necessarily in pairs.

△ This bright light was photographed over São Paulo, Brazil in 1984. It is one of many so-called UFOs – Unidentified Flying Objects.

COSMIC QUESTIONS

Impossible Questions

Throughout this book we have seen how astronomers observe our planet, our solar system, our galaxy and some of the billions of other galaxies beyond it. One day, in principle, we could learn every detail of the physical Universe. But there are still some questions that can never be answered with certainty. For example, what lies beyond or before our Universe? Why did the Universe begin? Why are we here in it? Astronomy, in discovering that the Earth is not the centre of the Universe, has pushed us further and further into what seems an insignificant corner. But some of the possible answers to these big questions could put us centre stage again.

△ *Every culture has proposed a god as the prime mover of the Universe. Scientists can offer few better explanations for the fundamental laws of the cosmos.*

Beyond the horizon

The furthest galaxies seem to be receding from us so fast that they are approaching the speed of light. We cannot see beyond them. The Universe may be infinite, or it may end just beyond this light horizon. We cannot tell. Perhaps our Universe is just one bubble in a whole foam of universes. Some may not have inflated, while others might have different physical laws or dimensions from our own Universe.

The living Universe

Perhaps, when a black hole forms in our Universe, it gives birth to another universe somewhere else. If the new universe can inherit the ability to make black holes, then universes might evolve and get better and better at making black holes. A universe, like our own, which is good at creating black holes is also good at making stars and ultimately planets and life itself.

▷ *Black holes may give birth to new universes. The coloured peaks in this computer simulation are other universes, each with its own physical laws.*

206

▽ The same force that makes apples fall also holds stars together. The same force that makes things radioactive blows the elements out from exploding stars to form new stars and planets. The same force that gives us electricity also makes the Universe transparent, enabling us to study it. It is as if we were meant to be.

Cosmic coincidences

Life may seem a lottery, the Universe a random accident. Perhaps the biggest coincidence of all is that our Universe is just right for life. If, for example, beryllium nuclei, made in the cores of stars, were a different size, they would not go on to form carbon and oxygen, elements essential for life. If the weak nuclear force was slightly different, stars would not explode as supernovae, spewing their elements out to form potential new stars and planets. But if the force of gravity was slightly stronger all stars would collapse into black holes. The list goes on, raising the question of whether our Universe is meant to be the way it is.

The ultimate question

The final question is why we are here? Cosmologists point out how the Universe is finely tuned to complexity and life. This is called the weak anthropic principle. More controversially it has also been suggested that this is more than coincidence and that the Universe *must* produce intelligent observers. Some even argue that observers are necessary to bring the Universe into being and that ultimately everything there is must be known. If that is true, astronomy has a bright future and we are back at the centre of the Universe.

▽ On a small, blue planet, the third rock from an average star in a typical spiral galaxy, a life form developed with the potential to understand the Universe. Why?

REFERENCE

Universal Facts

EARTH DATA

Equatorial diameter	12,756 km
Volume	1.084×10^{12} km^3
Mass	5.9742×10^{24} kg
Density	5.52 of water
Surface gravity	9.78 ms^{-2}
Day length	23.9345 hours
Year length	365.256 days
Axial inclination	23.44°
Age	4,700 million years approx.
Distance from the Sun	Min. 147 million km
	Max. 152 million km
Surface area	509.6 million km^2
Land surface	148 million km^2
Oceans cover	71% of surface
Atmosphere	Nitrogen 78%, Oxygen 21%, other 1%
Av. height of land	840 m above sea level
Av. depth of ocean	3,808 m
Continental crust	35 km av. thick
Oceanic crust	7 km av. thick
Lithosphere	75 km deep
Mantle	2,900 km thick
Outer core	2,200 km thick
Inner core	1,200 km thick

MAJOR EARTHQUAKES

LOCATION	YEAR	MAGNITUDE	DEATHS
Turkey	1999	7.8	17,118
Afghanistan	1998	6.1	4,000
N. Iran	1997	7.1	1,560
Russia (Sakhalin)	1995	7.5	2,000
Japan (Kobe)	1995	7.2	6,310
S. California	1994	6.8	60
S. India (Osmanabad)	1993	6.4	9,748
Philippines	1990	7.7	1,653
NW. Iran	1990	7.5	36,000
San Francisco	1989	6.9	275
Armenia	1988	7.0	25,000
Mexico City	1985	8.1	7,200
N. Yemen	1982	6.0	2,800
S. Italy	1980	7.2	4,500
NE. Iran	1978	7.7	25,000
Tangshan, China	1976	8.2	242,000
Guatemala City	1976	7.5	22,778
NE. Iran	1968	7.4	11,600
Nan-shan, China	1927	8.3	200,000
Japan	1923	8.3	143,000
Gansu, China	1920	8.6	180,000
Messina, Italy	1908	7.5	120,000
San Francisco	1906	8.3	500
Calcutta, India	1737	-	300,000
Hokkaido, Japan	1730	-	137,000
Shensi, China	1556	-	830,000
Antioch, Turkey	526	-	250,000

PROPERTIES OF COMMON MINERALS

NAME	TYPE	HARDNESS	CRYSTAL	OPTICAL
Talc	Silicate	1	Cubic	Pale green or grey; pearly lustre
Graphite	Element	1-2	Trigonal	Grey metallic lustre
Gypsum	Sulphate	2	Monoclinic	White to transparent
Calcite	Carbonate	3	Trigonal/ Hexagonal	Double refraction
Barytes	Sulphate	3-3.5	Orthorhombic	Pale, translucent
Fluorite	Halide	4	Cubic	Many colours, fluorescent
Pyrite	Sulphide	6-6.5	Cubic	Commonly known as "fool's gold"
Quartz	Oxide	7	Trigonal/Hexagonal	Translucent
Garnet	Silicate	7	Cubic	Various forms, often plum red
Tourmaline	Silicate	7-7.5	Trigonal/Hexagonal	Pink and green
Zircon	Silicate	7.5	Tetragonal	Often brown
Beryl	Silicate	7-8	Trigonal/Hexagonal	Many colours, emerald green
Spinel	Oxide	7.5-8	Cubic	Many colours
Corundum	Oxide	9	Trigonal/Hexagonal	Various forms incl. ruby & sapphire
Diamond	Element	10	Cubic	Transparent, sparkles if cut

A mineral's optical properties include not only its colour but also its transparency and lustre, or shine. Hardness is a scale based on ten minerals. These range from talc, the softest (1) to diamond, the hardest (10).

MAJOR VOLCANOES

NAME	HT(M)	MAJOR ERUPTIONS	LAST
Bezymyannaya, Russia	2,800	1955-56	1984
El Chichón, Mexico	1,349	1982	1982
Erebus, Antarctica	4,023	1947, 1972	1986
Mt Etna, Italy	3,236	Frequent	1991
Fuji, Japan	3,776	1707	1707
Hekla, Iceland	1,491	1693, 1845, 1947-48, 1970	1981
Helgafell, Iceland	215	1973	1973
Kiluea, Hawaii	1,247	Frequent	1991
Klyuchevskoy, Russia	4,850	1700-1966, 1984	1985
Krakatoa, Sumatra	818	Frequent, esp. 1883	1980
La Soufrière, St Vincent	1,232	1718, 1812, 1902, 1971-72	1979
Mauna Loa, Hawaii	4,172	Frequent	1984
Soufrière Hills, Montserrat	915	1995	2000
Nyamaragira, Zaire	3,056	1921-38, 1971, 1980	1984
Paricutin, Mexico	3,188	1943-52	1952
Mt Pelée, Martinique	1,397	1902, 1929-32	1932
Pinatubo, Philippines	1,462	1391, 1991	1991
Popocatepetl, Mexico	5,483	1920	1943
Mt Rainier, US	4,392	1st century BC, 1820	1882
Ruapehu, N.Zealand	2,796	1945, 1953, 1969, 1975	1986
Mt St Helens, US	2,549	Frequent, esp. 1980	1987
Santorini, Greece	1,315	Frequent, esp. 1470BC	1950
Stromboli, Italy	931	Frequent	1986
Surtsey, Iceland	174	1963-67	1967
Unzen, Japan	1,360	1360, 1791	1991
Mt Vesuvius, Italy	1,289	Frequent, esp. AD79	1944

PRINCIPAL ORE MINERALS

ORE OF	MINERAL	COMPOSITION	FEATURES
Aluminium	Cryolite	Na_3AlF_6	White, extracted by electrolysis
Copper	Chalcopyrite	Sulphide	Brassy yellow
	Cuprite	Oxide	Black
	Malachite	Carbonate	Green
Gold	Native	Metal	Golden
Iron	Pyrite	Sulphide	Brassy yellow
	Magnetite	Oxide	Black
	Hematite	Hematite	Black/reddish
	Siderite	Carbonate	Orange
Lead	Galena	Sulphide	Metallic black
Silver	Native	Metal	Silver
Tin	Cassiterite	Oxide	Black/brown
Titanium	Ilmenite	Oxide	Black opaque
Uranium	Uraninite	Oxide	Dull brown/black
Zinc	Sphalerite	Sulphide	Black

GEOLOGICAL TIMELINE

Mya	Period	Era
21	Quaternary	Cenozoic
	Pliocene	
	Miocene	
	Oligocene	
65	Paleocene and Eocene	
	Cretaceous	Mesozoic
135		
	Jurassic	
195		
	Triassic	
225		
	Permian	Paleozoic
280		
	Carboniferous	
345		
	Devonian	
395		
	Silurian	
430		
	Ordovician	
500		
	Cambrian	
570		
	Precambrian	
Mya		

Mya stands for Millions of years ago.

The changing fossil record (above) provides an effective means of dating rocks. So-called zone or index fossils have been picked as key markers for each time. The fossil record goes back to the Precambrian era which began 600 million years ago.

REFERENCE

THE PLANETS OF THE SOLAR SYSTEM

NAME	DISTANCE FROM SUN (Million km)	DIAMETER (km)	MASS (Earth=1)	ROTATION	YEAR	MOONS
Mercury	57.91	4,878	0.055	58.66 days	87.97 days	0
Venus	108.2	12,103	0.81	243.01 days	224.7 days	0
Earth	149.6	12,756	1.00	23.93 hrs	365.26 days	1
Mars	227.9	6,786	0.11	24.62 hrs	686.98 days	2
Jupiter	778.3	142,984	318	9.92 hrs	11.86 years	16
Saturn	1427	120,536	95.18	10.67 hrs	29.46 years	23
Uranus	2871	51,118	14.50	17.23 hrs	84.01 years	18
Neptune	4497	49,528	17.14	16.12 hrs	164.79 years	8
Pluto	5914	2,284	0.0022	6.375 days	248.54 years	1

BRIGHTEST STARS (in order of apparent brightness)

NAME	TYPE	LOCATION	DISTANCE (Light years)	APPARENT MAGNITUDE	ABSOLUTE MAGNITUDE
Sirius	White Major	Canis	8.6	-1.46	1.4
Canopus	Yellow Giant	Carina	1200	-0.72	-8.5
Alpha Centauri	Yellow	Centaurus	4.3	-0.27	4
Arcturus	Orange Giant	Botes	36	-0.04	-0.2
Vega	White	Lyra	25	0.03	0.5
Capella	Yellow	Auriga	43	0.08	-0.7
Rigel	Blue Giant	Orion	900	0.12	-7.1
Procyon	Yellow Minor	Canis	11	0.38	2.6
Achernar	Blue Giant	Erudanus	85	0.46	-1.6
Betelgeux	Red Giant	Orion	310	0.5	5.6
Agena	Blue Giant	Centaurus	460	0.61	-5.1
Altair	White	Aquila	17	0.77	2.2
Acrux	Binary	Southern Cross	360	0.83	-3.9
Aldebaran	Orange	Taurus	68	0.85	-0.3
Antares	Red Giant	Scorpius	330	0.96	-4.7
Spica	Blue Giant	Virgo	260	0.98	-3.6
Pollux	Orange Giant	Gemini	36	1.14	0.2
Fomalhaut	White	Piscis Australis	22	1.16	2.0
Deneb	White Giant	Cygnus	1800	1.25	-7.5
Beta Crucis	Blue Giant	Southern Cross	425	1.25	-5.0
Regulus	Blue	Leo	85	1.35	-0.6

Note: The lower the value of the magnitude, the brighter the star.

Apparent magnitude is how bright the star seems from the Earth.

Absolute magnitude is how bright it would seem if all the stars were the same distance from the Earth.

FIRSTS IN ASTRONOMY

- 1600BC Babylonian star catalogues compiled
- 270BC Aristarchos proposes the Earth revolves around the Sun
- 230BC Eratosthenes measures the Earth's circumference
- 135BC Hipparchos discovers that the Earth's axis wobbles
- AD127 Ptolemy develops the Earth-centred theory of the Universe
- 1054 Chinese observe the Crab supernova
- 1543 Copernicus revives the idea of a Sun-centred Universe
- 1609 Kepler describes the orbits of planets
- 1609 Galileo is first to use a telescope for astronomy
- 1655 Huygens discovers Saturn's rings
- 1668 Newton makes first reflecting telescope
- 1687 Newton publishes Theory of Gravitation
- 1705 Halley recognizes that comets orbit the Sun
- 1781 Herschel discovers Uranus
- 1838 Bessel measures the distance of a star
- 1846 Adams and Leverrier predict existence of Neptune
- 1912 Leavitt discovers Cepheid variable stars
- 1920 Slipher discovers that nebulae are receding
- 1923 Hubble shows that receding nebulae are galaxies
- 1938 Bethe and Weizsäcker suggest stars are powered by nuclear fusion
- 1963 Schmidt discovers the first quasar
- 1965 Penzias and Wilson discover microwave background radiation
- 1967 Jocelyn Bell discovers first pulsar
- 1992 *COBE* satellite identifies ripples in the microwave background

MAJOR TELESCOPES - optical/infrared

NAME	LOCATION	DIAMETER	FIRST LIGHT
Gemini	Hawaii, USA	8 m	1999
VLT	Chile	16 m equivalent	1998
Keck	Hawaii, USA	2 x 10 m	1990
Mt Hopkins	Arizona, USA	6.5 m	1999
Zelenchukskaya	Russia	6 m	1976
Hale, Palomar	California, USA	5 m	1948
Herschel	Canary Islands	4.2 m	1987
Cerro Tololo	Chile	4.0 m	1976
Mayall	Arizona, USA	3.8 m	1973
Anglo-Australian	Australia	3.9 m	1975
UK InfraRed	Hawaii, USA	3.8 m	1978
Hubble	Space	2.4 m	1990

MAJOR PLANETARY PROBES

NAME	NATION	LAUNCH	TARGET	RESULT
Mariner 2	USA	1962	Venus	First fly-by
Venera 3	USSR	1965	Venus	Crushed during descent
Mariner 4, 6 & 7	USA	1964, '69, '69	Mars	Fly-bys
Venera 7	USSR	1970	Venus	Landed. Survived 23 mins
Mars 2 & 3	USSR	1971	Mars	2: Orbiter, dropped flag 3: Orbiter and Lander
Mariner 9	USA	1971	Mars	Orbiter
Pioneer 10	USA	1972	Jupiter	Fly-by 1973
Pioneer 11	USA	1973	Jupiter and Saturn	Jupiter fly-by 1974 Saturn fly-by 1979
Viking 1 & 2	USA	1975	Mars	Orbiters and Landers
Voyager 1	USA	1977	Jupiter and Saturn	Jupiter fly-by 1979 Saturn fly-by 1980
Voyager 2	USA	1977	Grand Tour	Fly-bys: Jupiter 1979, Saturn 1981, Uranus 1986, Neptune 1989
Pioneer Venus	USA	1978	Venus	Orbiter
Venera 13	USSR	1981	Venus	Landed, lasted 2 hours
Venera 15	USSR	1983	Venus	Radar mapper
Vega 1	USSR	1984	Venus	Lander and balloon, plus
Magellan	USA	1989	Venus	Radar mapper
Galileo	USA	1989	Jupiter	Orbiter plus probe.
Pathfinder	USA	1996	Mars	Lander & rover
Global Surveyor	USA	1996	Mars	Mapping orbiter
Cassini	USA/Europe	1997	Saturn	Orbiter & Titan probe

FIRSTS IN SPACE

1957   *Sputnik 1* (USSR) first satellite launched
1958   *Explorer 1* (USA) discovers Van Allen radiation belts
1959   *Luna 1* (USSR) escapes Earth's gravity
1959   *Vanguard 2* (USA) takes first photos of the Earth
1959   *Luna 2* (USSR) hits the Moon
1959   *Luna 3* (USSR) returns first pictures of far side of the Moon
1960   *TIROS 1* (USA) first weather satellite
1960   *ECHO 1* (USA) first communications satellite
1961   *Vostok 1* (USSR) first manned orbital flight
1962   *Aerobee* (USA) x-ray satellite launched
1963   *Vostok 6* (USSR) carries first woman in orbit
1965   *Early Bird* (USA) commercial geostationary communications satellite
1965   *Gemini 6* (USA) manned rendezvous in space
1966   *Luna 9* (USSR) soft Moon landing
1969   *Apollo 11* (USA) manned lunar landing
1975   Apollo/Soyuz first international link-up
1978   Launch of *International Ultraviolet Explorer* (USA/EUROPE)
1981   *Columbia* (USA) first Space Shuttle flight
1986   Launch of *Mir* space station
1990   *Hubble Space Telescope* (USA/EUROPE) launched
1998   Launch of first component of *International Space Station*
1999   Launch of *Chandra x-ray Observatory* and *XXM-Newton x-ray Observatory*

REFERENCE

Glossary

Abyssal plain The flat floor of an ocean basin below a continental slope. Its surface consists of a layer of sediment covering uneven rock.

Accretion disc A disc of matter that builds up around a dense object as material spirals down towards it. It is believed that accretion discs often form around black holes.

Antarctic The region south of the Antarctic Circle, or simply the cold region around the South Pole – Antarctica and surrounding far southern parts of the Atlantic, Indian and Pacific oceans.

Antimatter Matter that shares properties with the fundamental particles but in reverse, such as an opposite electrical charge.

Arctic The region norht of the Arctic Circle, or the cold region around the North Pole. This includes the Arctic Ocean and surrounding far northern parts of Europe, Asia and North America.

Ash The name given to the fine, powdery material which is blown out by gas during a volcanic eruption. Ash can spread for thousands of kilometres and fall to form layers many centimetres thick.

Asteroid A rocky object, anything from a few metres to a few hundred kilometres across, in orbit around the Sun. Most asteroids are in the asteroid belt between the orbits of Mars and Jupiter, but some come in to the inner Solar System and, every million years or so, one collides with the Earth.

Astronomical Unit The average distance between the Earth and the Sun (149,597,870 km). It is a useful unit for expressing distances in the Solar System.

Atmosphere The thin layer of air, composed mostly of nitrogen and oxygen, that is held in place around the Earth by gravity.

Atoll A ring-shaped coral reef surrounded by open sea and enclosing an area of shallow, sheltered water called a lagoon. Atolls grow on the rims of volcanic islands.

Atom The smallest component of an element that retains its chemical properties. Even the biggest atom is only half a millionth of a millimetre across.

Aurora The display of what look like coloured curtains of light at high latitudes, caused by energetic particles from the Sun streaming in towards the Earth's magnetic poles and striking atoms in the atmosphere.

Basalt One of the commonest rocks in the Earth's crust. It is created by partial melting of the mantle and erupts as a runny lava from volcanoes. It is dark, dense and fine-grained.

Basin A depression in the Earth's surface containing an ocean. It also refers to the part of the ocean floor more than 2,000 metres below sea level.

Billion One thousand million (1,000,000,000).

Binary star A pair of stars in orbit around the common centre of gravity between them (i.e. around each other).

Biodiversity The full range of plant, animal and micro-organism species found in a particular habitat. The health of an ecosystem can be measured by the degree of its diversity.

Bivalves Soft-bodied animals living in a pair of hinged shells that they can open and close. Bivalves include clams, mussels and oysters.

Black hole A region of space-time where there is such a concentration of matter, and consequently gravity, that not even light can escape. Black holes can form when massive stars collapse. Others lie at the heart of active galaxies.

Bony fish A fish with a bony skeleton. Bony species, such as herrings and tuna, outnumber cartilaginous (gristly) species such as sharks and rays, by more than thirty to one.

Brown dwarf A small star of such low mass (less than 8 percent of the Sun's mass) that nuclear fusion reactions cannot begin. A brown dwarf shines only because of the faint heat released as it contracts.

Canyon A deep valley or gorge, often with near vertical sides. A canyon is carved by a river running through an arid, mountainous region.

Cartilaginous fish A fish with a cartilaginous, or gristly, skeleton. Cartilaginous fish include sharks and rays. Unlike bony fish, they lack a swimbladder – if they stop swimming they sink.

Cepheid variable A star that varies its brightness in a regular period between one and fifty days.

CFC Chlorofluorocarbons are the chemicals which once were widely used in aerosol sprays and refrigerators and which, when released into the atmosphere, damage the ozone layer. Their use is now strictly limited by international agreement.

Cluster A group of stars or galaxies affecting each other by their gravitational attraction.

Comet An object made of ice, dust and other material. There may be billions of comets beyond the orbit of Pluto. Some come nearer the Sun, on elliptical orbits, leaving spectacular tails of gas and dust.

Constellation A grouping of stars in the same direction in the sky, though not necessarily associated with each other.

Continent Great land mass on the surface of the Earth. There are seven continents.

Continental crust The Earth's crust forming the continents.

Continental rise A gentle slope formed by sediments at teh foot of a continental slope.

Continental shelf The rim of a continental landmass. it slopes gently down to about 180 metres and ends at the continental slope.

Copepod A tiny shrimp-like creature forming part of the zooplankton.

Core The innermost 7,000 kilometres of our planet, composed mostly of iron with traces of nickel and other minerals. The central 2,400 kilometres is solid, but the outer core is molten and slowly circulating. Electrical currents within the core generate the planet's magnetic field.

Corona The outer atmosphere of the Sun, extending many millions of kilometres above the visible surface. The corona can reach 2,000,000°C and is visible during eclipses.

Cosmic background radiation Microwave radiation coming from all directions in the sky and thought to be the cooled remnant of the fireball of the Big Bang in which the Universe began.

Cosmology The study of the structure and origin of the Universe.

Crater Circular depression on a planet, moon or asteroid, usually resulting from the impact of another body.

Current An ocean current is water flowing through the sea. Winds drive surface currents. Deep-sea currents occur where dnese water sinkds and spreads over the seabed.

Dark matter Matter known to exist, but mostly invisible. It might be normal matter in the form of brown dwarfs or black holes, or it could be ghostly, unidentified particles.

DNA An abbreviation of deoxyribonucleic acid – the chemical which carries the genetic code of life. It is made up of a long chain that forms a double helix or spiral structure.

Earthquake An often violent shaking of the Earth caused when two of the plates that make up the Earth's crust crack as they scrape past one another. Earthquakes are most frequent along plate boundaries.

Echinoderm A spiny-skinned marine invertebrate such as a sea urchin, starfish or sea cucumber.

Eclipse A shadow cast by one celestial object on another. For example, the Earth's shadow falling on the Moon causes a lunar eclipse. The Moon's shadow falling on the Earth is seen as a solar eclipse.

El Niño The Spanish name given to the warm ocean current that occasionally flows towards the coast of Peru, disrupting fisheries and wildlife and bringing droughts to some parts of the world and storms and floods to others.

Epicentre The point on the Earth's surface directly above the focus of an earthquake, the place where the ground cracks.

Erosion The process by which rocks are worn away over time, usually as a result of the action of water, wind or ice.

Escape velocity The velocity that a projectile must reach if it is to escape from the gravity of an astronomical object without further propulsion.

Estuary The place where a river widens and slows downs as it flows out into the sea. As the water slows, it can deposit the sediments it is carrying to form a delta.

Event horizon The boundary around a black hole from within which neither matter nor radiation can escape.

False-colour Colour added by computer to enhance the details of an image.

REFERENCE

Fault A crack in the Earth's crust that forms during an earthquake as a result of stresses within the rock.

Fold A region of rocks that have been deformed or bent by movements in the Earth's crust.

Fossil The traces of a prehistoric plant or animal preserved within rocks or sediments. Fossils can be made up of the original hard parts of the organism or they can be replaced by other minerals.

Fossil fuel Fossil fuels include coal, oil and natural gas, all produced from the decay, burial and fossilization of organic remains. Fossil fuels have taken millions of years to form, but humans have almost exhausted them in just a few centuries.

Galaxy A celestial city of millions or billions of stars, gas and dust bound together by their gravitational pull.

Gamma rays The most energetic radiation in the electromagnetic spectrum.

Glacier Literally, a river of ice that builds up in a mountain valley as a result of the compression of snow. A glacier can flow slowly downhill, gouging out a deep U-shaped valley.

Global warming A general warming of the Earth's climate brought about by increasing levels of so-called greenhouse gases such as carbon dioxide in the atmosphere. It is predicted that human activity will result in global warming of several degrees over the next century.

Globular cluster A spherical cluster of between a few thousand and a million stars. Globular clusters form the halo of our galaxy and contain very ancient stars.

Gondwanaland The name given to the great southern continent that resulted from the break up of the supercontinent Pangaea. It included present day Africa, South America, Australia, Antarctica and India.

Granite A crystalline igneous rock produced by the upwelling, or intrusion, of molten crustal rocks. It contains the minerals quartz, mica and feldspar.

Gravitational lens A region of mass, such as a cluster of galaxies, which bends light from more distant objects.

Gravity Gravity is the force that makes objects attract one another. It holds us on the surface of the Earth, keeps the Moon in orbit around our planet and the Earth in orbit around the Sun.

Greenhouse effect The greenhouse effect is caused by gases such as water vapour and carbon dioxide in the atmosphere which allow sunlight into the Earth's surface but prevent the escape of heat. As a result, the gases act like a blanket, keeping the planet warm in the same way as the glass in a greenhouse keeps plants inside warm.

Hot spot A hot spot is a place on the surface of the Earth above an upwelling plume of hot mantle material. Hot spots are often the site of intensive long-term volcanic activity. Examples include Hawaii and Iceland.

Hubble constant The rate at which the Universe is expanding. As the galaxies move further apart, this causes redshift which can be used to measure the rate of expansion.

Hurricane A tropical Atlantic storm with winds up to 170 kilometres per hour. The Pacific Ocean's typhoons and the cyclones in the Indian Ocean are similar storms.

Hydrothermal vent Where volcanic forces rise beneath the ocean crust, for example along the mid-ocean ridges, they can heat groundwater so that it jets out of underwater springs or vents.

Ice age An ice age is a prolonged period during which the Earth's climate cools and ice sheets and glaciers spread from the poles. It may be triggered by periodic variations in the Earth's orbit around the Sun. There have been four ice ages in the last two million years and there may be more to come.

Iceberg A mass of ice broken off a lnad-based glacier or ice sheet and floating in the sea. Most icebergs come from Antarctica and Greenland.

Igneous Igneous rocks are produced by the melting of material deep within the Earth's crust or upper mantle. They are of two main types – extrusive igneous rocks which come out of volcanoes and cool quickly, so they are usually fine-grained, and intrusive igneous rocks which bulge up in large masses within a continent. They cool more slowly and as a result are sometimes crystalline.

Infrared radiation Electromagnetic radiation with a longer wavelength than red light but less than radio.

Invertebrate An animal without vertebrae – the bones forming a backbone. Animals with a backbone are known as vertebrates.

Krill Small shrimp-like crustaceans. Krill teem in polar seas where they form much of the food consumed by various baleen whales.

Laurasia The great northern continent formed from the break up, 200 million years ago, of the supercontinent Pangaea. It was made up of present-day Europe, North America, Greenland and Asia.

Lava The molten rock which flows out of a volcano and then solidifies.

Light year The distance that light travels in one year (9,460,700,000,000 km).

Local Group The grouping of about 30 galaxies in which our own galaxy is found.

Magma Molten rock under the Earth's surface. Sometimes it rises within a volcano to flow out as lava.

Magnetometer A highly sensitive instrument used by geologists to measure the Earth's magnetic field.

Magnetosphere The magnetic bubble around the Earth or another planet in which ionized gas is controlled by the planet's magnetic field.

Main sequence The range of temperature and brightness at which the majority of stars spend most of their lives.

Mantle The thick layer of dense silicate rocks that forms the bulk of the Earth beneath the thin crust and above the iron core. Although virtually solid, it carries heat from the interior of the planet and produces volcanic activity on the surface.

Metamorphic Metamorphic rocks are rocks which have been changed by heat and pressure. They can be derived from either igneous or sedimentary rocks. The heat and pressure can turn shale into slate, limestone into marble and sandstone into quartzite.

Meteor A brilliant streak across the sky caused by objects, such as specks of dust or rocks, burning up as they enter the Earth's atmosphere. Meteors are popularly known as shooting stars.

Meteorite A lump of rock or metal that has fallen to the Earth from space. The largest meteorites create craters on impact.

Mid-ocean ridge The long range of underwater mountains that runs down the centres of many of the world's oceans. It forms lines of undersea volcanoes from which new ocean crust is spreading.

Mineral A naturally formed chemical substance with a precise molecular structure. Minerals are the building blocks of rocks. Mined natural substances, such as coal and oil, are also known as minerals.

Mollusc A soft-bodied invertebrate, usually with one shell or two shells. Molluscs include gastropods such as sea slugs and whelks, cephalopods such as squid and octopuses, and bivalves such as mussels and oysters.

Moraine The lines and piles of stones and mud deposited along the sides and at the end of a glacier.

Nebula A cloud of gas or dust in space.

Neutrino A particle with no charge and little or no mass.

Neutron star A star that has been so compressed that electrons and protons have been squashed together to make neutrons. It has the mass of a star but the size of a city.

Ocean The salt water covering two-thirds of the Earth, or one of its four major divisions – the Atlantic Ocean, Indian Ocean, Pacific Ocean or Arctic Ocean.

Oort Cloud A cloud of millions or even billions of dormant comets thought to lie beyond the orbit of Pluto.

Ooze Soft, wet mud on the deep ocean floor. The contents of deep-sea oozes include dust and the remains of billions of tiny organsims.

Orbit The path of one body around another, such as the Moon around the Earth or the Earth around the Sun. It may be circular, or more often, elliptical.

Ore A mineral rich in a particular useful substance such as a metal, for example, and used in commercial quantities for producing that material.

Ozone A form of oxygen molecule that contains three oxygen atoms. It forms naturally in a thin layer in the stratosphere, about 20 kilometres above us, where it filters out potentially damaging ultraviolet radiation from sunlight. However, it is destroyed by chemicals such as CFCs.

REFERENCE

Pangaea The supercontinent containing all the world's land masses. It existed between about 250 and 200 million years ago and broke up to form Gondwanaland and Laurasia, with the Tethys Ocean in between them.

Parallax The apparent motion of an object against a more distant background caused by a changing viewpoint. It provides a basis for calculating the distances to nearby stars.

Perihelion The closest point to the Sun in the orbit of a body such as a comet or planet.

Permian The geological period between about 280 and 225 million years ago. Some of the first large reptiles lived during the Permian period. However, it ended abruptly with the extinction of many species.

Photon The smallest particle of energy that can be carried as light.

Pillow lava Deposits of volcanic lava shaped like a series of pillows. They erupted underwater and were quickly quenched and solidified by the water before they could flow far.

Planet A body in orbit around the Sun or another star, shining in reflected light only. Bodies over 1,000 km across are normally considered to be planets. Smaller objects are called minor planets.

Planetary Nebula A cloud of gas that can have the appearance of a planet but really consists of expanding shells of gas thrown off by a star close to the end of its life.

Plankton The various tiny organisms that drift near the surface of sea water. Plankton provides the food that most marine creatures depend on, directly or indirectly.

Plate A unit of the rocky lithosphere – the crust and hard top to the mantle – that can slide intact over the Earth's surface as a result of continental drift.

Polar Relating to the world's far north or far south – the regions around the North Pole or the South Pole.

Polyp A sea anemone, coral or other form of coelenterate. These organisms have a stalk-like body fixed at one end to a rock or other underwater object. The other end has a mouth surrounded by a ring of tentacles.

Predator An animal that preys on others.

Protostar An early stage in the formation of a star before nuclear fusion has begun.

Pulsar A spinning neutron star emitting bursts of radiation, like a flashing lighthouse beam, often many times a second.

Pyroclastic flow A deadly flow of lava, ash, super-heated steam and gas that can race downhill from a volcanic eruption, scorching everything in its path.

Quasar The energetic core of an active galaxy. Quasars give out as much energy as a big galaxy from a region no bigger than our solar system. Quasar is short for quasi-stellar object.

Red dwarf A small, dim red star with a surface temperature of between 2,500°C and 5,000°C.

Red giant A bright red star up to 100 times the diameter of the Sun and thought to be near the end of its life.

Redshift The stretching of light from an object, such as a galaxy, that is moving away from us. Because the Universe is still expanding, the higher the redshift, the more distant the object.

Ridge A long, narrow, raised, steep-sided area of the Earth's crust. Spreading ridges on the ocean floor are formed where the Earth's plates diverge.

Rift A valley formed where a mass of rock slid down between two plates that were moving apart. Rift valleys can also be found along the crest of a mid-ocean ridge.

Satellite Any object in orbit around another object. The term is normally applied to a moon or an artificial craft orbiting around a planet.

Sea ice Ice formed from frozen seawater.

Sediment Loose particles deposited by water or wind. Out at sea, inshore sediments include gravel and boulders. Deep-sea sediments are made up mainly of fine clays.

Sedimentary Sedimentary rocks are rocks laid down, usually in layers, by water or by wind, ice and vegetation. They are mostly formed from the erosion of other rocks, and these so-called clastic rocks include shale and sandstone. Others are chemical deposits such as limestone and gypsum.

Seismic wave A wave running through the Earth usually produced by an earthquake.

Seismograph An instrument for measuring seismic waves.

Silicate One of the group of minerals containing silicon and oxygen atoms bound to other elements such as metals. Silicates are the main rock-forming minerals of the planet.

Smelting The process in which an ore is heated to extract a metal from it.

Solar wind The stream of electrically-charged particles blowing from the Sun. When it strikes molecules of air in the Earth's atmosphere, it produces an aurora.

Space-time The combination of the three dimensions of space plus one of time. Space-time makes up the fabric of the Universe.

Spectrum The rainbow band of electromagnetic radiation of different wavelengths. The light from a star or galaxy, split up into wavelengths of different colours.

Spring tide A tide when the difference between high and low water is greatest.

Stalactite A deposit of calcium carbonate hanging like an icicle from the roof of a cave.

Stalagmite A column of calcium carbonate rising up from a cave floor, often beneath a stalactite and formed by a similar process.

Submarine canyon A deep, narrow steep-sided, underwater valley created by a slide of sediment.

Sub-atomic physics The study of the fundamental particles that make up atoms, and the forces that act between them.

Submersible A manned or remotely operated submarine designed for research in deep water.

Sunspot A dark spot on the surface, or photosphere, of the Sun, caused by a magnetic disturbance. A sunspot is slightly cooler than the surrounding area.

Supercluster A grouping made up of clusters of galaxies. Superclusters can be hundreds of millions of light years across.

Supernova An exploding, massive star torn apart by an intense flash of radiation. This happens when the core of a star collapses.

Tide The regular rise and fall of sea level caused by the gravitational pulls of the Moon and the Sun on the Earth.

Tornado A small but extremely violent storm in which a funnel-shaped column of cloud rotates rapidly as warm air rises within it. Tornadoes can reach speeds of several hundred kilometres per hour and are common in parts of the US and Australia.

Trench A deep, narrow trough in the ocean floor.

Tsunami Sometimes known as a tidal wave, a tsunami can be triggered by an underwater earthquake or landslide. In open ocean it may be only a few centimetres high, but it can travel great distances, and as it reaches the shore, can build into a wall of water tens of metres high.

Ultraviolet radiation Electromagnetic radiation of shorter wavelength than the blue end of the visible spectrum.

Universe Space-time and everything contained within it. In theory, there might be universes other than our own, but we could have no direct knowledge of them, or they would be part of our own universe.

Van Allen belts Belts of radiation around the Earth caused by charged particles trapped in the Earth's magnetic field.

Vertebrate An animal with a backbone. Vertebrate species include fish, amphibians reptiles, birds and mammals as well as humans.

Volcano A place where molten magma rises to the surface of the planet and is released, often with violent results. A volcano can build into a mountain thousands of metres high.

Water cycle The continual flow of the Earth's water. Water vapour from the sea and the land rises into the atmosphere, becoming rain, hail or snow. These fall on the sea or fill rivers flowing to the sea.

Wavelength The distance between successive peaks (or troughs) in a wave, such as electromagnetic radiation.

White dwarf A hot, compact star no heavier than 1.4 times the mass of the Sun. With most of its nuclear fuel used up, the star contracts until it is very dense and hot.

X-rays Electromagnetic radiation of shorter wavelength than ultraviolet radiation.

Zooplankton The animals forming part of the plankton. They feed upon one-celled algae called phytoplankton.

Index

A
abyssal hills 94
abyssal plains 94
Adams, John Couch 168
Africa 17, 28, 40
air pressure, weather 44
algae 10, 13, 61, 88
aliens 204-205
Alps 40-41
Alvarez theory 72
amino acids 60
amphibians 67, 69
Anaxagoras 126
Andromeda galaxy 181, 188, 189, 191
animals
    conservation 86
    dinosaurs 68-73, 76
    evolution 66-67, 73
    extinctions 72, 88, 90
    fossils 58-66, 68, 70, 74
    mammals 70, 71, 73, 74, 76-77
    sea mammals 102-3
Anning, Mary 68
Antarctica 55, 56, 77
Apollo programme 134-135
Archaeopteryx 74-75
Arctic Ocean 92, 93
Arecibo 204
Ariane rocket 137
Ariel 167
Aristotle 126
Asia 36, 40, 44
asteroids 144, 156-157, 171
    asteroid belt 156
    Earth hit by 8, 9, 12, 157
    Jupiter's moons 160
    and mass extinctions 90, 91, 156
    minerals 83
    Moon hit by 150
asthenosphere 14
astronauts 11, 133, 134,135, 142
    Mars missions 155
    on the Moon 134-135, 151
    space shuttle 136-137
    space stations 138-139
astronomers 126
Atlantic Ocean
    explorers 112, 114, 115
    formation 17, 29
    size 92, 93
    Titanic sunk 123
atmosphere 10
    dawn of life 60
    formation of 9, 12, 13, 177
    greenhouse effect 48, 50-51, 88
    ice ages 56
    Jupiter 12, 158, 159
    Mars 10, 152, 154, 155
    Neptune 168
    oxygen 59
    Saturn 162, 163
    Titan 164
    Uranus 166, 167
    Venus 10, 11, 65, 148, 149
    weather 44
    winds 42-43
atolls 124
atoms 8
auroras 23

B
bacteria 10, 18, 61, 80
basalt 18, 24, 28, 29
beaches
    rocky shores 108
    sandy beaches 97, 110-111
    waves 99
Big Bang 193, 196-199
Big Crunch 200, 201
birds
    dinosaurs and 71
    evolution 74-75, 76
    extinction 88
    migration 116
black holes 184-185, 187, 194-195, 200-201, 206-207
black smokers 18-19
boats *see* ships
bores 97
Botticelli, Sandro 119
Brahe, Tycho 172
Braun, Wernher von 132
Britten, Benjamin 118
brown dwarf stars 200, 201
Burgess Shale 63

C
calcium carbonate 64-65
Callisto 160, 161
Cambrian period 62-63
canyons 53
carbon 8, 64, 80, 82, 84-85
carbon dioxide
    carbon cycle 64
    climate change 49, 50, 51
    in Earth's atmosphere 10, 13, 177
    and erosion 52
    fossil fuels 80
    Martian atmosphere 152, 155
    and origins of life 60
    rainforest destruction 88
    Venusian atmosphere 65, 148, 149
Carboniferous period 80
Caribbean Sea 115
caves 52
Cepheid variables 181, 188
Ceres 156
Challenger space shuttle 137
Challis, James 168
Charon 170, 171
charts *see* maps
chlorophyll 10
Christy, Jim 171
civilization 86
Clarke, Arthur C. 140
cliffs 108, 110
climate 10, 44, 48-51, 91, 124
    see also weather
clouds 44, 47, 52, 54
coal 50, 80, 81, 84
coasts *see* beaches; shores
COBE satellite 196, 197
Columbus, Christopher 114, 115
comets 9, 144, 145, 172-173
    cores 172
    Earth hit by 8

Halley's Comet 172
Jupiter hit by 159
Kuiper belt 171
and life on Earth 61
mass extinctions and 90
Oort Cloud 173
and Saturn's rings 162
water brought to Earth by 12, 13
Compton Gamma Ray Observatory 131
continental shelf 94
continental slope 94
continents 14, 15, 16-17, 24, 34, 40-41
Cook, Captain James 115
Copernicus, Nicolaus 126
corals 55, 65, 68, 104-105
Cordelia 167
core, Earth's 9, 14, 15, 20, 22-23, 90
Crab Nebula 183
crabs 108, 111
craters
  on Callisto 160, 161
  on Earth 156, 157
  on Mercury 146, 147
  meteorites 72
  on the Moon 150, 156
  on Venus 149
  volcanoes 26, 28
Cretaceous period 70, 72, 75, 76
crust, Earth's 14
  boreholes 20
  continents 16
  earthquakes 34
  mid-ocean ridges 17, 18, 19

mountain-building 41
currents 124
cyanobacteria 13

D
Da Gama, Vasco 114, 115
dams 54, 83
dark matter 200, 201
Darwin, Charles 60, 117
deep-sea life 106-107
deltas 52, 124
deserts 42, 48, 50, 77
diamonds 84-85
Dias, Bartholomew 114, 115
dinosaurs 68-73, 76
Dione 165
DNA 60, 71
dolphins 103
droughts 51, 54, 55
dunes 110

E
Earth
  age of 58-59
  ancient theories of 126
  asteroid collisions 156-157
  atmosphere 177
  birth of 8-9, 12-13
  climate 48-51
  continents 16-17
  core 22-23
  earthquakes 34-39
  end of 90-91
  fuels 80-81
  gems 84-85
  humans and 86-89
  ice 56-57
  life on 10, 13, 60-79

mantle 14-15
metals 82-3
Moon 150
mountains 40-41
satellites 140-141, 142
Solar System 144, 145
volcanoes 24-33
water 52-5
weather 44-47
winds 42-43
see also oceans
earthquakes 18, 21, 22, 26, 34-39, 98, 208
eclipses 175
Einstein, Albert 127, 195, 198, 202
electricity 96, 99
elements 183
emeralds 85
Enceladus 165
energy
  fossil fuels 80
  Sun 174
equator 20, 48
erosion
  coastline 108, 110
  glaciers 56-57
  mountains 41
  water 52, 53
  wind 42-43
Etna, Mount 26-27, 33
Europa 160, 161
Europe 29, 40, 50, 56
evolution 60-61, 63, 66-67, 73, 76-77
explorers 112-115
extinctions 63, 72-73, 88, 90
extra-terrestrial life 204-205

F
faults 34, 35, 39
feathers 74-75, 76
fish 100-101
  coral reefs 104
  deep-sea fish 106-107
  evolution 67
  fish farms 124
  fishing 96, 120-121
  fossils 74
  sandy beaches 111
fjords 57
floods 54, 55, 124
forces 198, 207
forests 50, 51, 66, 80, 88
fossil fuels 50, 80-81
fossils 20, 58-66, 68, 70, 74, 102
fronts, weather 44

G
Gagarin, Yuri 133
Gaia 10, 89
galaxies 126, 127, 186-195
Galileo, Galilei 126, 128, 160, 162
gamma rays 131
Ganymede 160, 161
gas, natural 80, 81
gems 84-85
genetics 60, 70, 71
geological time 209
geostationary satellites 140, 141
Giant's Causeway 24
glaciers 41, 56-57
Glenn, John 133
global warming 48, 50-51, 55, 73, 124

219

globular clusters 181
Goddard, Robert 132
gold 82, 83, 84
Gondwana 68
Grand Canyon 53
granite 16, 85
gravitational lenses 195
gravity 20
   black holes 184-185, 207
   and comets 173
   Earth's formation 8
   galaxies 191
   Jupiter 161
   Moon 150, 151
   rockets 132
   star death 182
   superforce 198
Great Attractor 190, 191
greenhouse effect 48, 50-1, 148, 177
Gulf Stream 48, 50
guyots 94

H

Hadley cell 44
hailstones 46, 47
Halley's Comet 172
Hawaii 28, 29
Henry the Navigator 114
Herschel, William 128, 166
Heyerdahl, Thor 113
Himalayas 40-41, 44
Hindus 8
Hodges, William 118
Hokusai 118
Homer, Winslow 118, 119
Homo erectus 78, 79
Homo sapiens 79, 86
Hoyle, Fred 142, 196

Hubble, Edwin 127, 190
Hubble Deep Field 193
Hubble Space Telescope 130-131, 137, 141, 152, 159, 162, 170, 171, 178, 179, 182, 189, 192, 193, 194
human ancestors 78-79
hurricanes 45, 98
Huygens, Christiaan 162, 164
hydrogen
   birth of the Earth 8, 12, 13
   on Jupiter 158, 159
   and life 60
   on Saturn 163
   in stars 180, 182
   in the Sun 91, 174, 177
hydrothermal vents 18-19

I

Iapetus 165
ice 49, 52, 56-7, 61, 93
   comets 172, 173
   on Europa 161
   glaciers 56, 57
   and greenhouse effect 48, 55
   ice ages 49, 56, 76-77
   ice caps 56, 124
   icebergs 56, 57, 122, 123
   on Titan 164
ichthyosaurs 68, 69
igneous rocks 82
Indian Ocean 92, 93
Indian sub-continent 40, 41
infrared radiation 131
Infrared Space Observatory 130, 131
insects 66, 70, 71, 75

International Space Station 138, 139
International Ultraviolet Explorer 131
invertebrates 62
Io 12, 160, 161
iridium 72
iron 9, 14, 15, 22, 23, 61, 83
Irwin, James 134
islands
   explorers 112, 113, 115, 117
   and global warming 55
   island arcs 95
   volcanic 19, 28, 29

J

jet streams 44
Jupiter 11, 158-161, 166
   asteroid belt 156
   atmosphere 12, 158, 159
   formation 8
   moons 126, 128, 160-161
   Solar System 144, 145
Jurassic period 68, 69, 74

K

knowledge 87
Kobe earthquake 36
Kon-Tiki 113
Korolev, Sergei 132
Krakatoa 25
krill 124
Kuiper Belt 170, 171

L

lahars 33
lakes 54
lapis lazuli 84
Larissa 169
latitude 116, 117

Laurasia 68
lava 15, 18, 24, 26, 28, 29, 32, 33
Leverrier, Urbain 168
life 58-79, 207
   on Earth 10, 13, 60-79, 204
   on Europa 161
   extra-terrestrial 204-205
   fossils 58
   greenhouse effect and 48
   on Mars 154-155
   mass extinctions 88
light
   daylight 46
   gravitational lenses 195
   speed of 202
   telescopes 129
light years 181
lightning 47, 60
limestone 52, 64-5, 68, 74, 83, 84
lithosphere 14, 15
lobsters 120
Local Group 188-189
Loma Prieta earthquake 36, 37, 38
longitude 116, 117
Lovelock, James 89
Lowell, Percival 170
Lucy 78
Lyell, Sir Charles 58

M

Magellan, Ferdinand 115
magma 18, 19, 26, 27, 28, 30, 31
magnetic field 9, 15, 22, 23
mammals 70, 71, 73, 74, 76-77, 102-103

mammoths 76, 77
manganese nodules 124
mangroves 124
Manned Manoeuvring Units (MMUs) 136
mantle, Earth's 14-15, 23
    continents 16
    earthquakes 34
    formation of Earth 9
    gems 84
    mid-ocean ridges 19
    volcanoes 24
maps 115, 116, 117
Mars 11, 46, 152-155, 166
    asteroid belt 156
    atmosphere 10, 152, 154, 155
    life on 155
    meteorites 154
    Solar System 144, 145
    space probes 153, 154
Mediterranean Sea 112, 114
Melville, Herman 118
Mendelssohn, Felix 118, 119
Mercalli scale 35, 37
Mercator, Gerardus 116
Mercury 144, 145, 146-147, 166
metals 82-83
meteor showers 173
meteorites 61, 72-73, 84, 154, 155, 157
meteorology 45, 48, 50
methane 13, 50, 60, 80
Mid-Atlantic Ridge 19
mid-ocean ridges 17, 18-19, 24, 94, 124
migration 116
Milky Way 9, 144, 186-187, 188, 190

Miller, Stanley 60, 61
Milne, John 39
Mimas 165
minerals 82-3, 84-5, 124, 208-9
mining 80, 83
Mir space station 138, 139, 141
mirages 46
Miranda 167
monsoon 44
Montserrat 33
Moon 20, 93, 126, 128, 150-151
    astronauts on 134-135
    craters 150, 156
    creation of 8, 9, 150
    eclipses 175
    future of 90
    haloes 47
    tides 96
moons 144
    Jupiter 126, 128, 160-161
    Mars 152
    Neptune 169
    Pluto 170, 171
    Saturn 164-165
    Uranus 167
mountains 15, 16, 17, 40-41, 53, 94
mudflows 33
music, sea in 118

N
national parks 89
navigation 114, 116-117, 122
Neanderthals 79
neap tides 96, 97
nebulae 178-179, 182
Neptune 144, 145, 167, 168-169
Nereid 169
neutrinos 201
neutron stars 90, 182, 183, 184
Newton, Isaac 20
El Niño 51
nitrogen 13, 50, 60
North America 41, 56
North Atlantic Drift 124
North Pole 23
nuclear power 80

O
Oberon 167
oceans
    and the arts 118-119
    and climate 48
    coral reefs 104-105
    currents 48, 50-51
    deep-sea life 106-107
    exploring 112-115
    fish 100-101
    food from 120-121
    formation of 12, 13, 16
    future prospects 124
    global warming 55
    ice 56
    Jurassic period 68
    minerals 83
    navigation 116-117
    pollution 88
    sea floor 18-19, 94-95
    sea mammals 102-103
    shores 108-111
    tides 96-7
    water 54
    waves 53, 98-99
    and weather 44
    wrecks 122-123
oil 29, 50, 80, 81, 88, 89, 123

oil rigs 122
olivine 21
Oort Cloud 173
Ophelia 167
orbits
    planets 144
    satellites 140-141
Ordovician period 66-67
ores 82-83, 209
Orion Nebula 178, 179
oxygen 8, 10, 13, 22, 59, 80
ozone layer 10, 90, 91, 142

P
Pacific Ocean
    explorers 112, 113, 115
    hurricanes 98
    El Niño 51
    size 92, 93
    volcanoes 24, 28
paintings, sea in 118-119
Pangea 17, 68, 77
parallax 180
particles 198-199, 201, 202
peat 80
pebbly beaches 110
Pelée, Mont 33
Philippines 30-31, 32
Phobos 152
Phoebe 164
photosynthesis 13
phytoplankton 106
Pinatubo, Mount 30-31
pirates 123
Planet X 170, 171
planetary nebulae 182
planets 9, 208, 210
    ancient theories 126, 128
    creation of 8
    Earth 10-11
    extra-terrestrial life 204
    Jupiter 158-161

221

Mars 152-155
Mercury 146-147
Neptune 168-169
Pluto 170-171
Saturn 162-165
Solar System 144-145
space probes 211
Uranus 166-167
Venus 148-149
plankton
    fishing grounds 120
    as food 102, 110, 111
    Jurassic period 68
    phytoplankton 106
plants 10, 64, 66, 70, 72, 75, 88
Pleiades 180, 181
plesiosaurs 68, 69
Pluto 144, 170-171, 173
polar ice caps 56, 64, 68, 77
pollution 83, 86, 88, 89, 123
Pompeii 32, 33
prairies 42
Pre-Cambrian period 61
Proteus 169
Proxima Centauri 181
Ptolemy 126
Puck 167
pulsars 183
pyroclastic flows 30, 31

Q
quartz 82, 84, 85
quasars 194, 195

R
radar 116, 117
radiation 90
radio telescopes 129, 197, 204
rain 44, 47, 48, 52, 54, 55
rainbows 47
rainforests 88
red dwarf stars 180
red giant stars 177, 180, 182, 183
redshift 190, 191
reefs 122, 123
    see also coral
reptiles 68-69, 70, 74, 76
Richter scale 34, 35, 37
rift valleys 94
Ring of Fire 28
rings
    Jupiter 158
    Neptune 169
    Saturn 162, 164
    Uranus 166
rivers 41, 52, 54, 55
RNA 60
rockets 132-133
    Ariane 137
    Saturn V 132, 133, 134
    space shuttle 136, 137
rocks
    continents 16
    earthquakes 34
    erosion 52, 53, 56-7
    fossils 58-59, 62-63, 64-65, 74
    gems 84-85
    and gravity 20
    mantle 14-15
    meteorite collisions 72, 73
    minerals 82-83
    mountains 40
    oil and gas 81
    sedimentary rocks 58, 62, 85
    seismic waves 21
rocky shores 108-109

S
St Helens, Mount 31
Salyut space station 138
San Andreas fault 16, 35, 37
San Francisco 36, 37
sand
    beaches 97, 110-111
    dunes 42
    sandbanks 122
satellites 11, 140-141, 142
    communications satellites 141
    COBE 196, 197
    continental drift 34
    geological surveys 20, 143
    navigation 116
    orbits 140, 141
    repairing 138
    space junk 140
    space race 132
    space shuttle 136, 137
    spy satellites 143
    weather satellites 45, 142
Saturn 11, 162-165, 166
    formation of 8
    moons 164-165
    rings 162, 164
    Solar System 144, 145
    space probes 163
    winds 46, 162
sea *see* oceans
sea defences 124
sea floor 94-95
sea level 96, 124
seamounts 94
seawater 93
seaweed 108, 109
sedimentary rocks 58, 62, 85
sediments 52, 54, 80, 94, 95
seismic waves 17, 21, 22, 38, 39
seismographs 38, 39
Severin, Tim 112
Severn Bore 97
sharks 100, 101, 106
Shepherd, Alan 133
ships
    explorers 112-113, 114, 115
    fishing boats 120
    navigation 116
    wrecks 122-123
shores 53, 108-9
silica 9, 22, 24, 65, 82, 84, 85
Sirius 180, 181
sky, colour 46
Skylab 138, 175
smelting 82
Smith, William 58
snow 44, 52, 53, 56
solar nebula 144-145, 150
Solar System
    comets 172, 173
    formation of 144-145
    size 186
    Sun 174, 176
solar wind 173, 175, 176
sonar 120
South America 17, 36, 37, 51
South Pole 23
space junk 140
space probes 211
    comets 172
    Jupiter 159
    Mars 152, 153, 154-155
    Mercury 146
    Saturn 162, 163

extraterrestrial life 204
   Sun 175
   Titan 164, 165
   Uranus 166
   Venus 148, 149
space shuttle 136-137, 138, 139, 141, 143
space stations 138-139
spring tides 96, 97
spy satellites 143
stalactites and stalagmites 52
stars 8, 82, 126, 178-183, 210
   birth of 178-179, 193
   black holes 184, 185
   death of 182-183
   distance 180-181
   galaxies 188-189, 192-193
   Milky Way 186-187
   Sun 174-175
   supernovae 90
   types of 180-181
stone tools 78, 79
Stonehenge 126
storms 45, 47, 51, 54, 98, 108, 159, 162
stromatolites 13
submarine canyons 94
submarines 122
sulphur 18, 19, 22, 28
Sun 9, 127, 174-177
   ancient theories 126
   birth of 8, 12
   and climate 48, 49
   eclipses 174, 175
   energy 174, 175
   fossil fuels 80
   future of 90, 91
   heat 14
   observing 175

rainbows 47
solar power 81
Solar System 144-5
sunset 46
sunspots 49, 176, 177
water cycle 52
and weather 44
superclusters 189, 199
supernovae 182, 183, 186, 207
swells, ocean waves 98
Swigert, Jack 135

T
telescopes 128-131, 180, 201, 204, 211
   asteroid searches 157
   gamma ray telescopes 131
   Hubble Space Telescope 130
   infrared telescopes 131
   invention of 128
   on the Moon 151
   radio telescopes 129
   solar telescopes 175
   ultraviolet telescopes 131
   Uranus 166
terraforming 155
Tertiary era 76
Tethys Ocean 17, 40, 68, 165
thunderstorms 47
tidal waves 25, 37, 72
tide pools 108
tides 96-197, 108
time 184, 202-3
Titan 162, 164
Titania 167
Titanic 122, 123
Tombaugh, Clyde 170, 171

tornadoes 42, 43, 47
trees 48, 50, 51, 88
trenches 94, 95
Triassic period 69
trilobites 62, 63
Triton 169
tsunamis 37, 98
tundra 76
Turner, J.M.W. 118
turtles 104

U
ultraviolet radiation 131
Umbriel 167
Universe 8, 206-207
   ancient theories of 126
   Big Bang 196-199
   Big Crunch 200, 201
   black holes 184-5, 194
   comets 172-3
   expansion 190-1
   extraterrestrial life 204-5
   galaxies 188-189, 190, 191, 192-5
   Milky Way 186-187
   planets 146-171
   quasars 194-195
   size 127, 190
   Solar System 144-145
   space travel 132-141
   stars 178-183
   Sun 174-177
   telescopes 128-131
   time 202-203
Uranus 166-167
   discovery of 166
   moons 167
   orbit 167, 168, 170, 171
   rings 166
   Solar System 144, 145
   space probes 166

V
valleys 15, 52, 53, 57
variable stars 181, 188
Venus 46, 148-149, 166
   atmosphere 10, 11, 65, 148, 149
   greenhouse effect 10, 148
   Solar System 144, 145
   volcanoes 148, 149
Verne, Jules 18, 20
Vesuvius, Mount 32, 33
Vikings 112
Virgo cluster 188, 189, 191, 194, 195
volcanoes 14, 16, 209
   on early Earth 12, 13
   eruptions 24-7, 30-3
   hot spots 28-9
   islands 19, 28, 29, 95
   on Mars 152, 153
   ocean floor 18
   seamounts 94
   on Venus 148, 149

W
water 64
   erosion 52-53
   floods 54-55
   formation of the Earth 12, 13
   on Mars 152, 153, 154
   see also oceans; seawater
water vapour 10, 44, 49, 52
waves 53, 98-99, 108, 110
weather 42-48, 98, 124
weather satellites 45, 142
whales 102-103, 118, 124
white dwarf stars 180, 182
winds 42-3, 44, 45, 81, 98, 110
wormholes 202, 203

223

Acknowledgements

The publishers would like to thank the following illustrators for their contributions to this book: Julian Baker, Julian Baum, Jim Burns, Tom Connell, Debbie Cook, Anthony Duke, Tim Duke, James Field, Gary Hinks, Richard Holloway, Rob Jakeway, Dave Kesarisingh, John Lawrence, Ceri Llewellyn, Kevin Maddison, Mark Preston, Bernard Robinson, David Webb, ZAP ART.

The publishers would also like to thank the following: Clarissa Claudel, Peter Clayman, Dougal Dixon, Jo Fletcher-Watson, Ian Graham, Dr Paul Murdin, Pauline Newman, Robin Redfern, Dr Denise Smythe-Wright, Marc Wilson.

Key: b = botton, *c* = *centre*, *l* = *left*, r = right, t = top;
The publishers would like to thank the following for supplying photographs:
8-9 *b* The Bridgeman Art Library, London, New York/Vatican Museum & Galleries, Rome **9** *b* The Bridgeman Art Library, London, New York/San Marco, Venice/Francesco Turino Bohm **10** *tl* SPL/NASA GSFC/Gene Feldman, *bl* SPL/CNES, 1995 Distribution Spot Image **10-11** SPL/Royal Observatory, Edinburgh, *c* Powerstock/Zefa/Panther **11** *c* SPL/US Geological Survey, *cr* SPL/NASA, *bc* SPL/Space Telescope Science Institute/NASA, *br* SPL/NASA **12** *tr* SPL/NASA **13** *tr* PEP/ Georgette Douwma **14** *tl* Mary Evans Picture Library **15** *tr* Robert Harding Picture Library **16** *cl* OSF/Matthias Breiter, *br* SPL/David Parker **17** *cl* Robert Harding Picture Library, *br* SPL/David Parker **18** *tl* Mary Evans Picture Library **19** *tr* National Geographic Society/ Cartographic Computer Lab/INGS Image Collection **20** *tl* Jean-Loup charmet, *bl* SPL/NASA **21** *br* Geoscience Features Picture Library **23** *tr* SPL/Pekka Parviainen **24** *tl* SPL/Simon Fraser, *bl* SPL/Simon Fraser **24-25** *b* Tony Stone Images/Wayne Eastep, **25** *tr* FSP/NASA/Liaison/*b* B. Ingalls **26** *tl* AKG London, *bl* Martin Redfern **27** *br* FSP/Gilles Bassignac **28** *tl* Werner Forman Archive/British Museum, London, *cl* Robert Harding Picture Library/D. Peebles **29** *tc* FSP/B. Lewis/ *tr* PEP/Bourseiller & Durieux, *c* FSP/A.P.I., *cr* PEP/ Verena Tunnicliffe **30** *tl* PEP/Bourseiller - I & V **30-31** Katz Pictures/Alberto Garcia/SABA **31** *tr* FLPA/USDA Forest Service, *cr* FLPA/USDA Forest Service, *br* FLPA/ USDA Forest Service **32** *tl* Topham Picture Point, *tr* Popperfoto/Reuters/Ted Aljibe, *cl* ET Archive/Royal Society, *bl* PEP/Bourseiller - I & V **33** *tl* Corbis UK/Library of Congress, *tc* Corbis UK/Library of Congress, *tr* Corbis UK/Library of Congress, *cr* FSP/Kevin West, *br* PEP/ Krafft - I & V **34-35** *c* TRH/US Navy **35** *cl* SPL/David Parker, *c* Popperfoto/Reuter, *bc* Popperfoto/Reuters/Reinhard Krause **36** *t* Rex Features/Sipa Press, *tl* Peter Newark's Pictures, *clt* John Frost Historical Newspaper Service, *cl* John Frost Historical Newspaper Service, *bl* Popperfoto/Reuter, *br* Popperfoto/Reuter **36-37** *t* Popperfoto/Reuter **37** *tr* Tony Stone Images/Warren Bolster, *b* Tony Stone Images/Ed Pritchard **38** *tl* SPL/Science Museum **38-39** *b* Popperfoto **39** *br* SPL/David Parker **40** *tl* SPL/Martin Bond, *bl* Tony Stone Images/Monica Dalmasso **42** *tl* Tony Stone Images/Gary Irving, *cr* Corbis UK/Library of Congress **43** *tl* FSP/Shamsi-Basha, *tr* FSP/Gamma/ Schofield /Liais, *cl* OSF/M.P.L. Fogden, *cr* NHPA/Jany Sauvanet, *br* Sygma/Palm Beach Post/Waters **44** *tc* OSF/Scott Camazine, *tr* Popperfoto/Reuters/Peter Morgan, *cl* SPL/NASA, *bl* SPL/NASA **45** *tr* OSF/E.R. Degginger, *cl* The Met Office, *br* Sygma/Bleibtreu/John Hillelson Agency **46** *tl* Rex Features/Sipa/Oliver Monn, *bl* SPL/Pekka Parviainen **46-47** Popperfoto **47** *br* FLPA/Martin B Withers **50** Image Bank/Mancle Isy Stewart, *tl* Tony Stone Images **48-49** *c* PEP/J.P. Nacivet, *bc* Tony Stone Images/Frans Lanting **49** *br* NHPA/Anthony Bannister **50** *tl* SPL/Dr Jeremy Burgess, *bl* SPL/NASA **51** OSF/Paul Franklin **52** *tl* Tony Stone Images/Glen Allison, *bl* Tony Stone Images/Demetrio Carrasco **53** *c* Tony Stone Images/Cameron Davidson **54** *bl* Panos Pictures/Liba Taylor **55** *c* SPL/Earth Satellite Corporation, *cr* SPL/Earth Satellite Corporation **56** *tl* Mary Evans Picture Library, *bl* Tony Stone Images/Tom Bean **57** *tr* Tony Stone Images/Arnulf Husmo, *br* PEP/John Lythgoe **58** *tl* NHPA/George Bernard, *bl* PEP/Jon & Alison Moran **58-59** *c* SPL/Martin Dohrn **59** *bc* FSP **60** *tl* Mary Evans Picture Library, *c* The Royal Geographical Society **61** *tl* Corbis UK/Jim Sugar Photography, *cr* NHM, London, *br* Auscape International Photo Lib. **62** *cr* Corbis UK/James L. Amos **63** *cl* Simon Conway Morris University of Cambridge **64** *tl* PEP/Steve Hopkin **64** *tc (background)* SPL/Kaj R. Svensson **64** *bl* PEP/A.S. Edwards **64-65** *t* OSF/Manfred Kage **64-65** *b (background)* SPL/Kaj R. Svensson **65** *tc (background)* SPL/Kaj R. Svensson **65** *tr* SPL/Sinclair Stammers **65** *br* OSF/Marshall Black **66** *tr* PEP/Peter Scoones **67** *cl* PEP/Ken Lucas **68** *cl* NHM, London, *cr* SPL/Sinclair Stammers **69** *cl* SPL/Sinclair Stammers **70** *c* SPL/Vaughan Fleming **71** *cr* The Ronald Grant Archive, *bc* NHM, London **72** *tl* SPL/Geological Survey of Canada/Mark Pilkington, *bl* SPL/NASA **75** *cl* Alessandro Montanaii **77** *cl* Corbis UK/Ecoscene/Sally A. Morgan, *cr* NHM, London **78** *tl* Novosti **79** *cl* NHM, London, *cr* NHM, London **78** *tl* Powerstock/Zefa, *tr* NHM, London **79** *tl* Powerstock/Zefa/Bond, *c* NHM, London, *cr* NHM, London, *bc* NHM, London, *br* NHM, London **80** *cl* SPL, *bl* SPL **81** *cl* SPL, *br* SPL **82** *tl* SPL/KAJ R. Svensson **82-83** *t* SPL/Rosenfeld Images Ltd **83** *br* Tony Stone Images/Lester Lefkowitz **84** *tl* SPL/Vaughan Fleming, *cr* NHM, London, *br* The Bridgeman Art Library, London, New York/Derby Museum & Art Gallery **85** *c* NHPA/Anthony Bannister, *cr* Popperfoto/W.U.W **86** *tl* Martin Redfern, *bl* Tony Stone Images/Philip H. Coblentz **88** *tl* Tony Stone Images/David Woodfall **89** *tr* Tony Stone Images/David Woodfall, *cl* Tony Stone Images/Robert Van Der Hils.Pages *co* The Bridgeman Art Library/British Library, London **92** *tr* SPL, *bl* SPL **92-93** *c* SPL **94** *b* SPL **96** *l* OSF **97** *tc* Images Colour Library, *cr* Images Colour Library, *bc* NHPA **98-99** *b* Image Bank **99** *b* Hulton Getty **100** *tl* BBC Natural History Unit Picture Library, *cl* OSF, *cr* Natural Science Photos **100-101** *b* NHPA **101** *t* Fred Bavendam, *cl* PEP, *cr* PEP **102** *t* Natural Science Photos, *cr* PEP, *bl* Natural Science Photos, *br* BBC Natural History Unit Picture Library **103** *t* Ardea London, *cl* PEP, *cr* Image Bank, *br* Bruce Coleman Collection **104** *tl* OSF, *c* PEP **105** *tc* (reef) FLPA, *tc* (snake) PEP, *tr* (reef) PEP, *cl* (lionfish) PEP, *c* (corals) OSF, *c* (reef) Robert Harding Picture Library, *cr* (nudibranch) Linda Dunk, *cr* (starfish) Bruce Coleman Collection, *bl* (grouper) PEP, *bl* (reef) NHPA, *bl* (sponges) NHPA, *bc* (corals) NHPA **106** *tl* OSF, *b* PEP **107** *tl* PEP, *tc* OSF, *tr* OSF, *cl* NHPA, *c* OSF, *cr* PEP, *bl* NHPA **108** *tr* PEP, *bl* Art Directors & Trip Photographic Library, *br* PEP **108-109** *c* PEP **109** *t* PEP, *cr* FLPA, *bl* PEP, *br* OSF **110** *cl* OSF, *bl* OSF, *br* OSF **110-111** *c* PEP **111** *c* Bruce Coleman Collection, *bl* OSF, *bc* OSF, *br* PEP **112** *t* Tim Severin **113** *cr* Rex Features, *b* Rex Features **114** *l* Corbis, *cr* Mary Evans Picture Library **115** *tr* Mary Evans Picture Library, *bl* Natural Science Photos **116** *t* Michael Holford, *bl* Mary Evans Picture Library, *br* The Bridgeman Art Library **117** *tl* Bridgeman Art Library, *tr* Michael Holford, *c* The British Museum, *bl*, Kos Picture Source Ltd, *br* The Bridgeman Art Library **118** *tl* The Art Archive, *cr* The Ronald Grant Archive, *bl* Michael Holford/Victoria & Albert Museum **118-119** *t* Metropolitan Museum of Art, **119** *cr* Bruce Coleman Collection, *bl* Superstock, *br* The Art Archive 120 *t* FSP, *c* PEP **121** *tl* OSF, *tr* Still Pictures **122** *tl* NHPA, *bl* FSP, *br* Hulton Getty **122-123** T Rex Features **123** *bl* NHPA, *br* Sygma **124** *tl* PEP, *tr* PEP, *bl* PEP, **125** *l* PEP **126** *tl* Powerstock/Zefa, *tr* SPL/Jean-Loup Charmet, *cr* The Bridgeman Art Library/British Library **127** *cl* SPL/Hale Observatories, *c* Corbis **128** *tl* Science & Society Picture Library, *tl* Scala/Biblioteca Nazionale, Firenze, *c* Mary Evans Picture Library **128-129** background Hulton Getty, *t* SPL/Peter Menzel, *b* Carnegie Institute of Washington **129** *tr* SPL, *br* FSP/Gamma **130** *t* PEP, *cr* NASA/Uni. of Washington/B. Balik, *bl* European Space Agency/PPARC **131** *tl* NASA/KSC, *cr* European Space Agency, *br* European Space Agency **132** *l* PEP, *tl*, The Art Archive, *tr* Popperfoto, *cr* Corbis/Bettmann/UPI **133** *tl* Novosti, *tc* SPL/Novosti *cr* FSP/Gamma **134** *bl* NASA/Portfolio Pictures, *bc* FSP/Gamma **135** *c* Genesis Photo Library, *cr* Genesis Photo Library/NASA **136** *tl* FSP/Gamma, *bl* Telegraph Colour Library **136-137** *c* FSP/Gamma, **137** *cl* SPL/Novosti, *c* European Space Agency, *br* SPL/NASA **138** *tl* SPL, *cl* SPL/NASA, *bl* NASA, *br* Novosti **138-139** *t* NASA/Portofolio Pictures **139** *tr* NASA/Portofolio Pictures, *c* SPL/NASA, *bl* SPL/NASA, *br* SPL **140** *tr* Popperfoto, *cr* European Space Agency, *bl* SPL, *bc* Popperfoto, *b* Popperfoto **141** *tl* NASA, *tc* NASA, *tr*, NASA, *cr* NASA, *b*l European Space Agency, *bc* PEP, *br* Tony Stone Images **142** *tl* European Space Agency, *c* SPL, *bl* SPL/ESA **142-143** *c* SPL **143** *cl* SPL, *c* PEP, *cr* FSP/Gamma **146** *tl* SPL/NASA, *cl* SPL **147** *tr* (insert) SPL **148** *tl* SPL/NASA, *cl* SPL/Novosti, *cr* SPL/NASA **148-149** *c (background)* SPL/NASA/David Anderson **149** *tr* SPL/NASA, *cl* SPL/NASA, *c* SPL/NASA **150** *t (background)* PEP, *tl* SPL, *c* PEP **150-151** *c* SPL/NASA **151** *b (background)* NASA **152** *tl* SPL/NASA, *cl* SPL/NASA, *bl* SPL/NASA **152-153** PEP *c*, SPL/U.S. Geological Survey **153** *tl* PEP, *tc* SPL, *tr* NASA, *c* SPL/NASA, *cr* SPL/U.S. Geological Survey, *br* PEP **154** *bl* SPL, *b (background)* SPL/NASA **155** *t (background)* The Ronald Grant Archive, *tl* PEP, *tr* SPL/NASA, *c* SPL **156** *cl* SPL/Novosti, *bl* SPL/Geological Survey of Canada, **157** TC Powerstock/Zefa, *tr* National Air Library of Canada, *cl* (3) SPL, *cl* (1) NHM, London, *cl* (2) SPL, *cl* (4) NHM, London, *bc* NHM, London, **158** background SPL, *cl* SPL/NASA/STSI, *bl* Jet Propulsion Lab/NASA, *br* SPL/J.Tennyson & S.Miller, University College, London, **159** *tl* Jet Propulsion Lab/NASA, *tr* PEP, *cr* Jet Propulsion Lab/NASA, *bl* SPL **160** *cr* PEP, *bl* PEP **161** *cl* PEP, *cr* SPL, *bc* SPL **162** *tl* PEP, *tr* SPL/STSI/NASA, *bl* SPL, *br* SPL/STSI/NASA **163** *tl* SPL/NASA, *b* Jet Propulsion Lab/NASA **164** *tl* SPL/NASA, *tr* (2) SPL/NASA, *tr* (4) Jet Propulsion Lab, *tr* (3) SPL/NASA **165** *tr* (1) SPL/NASA *tr*, (5) SPL/NASA **166** *tl* Telegraph Colour Library, *cl* SPL, *cr* SPL, *bl* SPL **167** *tl* SPL, *tr* (3) SPL/NASA *tr*, (2) SPL/NASA, *tr* (1) SPL/NASA, *cl* SPL **168** *tl* SPL, *cl* SPL, *bc* SPL **169** *cr*, SPL/NASA **170** *tl* SPL/NASA/STSI, *cl* SPL **171** *cl* SPL, *bl* PEP **172** *tl* Ann Ronan/Image Select, *tr* The Art Archive, *cl* SPL/David Parker, *c* SPL/ESA, *bl* SPL, *bc* SPL/Gordon Garradd **173** *br* SPL/Steven Jay **174** *cl* SPL/Pekka Parviainen, *cr* SPL/George Post **175** *tl* SPL/Jisas/Lockheed, *c* SPL/Dr. Douglas Gorgh, *br* SPL/David Parker **176** *c* Telegraph Colour Library, *b* SPL/NASA **177** *tl* Martin Redfern/Smithsonian Institute, *tr* SPL/Hale Observatories **178** *cl* SPL, *cr* Martin Redfern/NASA, *bl* SPL **179** *cl* Martin Redfern/NASA/Jeff Hester, Paul Scowen, *br* Martin Redfern/Protoplanetary Disks/C.R.O'Dell **180** *cr* SPL/ESA, *bl* SPL **181** *l* SPL/Luke Dodd, *br* Martin Redfern/NASA **182** *tl* SPL/STSI/NASA, *cr* NASA/Harvard-Smithsonran Centre of Astrophysics/Peter Garnavich, *bl* SPL/STSI/NASA **182-183** background Martin Redfern/Royal Observatory/Photolabs, *t* Martin Redfern/NASA/STSI **183** *tr* SPL/STSI/NASA, *cl* SPL/STSI **186** *tl* SPL/Dennis Di cicco/Peter Arnold Inc., *bl* SPL/NASA **187** *tr*, PEP, *c* SPL/Max Planck Inst. for Radio Astronomy, *cr* SPL/NASA, *br* Martin Redfern/Smithsonian Institute **188** *c* & *cr* SPL/STSI, *tc* SPL/Harvard College Observatory **188-189** *t* SPL, 189 *t* SPL, *c* SPL **190-191** *t* Department of Astrophysics, Oxford University/University of Oxford **191** *cl* SPL, *cr* Department of Astrophysics, Oxford University **192** *tl* SPL/Dr. Martin England, *cr* SPL/US Naval Observatory, *bl* SPL, *br* Martin Redfern **193** *tl* Martin Redfern/Smithsonian Institute, *cl* Martin Redfern, *cr* Martin Redfern/NASA **194** *bl* SPL **195** *tr* SPL, *c* SPL **196** *tc* SPL, *bl* Zap Art **196-197** *c* PEP **197** *br* SPL/AT & *t* bell Labs./R.Wilson & A.Penzias **198** *cl* Corbis **200** *bl* SPL, *bc* Martin Redfern/NASA **204** *tl* Martin Redfern/NASA/JPL, *cr* PEP, *bl* SPL/Peter Menzel **204-205** *t* SPL/John Reader **205** *bl* Fortean Picture Library **206** *c* Corbis **206-207** Pictor International Ltd

(NHM Natural History Museum; FSP Frank Spooner Pictures)

Every effort has been made to trace the copyright holders of the photographs.
The publishers apologize for any inconvenience caused.